ASTROLOGY

A HISTORY

Peter Whitfield

✳✴✳

Harry N. Abrams, Inc., Publishers

Library of Congress Cataloging-in-Publication Data

Whitfield, Peter, Dr.
    Astrology : a history / Peter Whitfield.
          p.   cm.
    Includes bibliographical references and index.
    ISBN 0-8109-4235-6
    1. Astrology–History. I. Title.

    BF1671.W55 2001
    133.5'09–dc21

                            2001022135

First published in 2001 by The British Library, London

Published in 2001 by Harry N. Abrams, Incorporated, New York

Printed and bound in Hong Kong

10 9 8 7 6 5 4 3 2 1

Harry N. Abrams, Inc.
100 Fifth Avenue
New York, N.Y. 10011
www.abramsbooks.com

CONTENTS

PREFACE

This book is the history of an idea, an idea both simple and profound, and which can be traced in many cultures and in many religions. The idea is that man is somehow related, organically linked, to the universe around him. In itself this is not a bizarre idea, and it is once again alive and well in some scientific and philosophical circles today. But in certain ancient civilisations, the idea was developed along rather special and unexpected lines. This was that a network of relationships existed between man and the heavens which, if correctly understood, gave a key to human character and destiny. The study of these relationships was the science of astrology. Whether some power in the heavenly bodies was responsible for shaping human destiny, or whether they acted merely as signs of it, was a matter of argument from the first. The most distinctive feature of this idea is that it was not employed to found a philosophy in the usual sense, but that it became the starting-point of a system, which was technical, mathematical and, in the context of its time, scientific. How exactly this supposed link between man and the stars came to be *mathematised* – elaborated into a complex system of geometric relationships – is now impossible to say. The history of astrology is like a distant landscape where the main features stand out clearly, but where the detail is always blurred or hidden in shadows, and there are fundamental puzzles as to when and why many of its key doctrines emerged. It is certain that the birth of astrology was dependant on the concept of the spherical model of the heavens; but who the individuals were who formulated its rules, and what their guiding principles were, is lost in history.

It has often been claimed that astrology is of immense antiquity, and that it existed in a mature form as much as 5,000 years ago in civilisations such as Egypt and Mesopotamia. But the essence of astrology is the ability to calculate the configuration of the heavens at any desired moment – above all at the moment of somebody's birth. This could only be done by using the rules of mathematical astronomy to determine where the Sun, Moon, planets and Zodiac signs stood at the chosen moment. Therefore is it axiomatic that true astrology could not and did not exist before the science of mathematical astronomy existed. That science developed not earlier than the fifth century BC, in the late phase of Babylonian civilisation, and it was given its distinctive *geometric* form some two or three centuries later by Greek mathematicians. Thus the astrology of the horoscope, and the calculated mapping of the heavens which lies behind it, are entirely Greek in character, although it built upon earlier Babylonian foundations. There was no equivalent system of mathematical astronomy in ancient Egypt. Astrology was born in the Hellenistic era, when so many other creeds and philosophies were also taking shape, and it spread throughout the ancient near east, eventually reaching Europe in the early middle ages through the intermediary of Islamic scholarship.

Astrology has perhaps two outstanding characteristics: its continuity and its protean nature. It was perfected as a system by the first century AD, and very little even in modern astrology would be unrecognisable to a practitioner of that era. The methods by which the figure of the heavens is determined, and the interpretation of that figure, follow certain principles first set down almost 2,000 years ago, and which have never been fundamentally altered. On the other hand, having begun as a pagan science it always contained a strongly religious element, and it proved capable of being harmonised with ancient mystery religions, Neoplatonic philosophy, Islamic and Christian theology and Renaissance occultism. It is this adaptability which claims our attention, for it suggests that astrology has refused to die because it springs from some perennial human need. It would be easy to argue that its motive was simply the desire to see into the future, but astrology has always made intellectual claims which were far higher than fortune-telling or crystal-ball gazing. The historical appeal of astrology is that it cuts a swathe through intellectual and social history, touching science, religion, philosophy, politics and art. Astrology was a mirror held up to the changing spirit of each age, an intellectual challenge to which few classical, medieval or Renaissance thinkers were indifferent. It underwent an intriguing process of democratisation; from being a religious art and a royal, political art, it became a universal guide to human character. Its demise under the impact of the new science of the seventeenth century ought logically to have been final, but the ancient idea of the link between man and the cosmos has proved too strong for logic, although astrology will probably never regain its position in the intellectual mainstream. Nevertheless it did for centuries enjoy such a position, half-way between a religion and a science, and this book attempts to explain some of the reasons why.

CHAPTER ONE

BABYLONIA:

THE DAWN OF ASTROLOGY

THE SACRED WRITING

The place is Nineveh, capital of the Assyrian Empire, the date is 672 BC. Esarhaddon the great king, conqueror of Egypt, and at that moment the most powerful man in the world, knows that his death is not far off, and he is agonising over the future of his vast empire. His health is failing, he is nervous of political intrigues, and even more nervous of omens and portents, especially those in the sky such as eclipses and falling stars. He is a religious and deeply superstitious man, and his mind had been scarred by the events of his youth, when his father Sennacherib was murdered by Esarhaddon's brothers, and civil war had resulted. The king is now determined to avoid a repetition of those traumatic events, and therefore he has taken counsel – not only with courtiers and ministers, but with his diviners and soothsayers. These men – the *ummanu*, the 'experts' or 'scholars' – wielded enormous influence in these Mesopotamian civilisations, combining the roles of priest and scientist, and without their daily advice, the king would not act in any matter of state importance. Together Esarhaddon and these counsellors now devised a scheme for safeguarding the future of the realm; one of his sons, Ashurbanipal, would succeed to the throne of Assyria, while the other, Shamash-shum-ukim, would be Prince of Babylon. One of the king's scholars greeted the plan with these words:

> Your majesty has done on earth what cannot be done even in heaven...
> You have clad your younger son in royal garments and handed to him the
> kingship of the land of Assyria. Your elder son you have installed as king in
> Babylon. To right and left, wherever you look, the opponents of your
> majesty among the lesser kings say that the king has done good to Assyria.
> But now the god Assur has given you the world from the rising of the sun
> to the setting of the sun. Look upon these gracious sons of yours and your
> heart will be happy.

And this plan was indeed highly successful – for a time. When Esarhaddon died in 669 BC, the dual succession was carried out smoothly, and for sixteen years the brothers rules in harmony. But then, for reasons unknown, internecine war broke out, and Ashurbanipal took up arms against his rebellious brother, who eventually died in 648 BC, amid scenes of terrible slaughter in the burning city of Babylon. Yet the years of peace had shown that the experts and soothsayers had been correct, and Esarhaddon had been wise to trust them. The tragic relapse into conflict sprang from the sinful nature of princes, for which the soothsayers were not answerable. So the influence of the experts was in no way diminished, and Ashurbanipal would claim that, as part of his regal training, he had 'mastered the hidden wisdom...to interpret the omens of heaven and earth...and participate in the councils of the *ummanu*.'

What precisely did the *ummanu* do, and why do they stand at the commencement of a history of astrology? The answers to these questions may be pieced together from thousands of omen-texts gathered by Ashurbanipal himself in his royal library at Nineveh between 660 and 630 BC. The task of these experts, these scholar-scientists, was to scan the face of nature in order first to find significant patterns there, and then significant departures from those patterns; then they would proceed to fathom what these things meant. The events which they scanned included the paths followed by birds in flight, the entrails of sacrificed animals, the movement of oil poured into water, and above all perhaps, the configuration of the heavens – conjunctions, eclipses, shooting stars, halos of light, comets, cloud-formations and so on. We know from diviners' manuals why they scanned nature in this way: it was because they believed that the gods placed signs in the natural world and in the heavens which served to warn mankind of events to come, both good and evil, and thus they offered man the chance to influence the future. The sky and the natural world were the pages upon which the gods

Assyrian king and sacred tree: the king's sacral role was to tend the tree which symbolised the link between earth and heaven. The roots of astrology lay in the interpretation – by means of omens in heaven – of the king's success or failure in this role.

Department of Western Asiatic Antiquities, The British Museum

wrote their decrees in a mysterious but systematic language. 'The signs on earth, just as those in heaven, give us signals', wrote one of the scholars. 'Sky and earth both produce portents; though appearing separately, they are not separate, for sky and earth are joined'.

There was thus in Mesopotamian thought an intimate connection between the divine realm and the realm of nature and man. Moreover there existed a received wisdom, a set of skills, a science, by which this connection might be understood, and that science was the province of the *ummanu*. But the *ummanu* were at this stage exclusively royal counsellors; neither their special wisdom not the events they studied were of concern to the population at large, but only to the king. The omens concerned his conduct, his family, his enemies, his kingdom, his harvests, and so on. There is here undoubtedly the seed of the doctrine that the microcosm and the macrocosm are linked, but that link was limited and concentrated in the person of the king. Why should this be so? In Mesopotamian thought, the king upheld the divine world-order, for he was the gods' representative on earth. The king's wisdom and just rule on earth mirrored that of the gods over the universe as a whole. The equilibrium of the secular kingdom required the purity of the king, his painstaking observance of religious and moral laws. This principle is well illustrated in the motif of the Sacred Tree, which reached between and linked earth and heaven, and which was tended by the king himself. It was recognised of course that the king, as a human being, might often err in his judgement or his conduct, and these royal sins were indeed offences against the divine order, which would provoke retribution from the gods. But – and this was the vital point – such retribution would not come without warning. The gods would use dreams, portents and omens to warn the king of his misdeeds and of his danger. This was precisely where the *ummanu* came in: it was their duty to scan nature for these omens, for anything which departed from the norm, for in this system any such departures must carry some meaning. Their second role was to instruct the king in the 'apotropaic' rituals – rituals which would cleanse the king of his sins, and thus avert the omen.

Where did these ideas of cosmic kingship, and the wisdom to interpret omens, both come from? Mesopotamian tradition – again texts in Ashurbanipal's library – tell us of divine teachers who dwelled on earth in ancient times, and who taught men science, philosophy, law and all manner of wisdom. In a manner which paralleled the Greek belief in Hermes, and the Egyptian cult of Thoth, the Mesopotamian scholars claimed that their learning had been revealed by these divine teachers.

The importance of the *ummanu* and the nature of their esoteric work is independently confirmed in certain passages in the Old Testament, from the period when the Israelites had ample opportunity to study these cults. The scornful words of Isaiah concerning the Babylonian stargazers and soothsayers are well known (*Isaiah* 47:12-13), but a still more striking passage appears in the Book of Daniel (*Daniel* 5:11-12)

> There is in your kingdom a man who has in him
> the spirit of the holy gods, a man who was known
> in your father's time to have a clear understanding and a godlike wisdom.
> King Nebuchadnezzar, your father, appointed him chief of the magicians,
> exorcists, astrologers and diviners. This same Daniel is known to have a
> notable spirit, with knowledge and understanding, and the gift of inter-
> preting dreams, explaining riddles and unbinding spells.

The victory stele of Naram-Sin, c.2100 BC. A victorious king leads his troops to a hill-top, perhaps to worship the astral deities who have blessed his campaign.
The Louvre

This is a remarkable external testimony to the work of the first astrologers, the *ummanu*; it confirms the belief in an esoteric learning which was divinely inspired and which enabled them to interpret the signs written by the gods on the face of nature; the biblical image of the 'writing on the wall' in Nebuchadnezzar's palace is in fact this very doctrine given a quite literal form. In what way then did these principles of cosmic kingship and divine, especially celestial omens, develop in Mesopotamia towards a form of proto-astrology?

THE GODS OF THE SKY

In a cuneiform text from the Old Babylonian period (*c*.1700 BC) we read:

> If the face of the sky is dark, the year will be bad.
> If the face of the sky is bright when the New Moon appears, and it is greeted with joy, the year will be good.
> If the north wind blows across the face of the sky before the New Moon, the corn will grow abundantly.
> If on the day of the crescent the Moon-god does not disappear quickly enough from the sky, disease will come upon the land.

The Babylonian year began when the first faint crescent of the new Moon appeared at the beginning of the spring month of *Nissanu*. The purpose of this text is to foretell, from the appearance of the sky at that moment, the character of the coming year. Notice that here astronomy is combined with meteorology: atmospheric effects of wind and cloud are considered to take place in the same realm as the Moon. Notice also that there is no claim that the Moon's appearance will directly *cause* the effects predicted. The Moon, wind and clouds are treated as *signs* which indicate to those who can read them what the future will be. This is the outstanding characteristic of the omen-culture of ancient Babylonia – that these signs were written by the gods on the face of nature for men to read. The heavenly bodies were the manifestations of cosmic deities, as were certain other forces of nature, such as wind and storm, rain and flood, earthquake and disease. The earth and the heavens were considered to be linked in a network of cosmic relationships, and the future intentions of these deities were therefore discernible from the signs which they placed in the sky. In astral omens, in the entrails of sacrificed animals, and in many other things, the gods might chose to write intimations of the future. A prayer before divination from the Old Babylonian period reads:

> Veiled is the night;
> The temple and the most holy places are quiet and dark...
> Oh great ones, gods of the night...
> Oh Pleiades, Orion and the Dragon,
> Ursa Major, Goat and Bison,
> Stand by and then
> In the divination which I am making,
> In the lamb which I am offering,
> Write the truth for me.

This system of divination by omens is alien to us, and extremely difficult to rationalise. Did it have any empirical basis? Had it once been observed that when the north wind blew before the New Moon, a good harvest had followed? How often must such an event have been observed before it was elevated into a divine omen? Or was it really believed that the meaning of these patterns had been divinely revealed? What is certain is that Mesopotamian scholars regarded any deviation from the norm as endowed with significance for man – anything unusual must *mean* something – thus confirming once again the unity of man and nature. But these signs seem always to have been seen as the expression of *arbitrary* power, not as indicating systematic cause and effect. The diviner examining the entrails of an animal was seeking malformations, departures from the norm, but showed no interest in the function of the organ or in the abnormality as a possible sign of disease. Likewise Babylonian physicians were of two distinct classes; the first observed symptoms purely as signs of divine disfavour, and never prescribed any remedy, while a second class specialised in trying to alleviate the sickness.

Divination of various kinds became firmly established in Babylonian life, and a large professional class of experts grew up – the *ummanu* – whose job it was to tabulate omens in their thousands, astral and otherwise, and elucidate their meaning.

It was a general characteristic of Babylonian science to accumulate exhaustive lists (of plants, medical symptoms, materials, weather patterns, stars and so on) but without building causal connections or laws of science from them. Omens of the heavens formed a large and important group, indeed the sky was thought to be a vast page for the gods to write on. At the early stage these omens were general and impersonal, and made no claims to foretell the life and fate of any individual. The exception to this were those omens which deal with the life and fortune of the king, for the religious reasons described above:

> When on the fifth of the month Nissan, the rising Sun appears like a red torch, white clouds rise from it and the wind blows from the east, then there will be a solar eclipse on the 28th or 29th day of that month; the king will die that very month, and his son will ascend to the throne.

Eclipses were considered to be especially powerful as signs, and often dangerous to monarchs, so much so that the astronomical advisers to King Ashurbanipal had recourse to this ingenious fiction:

> If an eclipse occurs but is not observed in the capital, such an eclipse is considered not to have happened... The great gods who live in the city of your majesty have covered up the sky and not shown the eclipse... This eclipse has no relation to your majesty or his country; on this account the King should be happy.

It was also the practice for dummy-kings to be enthroned during the period of an eclipse, while the true king hid himself away under the name of 'Mr. Small-Man' or 'Mr. Farmer' or something similar. Again, we cannot know whether this fear had some historical basis: was it that the sight of one heavenly body being obscured by another had acquired a dangerous symbolic meaning? Or had past conspirators deliberately chosen such a moment to attack and kill their King? What is clear from these evasion-techniques is that these omens were seen as warnings, not as decrees of immutable fate; it was evidently possible to avert the omen and to some extent to change one's destiny.

Aside from such exceptional events as eclipses, the heavenly bodies which most interested the Babylonians were the Sun, the Moon and the planet Venus. These three were manifestations of the powerful gods Shamash, Sin and Ishtar. The first two derived their primary importance from their role in time-measurement for their motions give the fundamental units the day, the month and the year. In the creation epic *Enuma Elish* the heavens are said to have been created in order to mark the passage of time, to give order to man's cosmos. But in addition to the absolute, if not simple, regularity of the Sun and Moon, other bodies had been observed whose motions seemed erratic – these were the five planets. By 1500 BC a series of astronomical texts had been compiled (known as the Venus tablets of Ammizaduga) which gave the rising and setting times of Venus over a period of twenty-one years, with omens relating to many of these timings:

> If on the fifteenth day of the month Shabatu, Venus disappeared in the west, remaining absent from the sky three days, and on the eighteenth day of the month Venus appeared in the east: catastrophe of Kings: Adad (weather god) will bring rains; Ea (river god) will bring subterranean waters; King will send greeting to King.

The Babylonians had identified Venus as being both the morning and evening star, and the complex movements of the planet were naturally of interest in their own right to any sky-watcher. But the real reason for this extended study was that the planet was believed to be a visible manifestation of the goddess Ishtar. Ishtar was a powerful but contradictory figure in the Babylonian pantheon; ruler of love and also of battle, of fertility and storms, of rejoicing and tears. Tracing the position of the planet in the sky was an essential requisite for divining her actions and interactions with the other gods and with the affairs of men. The

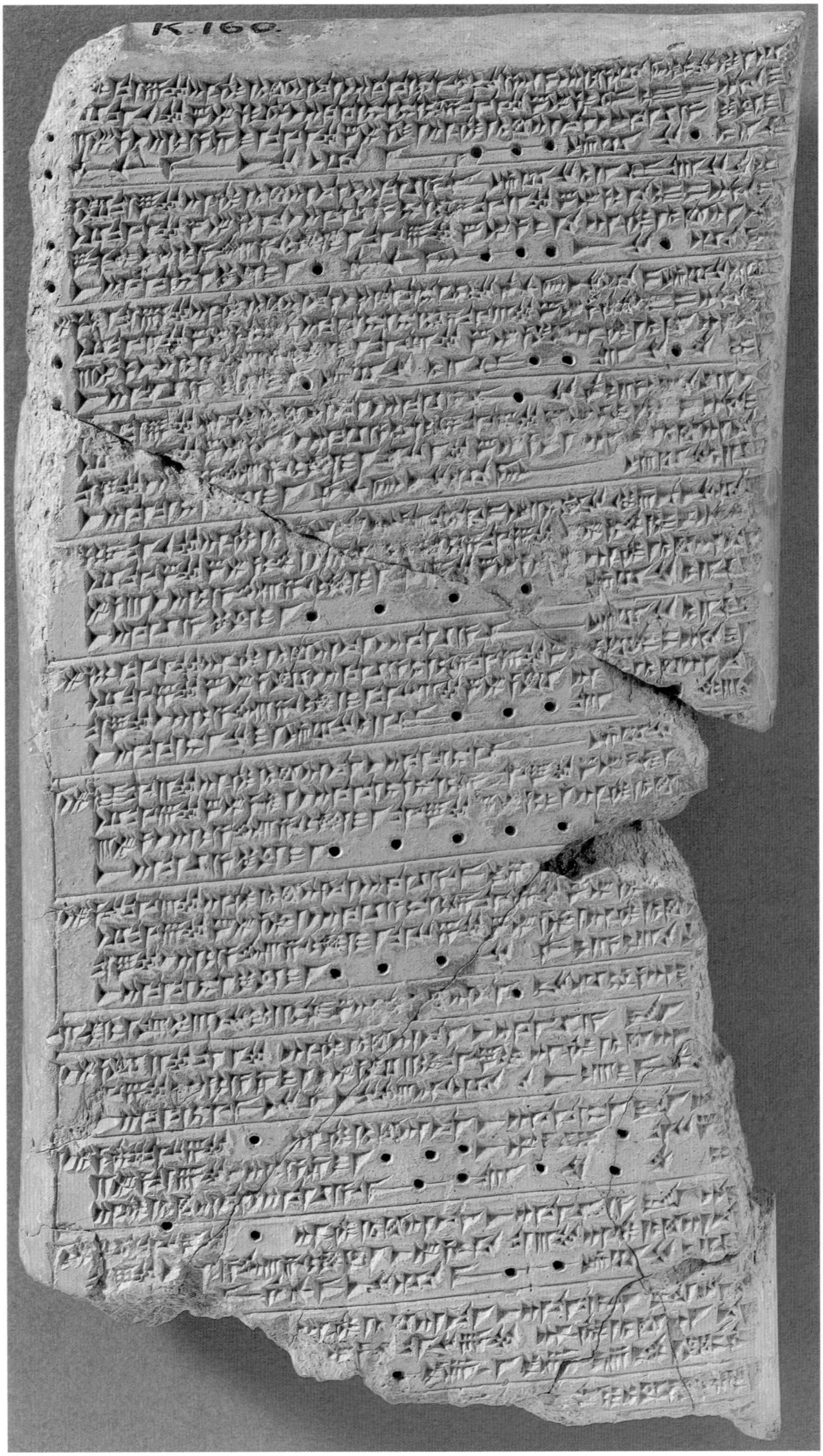
K.160

simplest example is the omen 'When Venus stands high, love-making will be pleasurable'. This is a central feature of the way in which Babylonian astronomy interacted with astral religion: the positions of the planets indicated the greater or lesser roles that the gods would play in earthly affairs at any given moment. The classical planets now familiar to us all had identifications with Babylonian deities, although their attributes were not always identical with the Graeco-Roman gods. Marduk was the planet Jupiter, creator and ruler of the heavens, and also the god of life and justice. Nergal was Mars, god of war but also the ruler of the under-world. Nabu was Mercury, god of writing and of all intellectual pursuits. Ninib or Ninurta was the god Saturn, but without sharing Saturn's role as ruler of time; instead he was the god of the hunt. This view that the planets were manifestations of personal deities was one of the motives behind the development of Babylonian

astronomy; if the planetary gods were responsible for determining what happened in love or war, in the harvest or the hunt, then the ability to predict celestial positions became tantamount to divining the gods' intentions. Thus if calendar-making was a first motive for mastering the movements of the heavenly bodies, astral religion, especially as it related to the king, was a close second. This motive has a logic of its own which was lost in later Hellenistic, and still more in medieval Christian, astrology, when men had ceased to believe in the planetary gods. Prediction based on *planetary position alone*, would require the operation of some kind of physical force emanating from the planet – which was indeed the theory advanced by Ptolemy in the second century AD, and widely accepted for centuries by Islamic and Christian astrologers.

THE ASTRONOMICAL FRAMEWORK

In what ways then did Babylonian astronomy develop so as to permit the earlier omen-culture to mature in the direction of systematic astrology? The needs of cal-endar-making and the astral religion outlined above both made it desirable to plot celestial positions in space and time, and the great achievement of Babylonian astronomy was to devise mathematical methods which made that possible. These methods were based on long, painstaking observations extending over decades, like those which lay behind the Venus tablets, and on mathematical analysis. The observatories from which these observations were made were the temple towers or ziggurats, examples of which are known to date from 1000 BC. The most important ziggurat of the high Babylonian period, from around 600 BC, was the Temple of Marduk in Babylon itself. Slightly later than the Venus tablets are another group of texts giving star positions. These texts have in the past been

Above:
The goddess Ishtar, from a Sumerian seal c.2300 BC. Ishtar – Venus – was the astral deity who most interested Mesopotamian priests. A complex deity, she presided over love and battle, fertility and storms.
Oriental Institute, University of Chicago

Facing page:
The Venus tablets of Ammizaduga. These tablets originated around 1500 BC, and give the movements and periods of visibility of the planet, with associated omens.
Department of Western Asiatic Antiquities, The British Museum

✴ Astral Religion in Babylonia ✴

IN THE YEAR 880 BC, the Babylonian king Nabu-apla-iddina began the rebuilding of the temple dedicated to Shamash the Sun-god, in the ancient city of Sippar (which stood south-west of modern Baghdad). During the excavation for this work, an ancient image of the god was discovered, which so impressed the king that he commanded that these events and the rededication of the temple should be recorded in stone. That stone tablet has survived virtually intact, and it graphically embodies for us some of the themes of the Babylonian astral religion from which astrology would later arise. The gigantic Sun-god is seen seated on his throne, while an image of the Sun is placed upon the altar before him. The king himself is touching the altar, watched by two attendant priests. Beneath the throne are two *apkallu* – the half-human, half animal figures whose legendary role had been to reveal divine wisdom to mankind. Above the god are symbols of the three planets Sun, Moon and Ishtar (Venus) which formed the great trinity of Babylonian astral religion. Shamash was the greatest of the three, upholder of order and justice in both the cosmic and the human realms. Shamash and his wife Aya produced two children: Kittu, who was justice, and Misharu who was law.

Shamash was the most easily-identifiable astral deity, but he was only one of many, for the cultures of Mesopotamia were unique at this period in regarding the planets as personal deities. Other nations venerated the Sun – Egypt for example – but only in Mesopotamia were the planets known as 'the gods of the night'. From this belief sprang the habit of seeing planetary positions and movements as endowed with meaning for mankind. Babylonian astronomers had mastered the regular patterns of celestial movements, and any unusual events – conjunctions, eclipses, comets, periods of invisibility and so on – were thought to be special signs from the gods. Atmospheric phenomena too, such as clouds, halos or lightning, were thought to take place on the surface of heaven and to have a similar transcendent significance. These signs were interpreted by a group of expert advisers to the king, who were thus the forerunners of the later astrologers. These signs had a very definite and restricted range of meaning: some related to the weather and the harvest, but they foretold above all the future well-being of the king. The king's role as the gods' representative on earth was constantly under divine scrutiny, and his moral and spiritual conduct would be rewarded or punished, but not before the appropriate warnings had been placed in the sky. Thus in Mesopotamian thought, the realm of mankind and the realm of the divine were intimately related, but the focus of that relationship was the king alone. The stars did not issue implacable decrees of fate, but omens which, correctly understood, would enable the king to avert evil. The movements of the heavenly bodies were in fact a form of language, through which the planetary gods spoke to mankind, and from the study of this language sprang the earliest phase in the history of astrology.

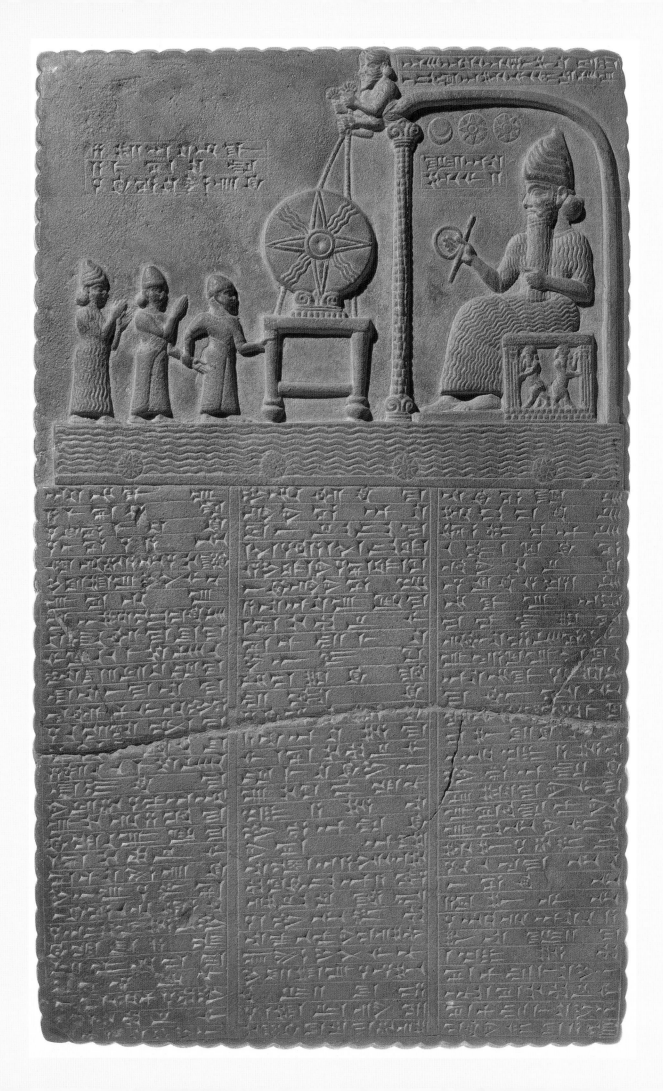

called, confusingly, astrolabes, but they are better referred to by their original name, which was 'Three Stars Each'. These tablets are circular diagrams, divided by radial spokes into twelve equal arcs representing the twelve months of the year. For each month, three stars are identified as rising and becoming visible immediately before dawn, following a period of invisibility – the 'heliacal rising'. Moreover the disc is divided horizontally into three rings or zones: that nearest the centre represents the northern sky, the next represents the central band of sky overhead, while the outer zone represents the southern sky. The whole diagram thus becomes a calendrical star-wheel. The function of the 'Three Stars Each' was to tie each month to an objective astronomical event – the heliacal rising of chosen stars.

This remarkable star-wheel was complete before 1000 BC, and it is intriguing

'Three Stars Each'. These tablets, dated from 1000 BC onwards, are a form of astronomical calendar, giving the pre-dawn risings of three stars in each month. They demonstrate the Babylonian mastery of stellar movements, but also that the Zodiac had not yet been identified.

Department of Western Asiatic Antiquities, The British Museum

for a number of reasons. First it raises the question whether Babylonian astronomers did think of the heavens as a disk or sphere. One of the puzzling gaps in Babylonian science is the absence of any cosmic theory or model which could explain the movements of the heavens, in the way that the later Greek theory of the celestial sphere did. The disk-formation of the 'Three Stars Each' tablets, with the northern point at the centre and the encircling southern horizon, functions as a rough celestial map, although without locating the stars in any precise framework. This inevitably suggests a circular model of the heavens, but such an idea is not found confirmed in any astronomical texts. The second point about these tablets is that they show that the yearly passage of the Sun through the constellations of the Zodiac had not been recognised at this date, for if it had, those star-groups would surely have been used to mark the months. It is certain from other texts that some star-groups had been designated – the Pleiades, Orion and the Great Bear for example. In addition there are Babylonian artefacts inscribed with images of lions and scorpions which almost certainly refer to the constellations. But awareness of the Zodiac band and its possible functions clearly lay still in the future.

The Venus tablets and the 'Three Stars Each' tablets taken together tell us that before 1000 BC the Babylonians had identified several dozen individual stars and had charted their yearly progress across the sky. They had recognised the more complex paths of the planets and, for some of them, had mastered the periodicity of their movements, their risings, settings and times of invisibility. They had begun the process of zoning the sky into three latitudinal bands, which they termed the paths of Anu, Ea and Enlil, after the three great gods of sky, water and air. What they had not done was to devise a framework or reference system within which celestial positions could be related to each other, as we would relate geometrically or graphically. The periodicity of planetary movements was worked out in ingenious arithmetical patterns , in which changes in longitude were tabulated against units of time. Planetary, including lunar or solar, velocities emerged as linear functions of time, which we would now plot as graphs, but which the Babylonians handled expertly in numerical columns. Somehow this periodicity failed to suggest to the Babylonians an orderly cosmic model on the Greek pattern. The celestial positions were computed points in a time-sequence, not components in a real geometric system, turning in space. However, despite being devoid of geometric paths, curves and circles, this system could chart and predict many celestial positions, centuries before Greek astronomy was born.

By the seventh century BC, the advances made by Babylonian astronomers are evident in a new series of tablets known as *Mul. Apin* (the name means simply 'the stars of Apin', which was a constellation approximating to our constellation Triangulum). *Mul. Apin* is virtually a complete compendium of the astronomy of its time, but the features which interest us are that the catalogue of individual stars has increased to around 70, with the dates of their heliacal risings, and that eighteen constellations are now designated as lying in 'the path of the Moon'. The Moon's path through the sky is close to that of the Sun, being inclined at roughly 5° to it, but it is easier to observe, and the eighteen constellations include our twelve Zodiac constellations. It seems therefore that the first movement towards a reference system in the sky made use of the path of the Moon, rather than the ecliptic, the path of the Sun. The history of the constellations is an intriguing but deeply obscure subject, so it is worth listing these star-groups that considered around 700 BC to be 'in the path of the Moon', with their modern equivalents:

Mul	the Mane	the Pleiades
Guanna	the Bull of Anu	Taurus
Sibzianna	Anu's shepherd	Orion
Sugi	the Old Man	Perseus
Gam	the Sickle Sword	Auriga
Mastabbagalgal	the Great Twins	Gemini
Allul	(meaning unknown)	Cancer + Procyon
Urgula	the Lion	Leo
Absin	the Furrow	Virgo
Zibanitum	the Scales	Libra
Girtab	the Scorpion	Scorpio
Pabilsag	the Archer	Sagittarius
Suhurmas	the Goatfish	Capricorn
Gula	the Great Star or Giant	Aquarius
Zibbati	the Tails	Pisces
Simmah	the Great Swallow	Pisces + part of Pegasus
Anunitum	the goddess Anunitum	Pisces + part of Andromeda
Luhunga	the Hired Man	Aries

How much significance was there in these images – the swallow, the furrow or the hired man, instead of the fish, the maiden and the ram? Were they mere images, or did they carry some cultic significance which was later forgotten?

The *Mul. Apin* texts also show an awareness of the general nature of the Sun's path, that it moved each year between two points of high and low altitude, with two median points, and that these four points therefore divide the astronomical year into four, corresponding to the four seasons on earth. These four points became known as the four corners of the sky, and they lay in the constellations Scorpio, Leo, Taurus and Aquarius, which are each 90° apart on the Zodiac circle. The four seasons would be characterised by the invisibility of those four constellations because the Sun was in them during the daytime. This realisation offers a further clue to Babylonian concepts of cosmology. In common with the Egyptians, the Babylonians envisaged the Sun spending the night hours in an underworld; a familiar Babylonian image shows the Sun-god Shamash sawing his way out of the depths of the earth at dawn, while the Gilgamesh epic refers to the gates by which the Sun enters and leaves the world. The stars likewise were believed to return to this underworld at sunrise. But if the Sun was understood to *share* the heavens with the stars, merely making them invisible in its light, then clearly some less mythical form of cosmic cycle must be envisaged – for example Sun and stars both moving in circular paths around the earth. However no such scheme is described in any Babylonian text.

Facing page, above. *A priest or worshipper performing a rite before a ziggurat, with an astral symbol above.* Vorderasiatisches Museum, Berlin

Below. *An astronomical text from the third century BC, from the city of Uruk. On the left is the planet Jupiter, with the constellations Hydra and Leo clearly visible.* Vorderasiatisches Museum, Berlin

ZODIAC AND HOROSCOPE

It was some time between the seventh and fifth centuries BC that the important step was taken of subdividing the path of the Sun into twelve zones or units, each marked by a constellation and corresponding to the passage of one month of the year. Historians and astrologers have been much exercised to provide a religious or mythological background for the Zodiac figures: did Virgo or Aquarius commemorate real people or forgotten deities, and did the Lion and the Bull have some cultic significance? Is some mythic cycle of birth and death, fertility and destruction, embodied in these ancient figures? The answers to these questions are probably beyond recall, and no Mesopotamian myths or legends have been recorded in which these Zodiac creatures appear. It is worth noticing, however, that some of the ancient sages who were supposed to have taught philosophy and law to mankind (see above, p.11) were described as having the forms of animals, or as being half-man and half-animal, like the centaur. It seems just possible that some of the constellations – the fish, the goats, the snakes, and so on – may represent memories of these mythical creatures. If the constellation figures do *not* embody astral myths which have vanished without trace, then we must assume that these images were purely mnemonic, that they served to name and designate star-groups and nothing more. Nevertheless the supposed characters of the Zodiac figures – gentle, warlike, creative, destructive, venomous, balanced and so on – were to be greatly elaborated in the imagination of later astrologers. The Zodiac circle, like all other circles in Babylonian mathematics, was divided into 360°, with each of the twelve arcs covering 30°. This now provided the element that had been missing from Babylonian astronomy: a referencing system within which to locate any celestial body. Any star or planet could be described as being at 10° of Aries, or at 15° of Leo, and so on. This system applied only to celestial longitude, and celestial latitude is mentioned much less frequently; but of course all positions relative to the Zodiac band are longitudinal, and are confined within a band of about 5° either side of the ecliptic. In a representative text of around 400 BC, we now find that twelve star-groups have been culled from the earlier eighteen which were in 'the path of the Moon':

Luhunga	=	Aries
Mul	=	Pleiades (Taurus)
Mas	=	Gemini
Kusu	=	Cancer
Ura	=	Leo
Absin	=	Virgo
Zibanitu	=	Libra
Girtab	=	Scorpio
Pa	=	Sagittarius
Suhur	=	Capricorn
Gu	=	Aquarius
Zib	=	Pisces

The boundaries of some constellations had obviously been redefined in the interval between *Mul.Apin* and this later text, and this must have happened during the laborious task of calculating where the invisible ecliptic line lay among the daytime stars. This must have been accomplished by systematically observing the eastern horizon immediately before dawn and the western horizon immediately after sunset, and noting which constellations rose and set closest to the Sun's position. Over the course of a year, a list of constellations would emerge which, in modern terms, trace out a great circle on the celestial sphere, and through which the Sun appears to move from west to east at the rate of one degree per day. It seems that Babylonian astronomers were verging on the discovery of a spherical celestial model, and a coordinate system of celestial latitude and longitude, but somehow failed to achieve it. It was in this late phase that Babylonian astronomy reached its culmination in the main cities – Babylon itself, in Uruk, Ur and Nippur. The names of outstanding astronomers were recorded for the first time, Naburimanni being active around 500 BC, and Kidinnu a century later; both these names were known to the Greeks, as experts in plotting the paths of the Moon and the other planets.

We have few Babylonian documents which discuss the theory of their astronomy, and none which explain its historical development. What we have are working texts from which we must deduce the theories that lay behind the practice. In the case of the Zodiac, we cannot say when or how its importance came to be recognised, but we do know that by 400 BC, astronomical texts were describing a planet's position as within one of the twelve constellations of the Zodiac now familiar to us. In addition to its role as a celestial reference system, the Zodiac band fulfilled an all-important calendrical role: there were twelve signs of 30° each to mark the passage of time through the solar year, which consisted of twelve equal months, this system now replacing the 'Three Stars Each' formula.

Here we must make an important digression about the structure of the Zodiac. It will immediately be obvious that a problem would arise in defining the boundaries of the twelve constellations. For example, where exactly did Scorpio end and Libra begin? And what of those constellations which plainly overlap each other in longitude, such as Aquarius and Capricorn? Moreover the twelve constellations do not extend over precisely 30° each. For example, Virgo is a much larger constellation than the adjacent Libra, while Aries and Taurus appear crushed together in virtually the same space as that occupied by Pisces. Thus the twelve constellations must really be understood as zones or markers on the Zodiac circle, while for the purposes of measurement in time or space, the concept of the Zodiac *sign* was born. The sign is a fixed arc of 30° on the ecliptic, approximating to but not identical with its parent constellation.

This separation of sign and constellation was to have great consequences for astrology. During the few centuries in which the Babylonians made active use of the Zodiac, around 400 BC to 100 BC, before their astronomical tradition became extinct, it seems that they failed to notice the problem of precession. The earth's axis is slowly oscillating, like the axis of a spinning top. The effect of this

A boundary stone with Zodiac and planetary figures, c.1100 BC. Treaties and contracts, including land boundaries were often placed under the protection of astral deities.
Department of Western Asiatic Antiquities, The British Museum

is to displace the apparent longitudinal position of the Sun against the background of the fixed stars by one degree every 72 years. In calendrical terms, the solar and sidereal years are increasingly out of step with each other. If around 400 BC the Babylonian year began with the spring month of Nissanu, then at the spring equinox the Sun would be in the first degree of the constellation Aries. But over the centuries, the equinoctial point, the point where the ecliptic crosses the celestial equator, would appear to move slowly anti-clockwise, until it would eventually leave Aries altogether and enter the constellation Pisces, where indeed it now stands. This effect is believed to have been analysed by the Greek astronomer Hipparchus in the second century BC, although he could not correctly explain its cause. It is one of the curiosities of astrological history that the post-Babylonian, western tradition of astrology regarded the Zodiacal signs as arcs that were *fixed* on the ecliptic, while their parent constellations drifted slowly away from them in this precessional movement. The result is that the sign of Aries is now occupied partly by the stars of Pisces and partly by those of Aquarius. It is difficult to say why this system was adopted, for there seems to be no reason why the signs should not have been measured from the first degree of the constellation Aries, and thus they would all have retained their link with their parent constellations.

If the astronomical history of the Zodiac is obscure, then our understanding of its astrological history is veiled in even greater darkness. How did these star-groups come to be regarded as entities, having different qualities and powers, just as the planets did, and able to influence human affairs in their various ways? In a general sense, this development is consistent with the Babylonian belief that the stars and planets were themselves divinities; but how the *characters* of the Scorpion, Lion, Crab and so on were elaborated, and their influences balanced with those of the planets, we cannot discover. There are no surviving theoretical texts to explain this.

There was at this time a parallel development of lists called hemerologies – lucky and unlucky days. These tablets indicate whether or not certain days will be propitious for undertakings such as a journey, a marriage, a business transaction, a festival and so on. Such lists are somewhat mysterious for no explanation is ever given why a certain day should be lucky or unlucky, and it is difficult to know how they related to other Babylonian beliefs. But in this context, it would seem to be a natural development that the birth-date of a child would be

seen as indicating something of its future. If the schemes of lucky and unlucky days were added to an observation of celestial omens on the same day, then a movement is started which is moving unmistakably in the direction of personal astrology.

That this movement did occur around 400 BC, linking the influence of the planets with the idea of lucky and unlucky days, is certain from the survival of the first cuneiform horoscopes. In these tablets, positions of planets are given within the Zodiac signs, and interpretations about the future life of the child are sometimes drawn out. A horoscope from 235 BC reads:

> Year 77 (of the Seleucid era), the fourth day, in the last part of the night, Aristokrates was born. That day: Moon in Leo, Sun in 12° 30° of Gemini, Jupiter in 18° Sagittarius. The place of Jupiter means his life will be regular, he will become rich, he will grow old, his days will be numerous. Venus in 4° Taurus. The place of Venus means wherever he may go it will be favourable to him. He will have sons and daughters…

In some of these early horoscopes, no predictions at all are given, just celestial positions, so perhaps the interpretation was given verbally. Where predictions do appear, they are extremely brief, and do not much resemble anything which we would regard as a personal horoscope. The number of these surviving cuneiform

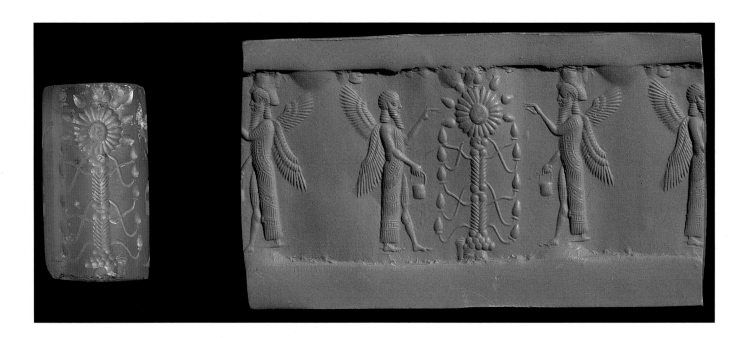

Apkallus tending the sacred tree. Babylonian mythology is full of winged genii, half man and half beast, who may represent the ancient divinities who were thought to have revealed the sciences, including astrology, to mankind.

Department of Western Asiatic Antiquities, The British Museum

horoscopes is very small, no more than a handful from the years 400–100 BC. But the important point is that they relate to an individual's moment of birth, which may have been calculated from a remote point in time, and from which long-term predictions are made. The omens of the earlier period were all short-term, never predicting events more than one year ahead, and often less. There is also an important broadening of the social scope of astrology: the fate of any individual, not merely kings or princes, might be read from the configuration of the heavens at the moment of birth. There was thus a movement towards a view of celestial influence which was sharper and more personal than before, and this carried with it the need to develop improved techniques of reading the heavens. We wonder what the social reasons for this widening of astrology may have been: did it reflect a more personal religious feeling among the people about the gods, or was it simply that astrologers realised that all men, not merely kings, longed to know their future, and were prepared to pay for that knowledge?

In this late phase then, Babylonian astronomical skills, primarily their key discovery of the periodicity of celestial events, became combined with their star-worship to produce the distinctive creation of the astrologer, the personal horoscope, albeit of a brief and rather primitive kind. Instead of singling out one or two general omens – a halo around the Moon, or the occultation of two planets – the entire heavens became a tapestry upon which complex patterns of celestial meaning were constantly being woven, and which the maturing skill of the astrologer attempted to interpret. And the crucial change was that these celestial patterns affected everybody – they were no longer tied to the king and his court. The charting of celestial positions, and the ability to draw out their meaning required special astronomical and divinatory skills, and it clearly implies the existence of a set of systematic beliefs about the power of the heavens over human life. This proto-astrology therefore combined aspects of exact science with religious or philosophical principles.

What the future course of Babylonian astrology might have been, having arrived at this important threshold, is now impossible to say, for political events in the fourth century BC and after, shifted the centre of scientific learning away from Babylonia. After the conquest of the Mesopotamian region first by the Persians and then by the Greeks, a flow of ideas and people was set up which deeply affected religion and science. The use of cuneiform ceased in government documents during the Achaemenian (Persian) period , when it was replaced by Aramaic and then by Greek. Only a few religious and astronomical texts continued to be written in cuneiform until around 100 BC. Greece was overpopulated in this period, and, following Alexander's conquests, a considerable process of Greek colonisation in Mesopotamia took place, bringing Greek language, thought and science with it. The Greeks in turn were often drawn to the eastern religions, which seemed deeper and more satisfying than their own. The subject of the horoscope mentioned above, Aristokrates, had a Greek name, and was almost certainly a member of an immigrant family.

It was in the period of Parthian domination from around 125 BC onwards that the last embers of Mesopotamian science and religion were extinguished. The astronomer-priests were no more, and cuneiform texts cease. There is a great scarcity of documents of any kind now, or of significant artefacts from this region. Local dynasts functioned autonomously, and the new cities of Ctesiphon, Deuro-Europos and Charax were without any intellectual tradition. The history of this dark period has to be written from the references in Greek authors, for indigenous sources are scarce. Virtually all recollection of the great civilisations of Mesopotamia was now wiped from human memory. Iranian and other oriental and mystery religions flourished, and the eastern gods would become identified with the gods of the Greek pantheon. The only system of mathematics and astronomy now available in the Hellenistic world was the Greek. The Babylonian tradition had withered and died, but not before vital elements of its astronomy and its astral religion had been carried through the Greek world, to Egypt for example, where they sprang into new and vigorous life.

CHAPTER TWO

GREECE:

THE SYSTEM PERFECTED

BABYLONIA AND GREECE

Political events played a major role in spreading astrology from its birthplace in Babylonia out into the wider world of the ancient near east. In 539 BC, the kingdom of Babylonia was seized by King Cyrus of Persia, and for the next two centuries it formed part of the Achaemenid Empire, which reached from Thrace and the Black Sea eastwards to the Indus and southwards into Egypt. In this context the cults of Zoroastrianism and Mithraism became diffused far beyond their Persian homeland, while the Persians in turn were exposed to the astral religion and the astronomical science of Babylonia. By 330 BC, the Achaemenid Empire had itself fallen to Alexander the Great, and the subsequent movement and resettlement of peoples throughout the entire region opened new channels of intellectual communication between east and west. The religions of Persia and Babylonia made a deep impression on the Greeks, while the mathematics of Greece provided a new language for the practitioners of the exact sciences throughout the ancient near east. The Hellenistic world in the three centuries before Christ witnessed a complex merging and re-shaping of religion, philosophy and science. The precise pathways by which knowledge and beliefs – astrology among them – were carried between Persia, Mesopotamia, Egypt, Asia Minor and Greece are impossible to trace, but certain key texts have survived which bear witness to the geographical spread of early astrology.

Consider this statement from Herodotus, describing what he had learned of Egyptian astrology when he visited that country around 450 BC:

> I pass to other inventions of the Egyptians. They assign each month and each day to some god; they can tell what fortune and what end and what disposition a man shall have according to the day of his birth. They have made themselves more omens than all other nations together; when an ominous thing happens they take note of the outcome and write it down, and if something of a like kind happens again, they think it will have a like result.

This obviously describes a fairly mature system of astrology, consisting of omens, lists of lucky and unlucky days, and perhaps even personal horoscopes. But the system is *Babylonian*; the astronomy and religion of ancient Egypt knew no such tradition, and it is clear that these beliefs must have been transmitted to Egypt from Babylonia during the Achaemenid period, that is in the century preceding Herodotus's visit. Such a well-informed writer as Herodotus was apparently ignorant of the character of Babylonian science, and he regarded astral divination as an invention of the Egyptians. By contrast, approximately a century later, the philosopher Theophrastus, the head of Aristotle's Athenian school, was referring to the 'Chaldean' art of predicting the future, and the mathematician and astronomer, Eudoxus of Cnidus, was repudiating the claims of the Chaldeans to foretell a person's character from his birth-date. In the Graeco-Roman world,

the term Chaldean became synonymous with astrologer, fortune-teller or magus; therefore the role of Babylonian science in this connection must have been recognised. Eudoxus penned the first known Greek description of the constellations, including all those of the Babylonian zodiac, but adding those relating to the Greek myths, the Perseus-Andromeda group, and it seems certain that he had made a personal study of Babylonian astronomy. Eudoxus's work on the constellations has not survived, but it was used as the model for another important work which has – the *Phaenomena* by Aratus of Soli. This is a description in verse of the forty-eight classical constellations, and it functioned as a handbook of popular astronomy throughout the Graeco-Roman period, and indeed into the middle ages. The Greek constellations, the *sphaera Graecanica*, did not replace all other celestial systems overnight, and elements of a *sphaera barbarica*, preserving Egyptian and Mesopotamian star-groups, were known to astronomers for many centuries.

Another key text in the history of Greek astrology is found in the Roman writer Vitruvius in the first century BC:

> It must be allowed that we can know what effects the twelve signs, and the
> Sun and the Moon and the five planets have on the course of human life,

The Farnese Atlas: the earliest known depiction of the classical constellations, including the Zodiac, appears on this sculpture of the first century BC.
Museo Nazionale, Naples

from astrology and the calculations of the Chaldeans. For the genethlialogical art is properly theirs, by which they are able to unfold past and future events from their astronomical calculations. And many have come from that race of the Chaldeans to leave us their discoveries, which are full of acuteness and learning. The first was Berosus, who settled on the island of Kos, and taught there, and after him the learned Antipater, and then Achinapolus, who however set out his genethlialogical calculations not from the date of birth but from that of conception.

Berosus was a well-known figure who, around 300 BC, wrote in Greek an account of the history and culture of Babylonia, which preserved virtually all that was known of that civilisation in the classical world. Pliny later cited Berosus's claim that Babylonian culture, including its astronomy, reached back 490,000 years! The tradition that Berosus migrated to Kos is well-attested, and it may be significant that Kos became the birth-place of the school of Hippocratic medicine, in

The celestial sphere, the fundamental model of the heavens in Greek thought, geometrically divided into poles, tropics, equator and ecliptic.
Private collection

which astrology played an important part. It may be that Berosus was indeed a pivotal figure in the westward spread of astrology; Pliny says that a statue of Berosus was erected in Athens, which had a golden tongue, as a symbol of his power to predict the future. However it is impossible to say how detailed Berosus's astrological writings may have been, because his work has survived only in fragmentary quotations, such as those of Vitruvius and Pliny. The testimony of Herodotus and Vitruvius, the case of Eudoxus and that of Berosus, all establish beyond doubt that there was a large-scale importation of astrological ideas from Babylonia into the Hellenistic world. Yet it is equally clear that, by the early years of the first century AD, the first astrological writer of Graeco-Roman world, Marcus Manilius, was describing a set of doctrines which had developed out of all recognition from these Babylonian origins. The changes undergone by astrology in the three centuries between Berosus and Manilius determined its whole character and its future; but they are virtually impossible to pin down in time and place, or to ascribe to individual thinkers.

In trying to understand astrology's transition from Babylonian cult to Greek science, two problems confront us, one technical and the other philosophical: what did Greek science bring to the technique of proto-astrology to make it more precise, more sophisticated and more convincing than it had previously been? And what was the intellectual appeal of the newer, scientific astrology, which caused it to flourish and spread throughout the Graeco-Roman world?

At the time when the great Babylonian star-catalogue *Mul.Apin* was taking shape, around 700 BC, Greek astronomy was on the level of folk-wisdom. From Homer and Hesiod it is evident that a few northern constellations were known but not the Zodiac, while the planets had purely descriptive names, the 'herald of dawn', the 'fiery star' and so on. The heavens were observed because they marked the passage of time for the farmer, and helped the seafarer to navigate. There was no written body of astronomical knowledge, and no celestial cults – the Greeks did not worship the Sun, Moon or other heavenly bodies as divinities. But the Greek approach to astronomy was to change profoundly over the next five centuries, and the result was some of the most enduring achievements of western science.

The central concept which emerged in Greek astronomy was that of the celestial sphere, which could be analysed and charted in geometric terms. The seeds of this cosmic model appeared first in the fifth century BC: Parmenides was probably the first to argue explicitly that the earth itself was a sphere, while in the school of Pythagoras it was an article of faith that the sphere was nature's most perfect shape, and that the heavens too must be spherical, and moving in circular motion. By the fourth century BC, the twin giants of Greek philosophy, Plato and Aristotle, were both speaking of the universe as a complex of interlocking spheres, upon which the Sun, Moon, stars and planets were carried in uniform circular motion about the earth, which formed the centre of the whole system. The Greek mathematicians, Eudoxus, Apollonius, Hipparchus and others, set out to show that the language of geometry could be applied to the observations of the astronomers, in order to build an accurate model of the movements of the heavens. In its early stages this spherical model was less precise and powerfully predictive than the Babylonian arithmetical functions. But the great difference was that it represented a cosmic model that could be visualised physically: it was coherent and comprehensible. It was accessible to the non-specialist, and it unified the movements of the heavens into a geometric system. Risings and settings, eclipses, retrograde motions – these could all now be seen as the visible effects of bodies moving in relation to each other in regular geometric paths. There is some evidence that by the third century BC, models of this cosmic system were being built, by Archimedes for example. Of course it had not the scientific status of a physical system; what the heavenly spheres actually were, and how they moved, could not be explained. But with the work of Hipparchus, and above all of Ptolemy of Alexandria, celestial geometry achieved the power to predict the position of any star or planet in any epoch, past, present or future. The model of the celestial sphere, inscribed with poles and tropics, equator and ecliptic, all measurable by means of latitude and longitude, became the fundamental working tool of the astronomer, his map of the universe.

The relevance of all this to astrology is clear: the movements of the heavenly bodies and the charting of horoscopes acquired a new, precise and agreed language to describe the configuration of the heavens. The horoscope chart could now be seen as a selective map of the heavens centred on the earth and charted for a specific moment in time. The boundary of this map, its outer circle, was the all-important ecliptic band, marked by the twelve Zodiac signs and divided into 360°. Within this circle, the astrologer could place the heavenly bodies which

The Sources of Indian Astrology

As early as the mid-first millennium BC, Babylonian astronomy of the kind found in the *Mul.Apin* texts had reached India, and with it the concept of celestial omens. Vedic texts of this period, for example the *Atharvaveda*, refer to *santi*, or pacification rituals designed to appease the gods who had sent the omens. The gods were of course the native gods of India, including Visnu and Soma, and among the omens they employed were shapes of animals seen in clouds, haloes around the Sun or Moon, meteors and comets: all of these omens are echoes of those found in Babylonian sources. These Indian omen texts date from shortly after the Achaemenid occupation of northern India, around 530 BC: thus the pathway by which Babylonian science and religious practices could reach India is clear. About a century later, evidence about the way omens had taken root in India comes from no less a figure than the Buddha himself. The Buddha preached a sermon, *Brahmajalasutta*, condemning the immoral activities engaged in by certain holy men in return for food, activities which encouraged occultism and superstition. These included exorcism and divination, and again the forms of celestial divination parallel exactly the Babylonian models. The Buddha (or at least the author of this sermon attributed to him) was evidently very familiar with omens derived from planets, stars, eclipses, earthquakes and atmospheric storms. Thus from the sixth to the third century BC, there was in India a programme of translation and adaptation of this aspect of Babylonian astral religion, and it was this which formed the basis of the Indian astrological tradition.

After the third century BC, military and then trading contacts between India and the Graeco-Roman world multiplied, permitting the new currents of Greek science to reach India, and to complete the structure of Indian astrology. Greek texts were now translated into Sanskrit, and resulted in a mature form of mathematical astrology on the Hellenistic pattern. A typical and very influential text was the *Yavanajataka* composed by Sphujidhavaja around 270 AD, a verse version of a Greek astrological treatise. In this work, a large number of astrological terms are simply transliterated from Greek into Sanskrit, clearly demonstrating that the writer was importing Hellenistic ideas for which there was no Indian equivalent. The terms decans, midheaven, trigon, horia and many others became components in an Indian version of the same form of technical astrology which are found in Manilius and Ptolemy. The *Yavanajataka* was in fact a seminal work of Indian astrology, which formed the basis of much of what followed. Certain concepts were however Indian inventions, such as interrogations and the system of lunar mansions. An interrogation was a type of katarchic astrology based on the interpretation of the heavens at the moment when a question was asked; it had no parallel in Greek astrology. The lunar mansions – *naksatras* – were 28 or 29 star-groups, each with its own characteristics, associated with the Moon rather than the Sun. These Indian ideas were later absorbed by Islamic astrologers, and transmitted in due course to the west. Interrogations became an important part of mainstream astrology, but the system of lunar mansions, while certainly known to many in the west, somehow failed to establish itself, perhaps because it functioned as an alternative Zodiac.

By the late fifth century AD, Indian astrological texts were multiplying, and Hellenistic techniques were firmly established. A key text in this period is the *Brhajjataka* by Varahamihira, composed around 550 AD. This is of special interest because it demonstrates the adoption of the Greek names for the Zodiac signs and planets, and again these take the form of direct transliterations. The Sanskrit *Aru* is Ares (Mars), *Asphujit* is Aphrodite (Venus), *Kona* is Kronos (Saturn), *Pathona* is Parthenos (Virgo), *Leya* is Leo, and so on. Indian astrology continued to add its own techniques and interpretative concepts, an example of the latter being the caste system. But its origin lay entirely in Babylonia and Greece, mirroring the transition which occurred in the Hellenistic world from astral omens to mathematical science. Astrology flourished in India for centuries, and since there was no scientific revolution there, it never suffered a catastrophic decline as it did in the west, but has played a unbroken role in Indian popular culture.

interested him, which were originally the Sun, Moon and five planets, although the chart would soon be enriched with a whole host of additional points of importance. The heavens came to be seen as an arena where competing forces,

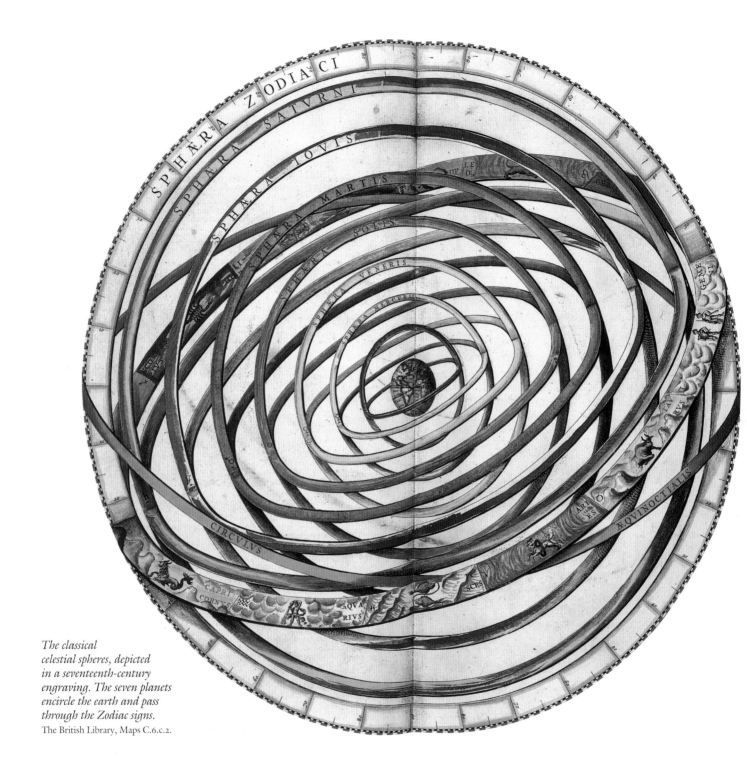

The classical celestial spheres, depicted in a seventeenth-century engraving. The seven planets encircle the earth and pass through the Zodiac signs.
The British Library, Maps C.6.c.2.

positive and negative, interacted and conflicted, not in a way which was chaotic, but in a way which might be rationalised by geometric measurement, and whose effects were capable of being predicted. The plotting of celestial positions, progressed forwards or backwards in time, was a demanding mathematical exercise, and the number of astrologers capable of performing the calculations themselves was never great at any time in history, so that the majority came to rely on tables of positions calculated by experts. As Greek astrology developed, it departed radically from its Babylonian roots; the techniques of astrology pre-supposed the Aristotelian cosmic structure, and the ability to compute precise positions on the celestial sphere.

THE PHILOSOPHICAL BACKGROUND TO GREEK ASTROLOGY

Before going on to examine how this new scientific understanding of the heavens was applied in detail to astrology, we must pause to ask why astrology should hold any appeal for the Greeks at all? Why did a people who were in the process of developing an unprecedented form of rational, analytical philosophy, and who had no tradition of astral religion, embrace astrology so fervently? Why, in the words of one historian, did astrology 'fall upon the Hellenistic mind as a new disease falls upon some remote island people '? The answer seems to be that, in addition to importing astronomy from the near east, the Greeks also found there a form of religious philosophy which was new to them, which appealed to them deeply, and which predisposed them to accept and develop the doctrines of astrology.

The early religion of the Greeks had little which we would recognise as spiritual in its makeup. Its cosmogony was crude, and its deities were simply human characters with superhuman powers; they could be as quarrelsome, selfish and deceitful as any mortal. These imperfect deities began their reign *after* the creation of the world, in which

Ahura Mazda, the principal deity of the Persian religion. The personal, spiritual religion of Persia greatly impressed Greek thinkers, and helped prepare their minds for astrology.

they had played no part, and they now dwelled not in the heavens but on Mount Olympus. Man was not even considered to possess an immortal soul: the dead in Hades, the virtuous as well as the sinful, were mere shadows, miserable reflections of their living selves.

From around 500 BC there is evidence that a very different form of cosmic religion had become an international phenomenon, and had arrived in the Greek world. The immediate source of this religion, in which man's destiny was believed to lie in his relationship to a transcendent heavenly power, was Persia, although its ultimate source may have been in Vedic India. The Persian religion ascribed to Zoroaster, which became the official religion of the Achaemenid state, worshipped a creator-god, *Ahura Mazda* ('great lord') who dwelled in heaven and who far transcended all human imperfections. Man possessed an immortal soul bound in an earthly body, and at death that soul would be released to ascend to its true home in the heavens. A subsidiary Persian deity, Mithra, became, by a process which is not understood, the focus of a mystery religion which spread throughout the Roman world, and whose promise was to liberate the souls of its adherents to find unity with the godhead.

There is no doubt that by the fourth century BC, Greek philosophers were well aware of this exciting new current of thought from the east. Followers of Pythagoras taught that he had been a personal pupil of Zoroaster in Babylon; Eudoxus, the great mathematician, was reported to have endorsed Zoroaster's teachings; Heraclitus's doctrine that fire was the element at the heart of nature was also said to have been borrowed from Persian religion. Perhaps the clearest sign of the Greek adoption of these ideas lies in the identification of their gods with those of Persia: in the second century BC in Asia minor, Zeus was being worshipped as 'Oromazdes', and Apollo as Mithra. Even more significant for the future of astrology was the Hellenisation of the Babylonian planetary deities. Traditional Greek names had been purely descriptive: Venus was 'the morning star',

Mars was 'the fiery star' and so on. The planets played no great part in religion or science, and the philosopher Democritus had even said that he was uncertain how many planets there were. Yet by around 400 BC, the era of Plato, the Greeks had re-named the five planets as the stars of Zeus, Kronos, Ares, Aphrodite and Hermes, corresponding directly to Babylonian gods Marduk, Ninib, Nergal, Ishtar and Nabu. The Greek names became, in their Latin equivalents, Jupiter, Saturn, Mars, Venus and Mercury. The identification of the planets with personal deities who were capable of swaying human destiny is, like the borrowing of the zodiacal constellations and the division of the circle into 360°, an unmistakable signature of Babylonian influence.

This new, more mature and spiritualised approach to religion and the cosmos became articulate in the fourth century BC in no less a figure than Plato. The whole tendency of Platonic thought was to seek the hidden, ideal, transcendent archetypes which were believed to lie behind and govern the world of nature. The very word by which Plato and his contemporaries designated the universe – 'cosmos' – signified an ordered, harmonious structure. Man could perceive and participate in this order because he possessed an immortal soul which was part of it. In his only extended work on natural science, *Timaeus*, Plato argued that the universe had been created by a rational power, which he called the *demiurge*, the 'craftsman'. This craftsman fashioned the human soul from the same material from which he made the stars, and indeed each human soul had originated in a star before being incarnated in human flesh. The stars were divine, living beings, and it was man's destiny to return to his place among them, indeed Plato went further and proposed that the parts of the cosmos were so interrelated that we must believe the universe to be a single living spirit, a world-soul. These extraordinary theories of cosmic sympathy were unlike anything previously known in Greek religion, but they show striking points of similarity with the eastern religions transmitted to Greece from Persia. They were to influence discussions about man and the cosmos among pagans and Christians, scientists and mystics, for almost 2,000 years. There is a passage in *Timaeus* which suggests that Plato was personally aware of the beginnings of astrology, for he speaks of the movements of the stars and the planets as 'the dance of the gods', and he says that their periodic conjunctions and oppositions 'have caused fear and anxious conjecture about the future to those not able to calculate their movements'. This implies that there did exist a group of people – astrologers – who *were* able to calculate these movements and foretell their effects.

While not sharing Plato's other-worldly stance, Aristotle too taught that the stars and planets were divine beings, whose eternal, regular motion was explicable only if they were impelled by will and intelligence. Aristotle's system of physics also contained a theory which was to have a deep and long-lasting influence on astrology. He had already formulated the doctrine that motion is the primary cause of change, and in his work *On Generation and Corruption*, he posited that the two great aspects of change in earthly things, coming-into-being and destruction, were caused by the Sun, and specifically by the Sun's advancing and retreating motion around the ecliptic. The very elements of which all the earthly realm was composed owed their existence to this motion, indeed Aristotle spoke of the four elements as being related to the heavens as tools are to an artificer. This theory contained many obscurities and threw up many problems; for example, why then does not all generation and decay take place within the cycle of a single year? Nevertheless Aristotle's authority ensured that this theory was widely known and discussed, and his weight was added to those philosophers who sought to link the natural processes which occurred on earth with those which occurred in the heavens.

One further strand in Greek philosophy helped to prepare the Greek mind for the doctrines of astrology: we know from many literary and philosophical works that there existed a cult of *tyche* – fortune or chance – and that the Greeks were tormented by the sense that humanity and history were at the mercy of blind hazard, making and unmaking lives and fortunes, beyond control or prediction.

Tyche, the classical goddess of fortune, surrounded by a Zodiac: there were obvious points of contact between the cult of Tyche and the astrological doctrine of destiny.
Cincinatti Art Museum

Chance was thought of as a more real and pervasive force even than the gods, indeed it seems that the cult of *tyche* served to undermine serious belief in the gods. As the Roman poet Lucan would put it:

> There are no gods; to say Jove reigns is wrong,
> Tis blind Chance that moves the years along.

Greek thinkers made great efforts to convert chance, the enemy of philosophy, into its ally. The most promising strategy was to shift the emphasis from chance to destiny, to build a picture of the events of human history as an ordered, purposeful flow. It was the Stoic school of philosophy which identified fate or destiny with divine reason. In this view, everything that happened in both the cosmic and human realms belonged in one indissoluble process. The task of the philosopher therefore was to teach acceptance of that process, and avoidance of the pain and striving which comes from resisting destiny. The Stoic ideal was *apatheia*, which was not apathy in the modern sense, but freedom from suffering. The Stoic philosophy became one of the leading intellectual forces in the Graceo-Roman world, and the sense that destiny was an objective reality pervading the world of nature and of man would clearly dispose its adherents to accept the arguments of the astrologers. Posidonius, who taught in Rhodes in the first century BC, was one of the leading thinkers responsible for spreading Greek Stoicism through the

The Planets as Gods

THE central doctrine of ancient astrology was that the planets shaped earthly events by the exercise of divine power, which in turn meant that the planets were themselves divinities. This belief was established in Babylonia by 1000 BC, and it formed part of the omen-culture which touched so many areas of Babylonian life. The Babylonian planetary gods were:

Saturn	–	Ninib
Jupiter	–	Marduk
Mars	–	Nergal
Venus	–	Ishtar
Mercury	–	Nabu

At this early stage, Greek observational astronomy was non-existent. In the texts which stand at the very beginning of Greek literature, the Homeric poems of the seventh or eighth century BC, only Venus was identified by name: as the morning star it was called Eosphorus, and as the evening star Hesperos. As late as 450 BC the philosopher Democritus not only knew nothing about the planets, but admitted that he was unsure even how many there were. However at the same period, writers of the Pythagorean school were describing the seven planets (including the Sun and Moon), and had given them descriptive names:

Saturn	–	Phainon
Jupiter	–	Phaeton
Mars	–	Pyroeis
Venus	–	Phosphoros
Mercury	–	Stilbon

All these names are rather general, meaning simply, 'shining' or 'light-bringing' or 'glittering'; only Pyroeis is specific, meaning 'fiery'. Yet if we move forward one century to the Platonic writings, we find that the planets are invariably given the names of the personal deities in the Greek pantheon:

Saturn	–	Star of Kronos
Jupiter	–	Star of Zeus
Mars	–	Star of Ares
Venus	–	Star of Aphrodite
Mercury	–	Star of Hermes

This was clearly a decisive intellectual step, for the Greeks had never previously regarded the heavenly bodies as divinities, nor practised any form of astral religion. Where then did it come from? The pseudo-Platonic dialogue *Epinomis*, probably written by a pupil of Plato, ascribes the discovery of these names to 'barbarians' who first observed 'the cosmic gods', and mentions Egypt and Syria as the sources of this wisdom. While the author was cor-

rect in supposing an eastern origin for these ideas, he wrongly followed the prevailing Greek belief that Egypt was their fountainhead, a belief which early Greek visitors to Egypt, such as Herodotus, had formed after learning about the Egyptian sky-deities. It is true that by this time – the fourth century BC – the Egyptians had identified the planets with their gods: Jupiter was the Star of Osiris, Venus the Star of Isis and so on. However this was a late Egyptian innovation, belonging to the Hellenistic period, and before this the Egyptians had in fact shown no interest in the planets, astronomical or astrological.

The true source of the idea that the planets were gods was undoubtedly Babylonian, and the link, the pathway taken by this idea from Babylonia to other cultures, was the Persian domination of Mesopotamia from the sixth century BC. This period of Persian hegemony made possible a flow of religious and intellectual ideas throughout the ancient near east, including Egypt. The Persians too accepted the Babylonian identification of the planets with gods: the Sun became Mithras, while Jupiter (the Babylonian Marduk) became Ahura Mazda, the 'Great Lord' of Zoroastrianism. In Syria and Asia Minor this name appeared as Oramazdes. Thus by the fifth century BC, at exactly the period when Babylonian astrology had reached its fullest development and was beginning to radiate across the entire region, this identification of planets with the divinities of the various pantheons is also found spreading to all neighbouring cultures, to Persia, to Egypt and to Greece.

The clear inference is that these two facts were intimately connected. Astrology could not function, could not command belief, unless some transcendent power could be shown to reside in the planets, and their elevation to the status of divinities obviously achieved this at a stroke. The appearance of planetary gods in cultures with no tradition of astral religion, such as Greece, or of planetary astronomy such as Egypt, was a necessary precondition for the acceptance of astrology. In the hands of later Greek theorists, a very different, quasi-scientific view of celestial influence would emerge; but there is no doubt that in this earliest phase, the planetary influence was understood to be purely the will of the gods, and therefore the planets and the gods must be one.

Roman world; his influence was acknowledged by, among others, Cicero and Seneca, and he believed that nature offered signs of future events to those who could read them.

We can now draw together these intellectual threads. First, a mature form of astronomy had been learned from Babylonia, central to which was the mathematical description of the movements of the heavens, but which also involved the firm belief that what happened in the heavens foretold in some way what was to happen on earth. Second, a more elevated and spiritual philosophy of man was evolving, drawn from eastern sources, in which man's soul was linked to transcendent powers which dwelled in the heavens. These ideas were articulated by the leading thinkers of the Greek world, Plato and Aristotle. Third, the Stoic school of philosophy sought to show that the processes of nature and history were not the result of blind chance but were the workings of a divine reason which shaped human destiny and which man must learn to accept. All these intellectual movements, in their different ways, carried with them a powerful motive to study the heavens in an attempt to uncover the link between man and the stars. If there was a divine reason shaping the destiny of man and the universe, how exactly could the heavens be read so as to make it accessible? Was there a code, a scientific language, which could unlock these secrets? This was the essential background to the development of astrology in the Greek world. The whole enterprise used a language which now appears mystical and overwhelmingly ambitious, but in the context of its time it was rational and scientific; it was an attempt to give meaning to existence, to escape from intellectual uncertainty and to rationalise fate. Throughout the Hellenistic and Roman periods, especially the latter, the strength of stellar religion would underpin the development of astrology.

MARCUS MANILIUS: THE FIRST ASTROLOGICAL TREATISE

By the first century BC, astrology had established itself in a fairly mature form in the Graeco-Roman world, that is in cities such as Antioch, Alexandria and Pergamum, as well as in Athens and Rome. Alexandria in particular was evidently the centre in which astrology developed most strongly, where philosophy and science met, and where some elements from Egyptian astronomy were merged with the Babylonian and Greek traditions. The evidence for the spread of astrology is threefold: there are the references to astrology made by classical writers (like that of Vitruvius given above, but also in poets and dramatists such as Ennius and Plautus); there is the considerable number of Greek horoscopes; and there are the first systematic treatises on astrology. These treatises, by Marcus Manilius and Vettius Valens, were written in the first century AD, but were evidently based on a mature body of teachings, and probably on written sources now lost. There are also the anonymous texts of uncertain date, but belonging in this period, known as the Hermetic writings, which deal on a mystical level with astrology, and also with Platonic philosophy, magic and alchemy. In all these sources we find a form of astrology which makes use of mathematical calculation and a technical language quite different from the proto-astrology of Babylonia. This language is often obscure or confused, but some of its general principles are clearly recognisable, for they still underpin the astrology of today.

The survival of almost two hundred papyrus horoscopes written in Greek and Demotic between the years 100 BC and 400 AD offers an insight into the practices and obscurities of Graeco-Roman astrology. A few of these horoscopes are accompanied by circular diagrams, the forerunners of the familiar nativity chart. More formally-structured horoscope diagrams would appear later, in Byzantine manuscripts, from which the classical western diagram would evolve. Some of these early texts are extremely brief, and give no predictions, only the astronomical

The celestial sphere in a Renaissance painting. The sphere bears the stars on its surface, and here it is turned by an angel, a Christianised version of Aristotle's prime mover.
The Vatican

positions, and these only in general terms:

> Nativity of Cyrus, 97th year of Diocletian,
> Menheir (month) 25, 9th hour of the day,
> Horoscopos in Cancer,
> Jupiter in Libra,
> Sun, Venus and Mercury in Pisces,
> Mars and Saturn in Taurus,
> Moon in Gemini,
> Lot of Fortune in Libra.

A Greek papyrus horoscope containing the elaborate horoscope for 1 April 81 AD.
The British Library, Pap.130

Brief as this is, we notice some unusual terms, which are evidently part of a technical astrological vocabulary – 'Horoscopos' and 'Lot of Fortune'. This technical language is still more in evidence in some of the longer, more discursive horoscopes, such as this one, datable to 1 April 84 AD:

> The divine and light-giving Moon, waxing in crescent, was running in Taurus 13 degrees; in the sign of Venus in its own exaltation; in the terms of Mercury, in a female and solid sign; like gold mounting the back of Taurus; in the second decan called Aroth; its dodecatemorion was shining about the sign place in Scorpio.

Here the words that strike us are 'exaltation', 'terms', 'decan', and 'dodecatemorion', and it is not clear at first sight whether the phrase 'female and solid' is a poetic metaphor, or whether it too represents some technical category. These terms and many more are also found in the horoscopes preserved in literary works, such the *Anthology* by Vettius Valens. This is the first of many such works which collected horoscopes of famous subjects in order to build up a picture of the qualities of the stars and planets, as exemplified in the lives of the famous and the infamous. This horoscope is datable to 24 January 76 AD, and is that of the Emperor Hadrian:

> There was a person having the Sun in Aquarius 8°, the Moon and Jupiter and the horoscopos, the three together, at the first degree of the same sign,

namely Aquarius; Saturn in Capricorn 5°, Mercury with it at 12°, Venus in Pisces 12°, and Mars with it at 22°; midheaven in Scorpio 22°... Such a person was adopted by a certain Emperor akin to him, and having lived with him two years, became Emperor about his 42nd year, and was wise and educated, so that he was honoured by shrines and temples, and he was married to one wife from maidenhood and was childless and had one sister, and he was at discord and conflict with his own relatives. When he reached his 63rd year he died, a victim of dropsy and asthma. And why it happened this way is explained as follows. He became Emperor because the two luminaries, Sun and Moon, were with the horoscope...and with Jupiter, which was also due to make its morning phase after seven days. And its (Moon's) attending stars were themselves found in favourable positions, Venus in her own exaltation, Mars in its own triangle...and besides the cosmos-ruling Sun was its (Moon's) attendant in the subsequent degrees, and had as attending stars Saturn in its own house, and Mercury, both at their morning rising. It is also a sign that the Moon was about to come into conjunction with a certain bright fixed star which is in the 20th degree of Aquarius. For it is necessary to look at the conjunctions of the Moon not only with the planets but also with the fixed stars.

It is evident that behind this horoscope lies the Greek geometric model of the heavens, in which the planets progress through the measured circle of the heavens. But is also evident that we have by this date a three-level system: first, the astronomical positions, measured in degrees around the ecliptic; second, a technical language, a series of criteria by which various points in that circle are judged to be of particular importance; and third, a body of rules by which the significance of these positions can be interpreted. In this horoscope we have some further examples of that technical language – 'midheaven', 'triangle', 'house', and 'conjunction'. Some of these terms entered permanently into the astrological tradition, and are still familiar today, but in order to understand how these ideas were used in their own time, and how that tradition was founded, we must turn to the explanations given by contemporary writers, primarily Marcus Manilius and Ptolemy of Alexandria. What we are never given however, is an explanation of the third level of the system: having established all the celestial positions and learned the technical language, what do they mean for the man or woman born under that configuration of stars? Vettius Valens's collection of horoscopes offers the system complete – the horoscope positions and their meanings, but no explanation of how we get from one to the other. If a planned programme of research had ever taken place to establish the consequences of certain celestial positions – in modern terms a statistical analysis – then no record of it has survived anywhere in astrological literature. What has survived is a body of rules or axioms, which foretell the probable results of various celestial positions, what we may expect if a planet is in a certain sign or house or aspect. These axioms were sometimes collected together to form texts in their own right, one of the most celebrated being a work known as *Centiloquium*, ('The Hundred Sayings') which was attributed to Ptolemy, but which was not actually his work. Such texts offered an instant guide to the way in which the powers of the planets were believed to wax or wane through the various points on the ecliptic, but they offered no evidence or justification in support of these rules. To give just one simple example from the *Centiloquium*: 'When a sickness begins when the Moon is in a sign in which at birth there was a malevolent planet...that sickness will be dangerous'. This has the appearance of a firm, empirical rule, but how it was arrived at, and how often its validity has been confirmed, the author does not attempt to explain. Nor were these rules fixed and immutable, and astrologers considered themselves free to develop different interpretations of celestial events. The apparently arbitrary nature of these rules is one of the cruxes of astrological history: they were the final weapon in the astrologer's armoury, by which he made sense of all his data, yet it seems impossible to discover how or by whom they were devised, or what their rational basis might be.

Nothing is known of Marcus Manilius, whose book *Astronomicon* was composed in the very earliest years of the Christian era, around 10–15 AD, but it is significant that the work springs from the reign of Tiberius, when astrology rose to its position of high influence in Roman thought. It is curious that the earliest full treatise on astrology from the Hellenistic period happens to be by a Roman author and not by a Greek. It seems almost certain that earlier works must have been written in Greek which have not survived, so that Manilius's place at the very beginning of astrological literature is a matter of accident. *Astronomicon* is in

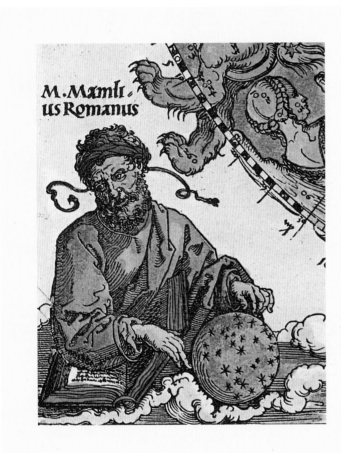

many places a difficult work, not least because it is written in verse; why should a treatise an astrology be written in verse? This has to be understood in the context of Latin literature: Virgil wrote a poetic treatise on agriculture, the *Georgics*, and in *De rerum natura*, Lucretius versified the scientific ideas of his day. Verse was thus a didactic medium, and it was part of the literary challenge to embody such alien material in poetry. Manilius was elegantly translated into English verse in the late seventeenth century by Thomas Creech, and the work has acquired an additional fame through its association with the scholar-poet, A.E. Housman, who devoted thirty years to editing Manilius's text.

Manilius opens with a *sphaera*, that is a description of the celestial sphere, in which he explains concepts such as celestial poles, tropics, equator and ecliptic, all described of course as if the earth were stationary and the heavens revolving around it. After expounding the physical background to astrology, Manilius sets it within a philosophical context:

Marcus Manilius, author of the first comprehensive treatise on astrology: an imaginary portrait drawn by Albrecht Dürer in 1515.
Private collection

The fates rule the world, and all things are established by a settled law; each long age is marked with its settled chances. At our birth we begin to die, and our end depends on our beginning. Hence flow wealth and power and poverty; hence all are given their skills and characters, their faults and virtues, their losses and their gains. No one can renounce what he is given, or possess what he is not given, nor can he grasp by his prayers the fortune denied him, or escape that which presses on him: each must bear his own lot.

This is pure Stoicism, and it might be found in a philosophical work rather than in a manual of astrology. But if man cannot alter his destiny, he can at least understand and predict it by reading nature's signs, by recognising the cosmic sympathy which Plato had propounded:

Nature is nowhere concealed; we see it all clearly and hold the universe in our grasp. We, being part of the universe, see it as our begetter, and being its children, reach to the stars. Surely no one doubts that some divinity dwells in our breasts, and our souls return to the heavens, and come from there; and that, just as the universe is constructed out of the four elements of air and fire and earth and water, the whole being a lodging for the governing Mind within, so we too possess bodies of earthly substance and spirits nourished by the blood, and a mind which governs all and controls every man. Is it so strange if men can understand the universe, seeing that there is a universe within themselves, and each is in small image a likeness of God?

The key to this understanding is the configuration of the heavens, and Manilius proceeds to explain how the myriad of celestial events, the ever-changing pattern

The planets in their domiciles, from a fifteenth-century manuscript. That each of the planets ruled one or more of the Zodiac signs was a fundamental doctrine of astrology, but no logical basis for these relationships has ever been identified.
Bibliotheque Nationale, Paris

in which the stars and planets move, form a complex but precise guide to earthly events and human character. Among the important technical ideas which Manilius expounds, or tries to expound, are houses, aspects, decans, lots, paranatellonta and dodecatemoria. One important point must be clarified at the outset: when Manilius, or any other writer in the astrological tradition, speaks of the subject of a horoscope being born under a certain sign or planet, they are referring to the presence of that sign at an important point in the horoscope, usually the ascendant. The emphasis on the position of the Sun at the moment of birth, the Sun-sign system of astrology now so familiar, is entirely a product of the twentieth century, and is unknown in classical astrology.

Manilius begins by discussing at length the qualities of the Zodiac signs. The later astrological tradition was to derive such qualities mainly from the planets, which were believed to exercise power over the signs – the domicile or house system, where each planet was the 'lord' of one or two signs, and was 'in exaltation' when it was in that sign. The origin of this doctrine, a central one in astrology, is completely mysterious, for no astronomical or mythological connection is detectable between the planets and their domiciles: what is the link between Venus and Taurus, or Mercury and Virgo? Manilius in fact seems unaware of those links, and he does not expound the now-familiar doctrine of planetary houses; in fact it is a general characteristic of Manilius that he gives far more weight to the Zodiac signs than to the influence of the planets. Instead he describes an unfamiliar system in which twelve great pagan gods or goddesses, not necessarily the planetary ones, are linked with each sign:

Aries – Minerva	Libra – Volcanus	Taurus – Venus	Scorpio – Mars
Gemini – Apollo	Sagittarius – Diana	Cancer–Mercury	Capricorn – Vesta
Leo – Jupiter	Aquarius – Juno	Virgo – Ceres	Pisces -Neptune

Manilius does not reveal the reasons, logical or traditional, for these links; they evidently have nothing to do with gender, although they do make male and female deities face each other across the Zodiac. The dwelling of the gods in these signs has powerful effects, as seen in the quality of Gemini, where Apollo is said to dwell:

> A softer inclination and gentler way of life comes from Gemini, through various kinds of singing and harmonious voices, and slender pipes, and words fitted to the natural sound of strings. Work itself is a pleasure to them. War's arms and trumpet they wish far from them, and bitter old age; they go lovingly through life in peace and perpetual youth. They discover the paths of the stars, and by understanding the mathematics of the heavens they complete the whole circle of the sky and pass beyond simple knowledge of the constellations. Nature is subject to their intelligence and at their service in all things. Of so many gains is Gemini said to be productive.

These might be termed spiritual qualities, and they were deduced, in ways which were never clearly explained, from the personal nature of the presiding deity. There were however other qualities which we encounter in Manilius and in other writers, which have no material basis in the signs but which are numerical. They result from looking at the signs as forming alternate pairs, or triplets or sets of four. These qualities include masculine-feminine, hot-cold, moving–fixed, nocturnal-diurnal. To give just one example, from Aries through to Pisces, each sign was considered alternately masculine or feminine, without reference to the nature of the constellation or the presiding deity. The obvious source for this idea lies in the Pythagorean doctrine that odd numbers were masculine while even numbers were feminine.

One of the fundamentals of the horoscope has always been the system of aspects, and Manilius gives a clear account of this doctrine. Within the circle of the horoscope, lines may be drawn from the centre – the earth – to any point on the ecliptic where a planet or any point of interest lies. The angle subtended at the centre of the circle by two such lines, or measured as an arc on the ecliptic, is the aspect which is said to exist between the two points, or between three or four points. These aspects are capable of producing a number of basic geometric forms: square, triangle or sextile, plus of course conjunction and opposition. These aspects were believed to reinforce or weaken the influence of the heavenly bodies concerned. A triangular aspect was always believed to produce harmonious results, while a square was unfavourable, producing conflict. Conjunction need not be precise and complete, in the sense of occultation, that is one body actually passing across another body. The theory was that each planet radiated a 'sphere of virtue' extending to several degrees in each direction; thus two bodies might be as much as ten degrees apart, but still be said to be in conjunction.

Equally fundamental was the division of the ecliptic into quadrants and into houses, which gave the horoscope its cardinal points and much of its interpretive

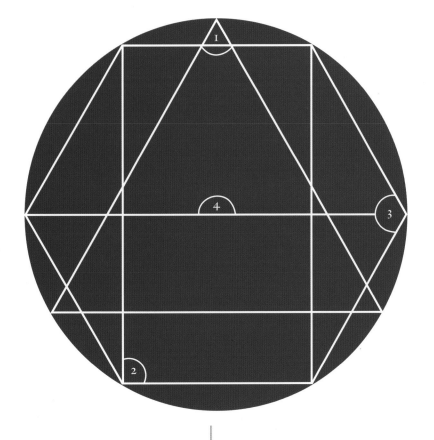

The four principal aspects.

The aspect is the angle between two planets or other points, and each aspect was considered to possess its own positive or negative qualities:
1. The Trine, an angle of 60°
2. The Square, an angle of 90°
3. The Sextile, an angle of 120°
4. Opposition, an angle of 180°

Midheaven

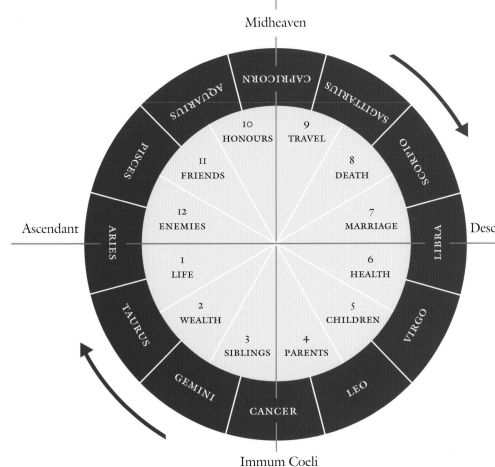

Ascendant

Descendant

Immum Coeli

The cardinal points, the Zodiac signs and the mundane houses.

The ecliptic and the twelve Zodiac signs rise in turn above the eastern horizon, the Ascendant; they culminate in the Midheaven, then set at the Descendant; the Immum Coeli is the lower Midheaven.
The planets are likewise moving in their paths, reaching points of exaltation and dejection in the Zodiac signs. The mundane houses however form a framework which is fixed about the earth, and through which the signs and planets move.

power. If the ecliptic were a visible band, from any point on the earth's surface it would take the form of a succession of degrees rising over the eastern horizon. Manilius, and all astrologers, regard the point that is momentarily rising as the most important in the entire horoscope – the ascendant, or *horoskopos*, literally the 'hour-observer'. The ascendant will be a sign of the Zodiac, or a particular degree of that sign, and it may also contain a planet or perhaps some other influential point (see below p. 48 the doctrine of Lots). Opposite this point is the setting degree, the descendant. The point culminating overhead was called the mid-heaven, the *medium coeli*, whose opposite point in turn was the lower midheaven or *imum coeli*. These four cardinal points divided the heavens into four quadrants, and it easy to imagine that these areas would become associated with the cycle of

ZODIAC SIGNS AND THEIR QUALITIES

Sign	Sex	Element	Planetary Ruler	Exaltation
Aries	M	Fire	Mars	Sun 19°
Taurus	F	Earth	Venus	Moon 3°
Gemini	M	Air	Mercury	
Cancer	F	Water	Moon	Jupiter 15°
Leo	M	Fire	Sun	
Virgo	F	Earth	Mercury	Mercury 15°
Libra	M	Air	Venus	Saturn 21°
Scorpio	F	Water	Mars	
Sagittarius	M	Fire	Jupiter	
Caporicorn	F	Earth	Saturn	Mars 28°
Aquarius	M	Air	Saturn	
Pisces	F	Water	Jupiter	Venus 27°

human life, with coming-into-being, maturing, decline and death; however the development of astrology was considerably more complicated than that .

In his discussion of the quadrants, Manilius involved himself in a problem that had far-reaching consequences. He described the two central axes, that from the ascendant to the descendant, and that from the midheaven to the lower mid-heaven, as dividing the heavens into four *equal* sections. But the cardinal points are those places where the horizon and the meridian cut the ecliptic, and the eclip-tic is not overhead, nor is the midheaven in the zenith. This would be true at cer-tain times of the day or year to an observer on the equator or anywhere between the two tropics. But to any other observer, one in the latitude of the Mediter-ranean for example, the midheaven is at some point well to the south of the zenith. Moreover the ecliptic is a great circle which is oblique to the equator, and not parallel to it, indeed the movement of the ecliptic across the sky can be spoken of as oblique ascension. To that Mediterranean observer, the ecliptic does not rise due east nor set due west. The consequence is that the Zodiac signs, although they are all arcs of 30°, will appear to rise at different rates, and the four quadrants of the heavens are not equal. This becomes vitally important when we consider the doctrine of the mundane houses, an absolutely central feature in interpreting the horoscope.

Manilius speaks of twelve 'places' on the ecliptic – he called them *loci*, not houses – each of which exercised a special influence over human life. These places are fixed in relation to the earth, and the Zodiac signs and all the planets move through them. The quadrants of the sky were to be trisected to form these places, and six of them were always above the horizon, the other six below. Manilius did not number them around the circle, as later became standard practice, but simply referred to them in relation to the cardinal points, and he does not ascribe to them clear and specific powers over the areas of life, such as wealth, family, friends, marriage and so on, as later became the practice. Instead he speaks of them as simply good or bad places, likely to lead to death or misfortune, and says that some of them *may* exercise special influence on certain areas of life. From this, we may conclude either that the system of mundane houses was not fully in place at this date, or that, for some reason, Manilius was not aware of it. To find the system in its developed form we must move forward approximately one hundred years to the works of Vettius Valens. Here the houses are numbered anti-clockwise around the ecliptic, beginning with the ascendant:

House   1. Life, the body
          2. Wealth and commerce
          3. Siblings, friends, power
          4. Children, family, private affairs
          5. Community, friends
          6. Enemies, health, suffering
          7. Marriage
          8. Death
          9. Travel, also religious matters
        10. Business, reputation
        11. Gifts, friends, ambitions
        12. Dangers, enemies

In some cases, 8 and 11 for example, these do coincide with the good-bad categories of Manilius, but in others they do not. The emergence of the doctrine of the mundane houses, sometime during the first century AD, is one of the enigmas of astrological history, for no source for it has ever been identified, logical, philosophical or literary. Why should planets affect bodily health if they are in one area of the sky, while in another they influence commercial matters, and in a third they have power over friendships? It has the appearance of a purely arbitrary system, but is it possible that such a system could arise and become universally accepted without some intellectual plan or basis?

In addition to these philosophical difficulties, the doctrine of mundane houses set up a formidable technical problem for all astrologers: given that the houses are assigned fixed areas in the sky, where exactly are they, and where are the boundaries between them? Since the house boundaries intersect the ecliptic, the houses must be thought of as sections of the heavens running north-south, their boundaries forming great circles which pass through both celestial poles. It would tempting to say that each house must occupy 30° of the ecliptic; but as in the matter of the quadrants, there are the twin problems of the obliquity of the ecliptic and the latitude of the observer. These two factors mean that the houses cannot be of equal length, so by what means can it be determined where one house ends and another begins? The solution to this problem is purely a matter a spherical trigonometry, and the method of dealing with it only emerged with Ptolemy in the second century AD. Before that date, various forms of mathematical progression must have been used, and their results cannot have been very accurate. Much later, long after Manilius and Ptolemy, the development of trigonometry led to four or five distinct methods of calculating the house divisions, each of which would give different results, that is, they would give conflicting definitions as to which stars or planets lay in which house. Few astrologers at any period of history have been equipped mathematically to master these methods and decide which was the most accurate, and it was common practice to follow pre-calculated tables. This meant that serious differences could arise if two astrologers used two different criteria of house division, or used two different sets of tables. This problem has never been resolved, and it has given powerful ammunition to the enemies of astrology, who have asked why astrologers could not agree on such a fundamental aspect of their science.

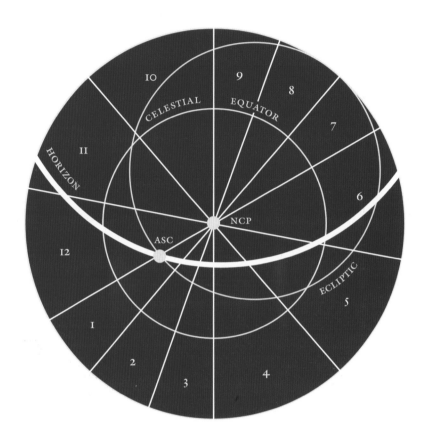

The mundane houses plotted in polar projection as on the rete of an astrolabe. The point where the ecliptic crosses the local horizon is the Ascendant, and gives the origin of the first house. The inequality of the houses results from the obliquity of the ecliptic to the celestial equator. The division of the celestial sphere into the twelve houses is a matter of spherical geometry, and the different possible methods may yield conflicting results.
By courtesy of J D North

The houses were the most important non-astronomical features of the astrologer's sky, but they were by no means the only ones. Manilius and Vettius Valens both describe the system of *sortes*, or lots, which were points on the ecliptic which stood in a purely mathematical relation to some celestial body or bodies. The most important was the Lot of Fortune, and the rule for determining its position is that it stands as far from the ascendant as the Moon is from the Sun, measured in degrees around the ecliptic. It was considered fortunate because it combined the influences of Sun and Moon together. There were other lots, places in the horoscope as distant from a selected point such as the midheaven, as two planets were from each other. Another such point was the prorogator, a point which could be used to predict the subject's length of life. The theories and calculations here were highly involved, but the prorogator, when found, was considered to travel at the rate of one degree per year towards one of the four cardinal points, giving the subject a general life-expectancy of up to ninety years.

Manilius describes one of the few ideas of Egyptian origin to be absorbed into the mainstream of astrology – the system of decans, which had functioned as an alternative Zodiac. The decans were thirty-six star groups lying just to the south of the ecliptic, which the Egyptians had identified, and which they used primarily for time-measurement from at least 1000 BC. Each group was observed in turn at its pre-dawn rising, and this rising was taken for ten days as the last hour of the night, until succeeded by the next group; we might think of this system as giving

thirty-six 'months' of ten days each. When the Babylonian Zodiac was transmitted to Egypt, the decans were added to it, making three 10° divisions of each sign. Visual representations of the Zodiac in Egypt, such as the well-known Zodiac of Dendera, show the smaller decanal figures surrounding the familiar twelve Zodiac creatures. It became standard astrological practice to assign each decan in turn to a planet, meaning that the planet would exercise additional influence if it

The Dendera Zodiac, an Egyptian temple ceiling of the first century BC, showing the 36 Egyptian decans around the outer edge, with the 12 classical Zodiac figures inside them.
The Louvre

were found in its own decan. Uniquely, Manilius offers a different scheme, where the decans are subject to the Zodiac signs in rotation. Thus the first 10° of Aries belongs to Aries, the second 10° to Taurus, the third 10° to Gemini; then the first 10° of Taurus belongs to Cancer, the second 10° to Leo, and so on. We are to imagine that the character of each zodiacal sign is modified by that of the decanal sign. In Hermetic and magical literature, the decans were to become personal semi-deities, wielding immense power in the governing of the universe, and they were portrayed in this personalised form in Islamic and western art.

The process of subdivision of the ecliptic continues with the curious system of dodecatemoria. This Greek word means twelfth part, and strictly speaking any twelfth part, for example one of the signs of the Zodiac, might be called a dode-catemorion. In practice the term became restricted to 2½° sections of the ecliptic, each one of which was considered to have special properties, and which formed part of the interpretation of the horoscope. The logical extension of this approach was to examine each degree of the ecliptic individually, to assign qualities to it, and to decide which planets worked favourably or unfavourably in which degrees. Manilius offers such a list, and classifies a large number of degrees as evil – he calls them *partes damnadae* – but such detailed judgements appear increasingly arbitrary, and no plan or system can be extracted from Manilius's list.

When the Zodiac signs were rising or progressing across the sky, it was of course always possible that they would be obscured by cloud, and that uncertainty about the time, the astrological moment, would result. At an early date, astronomers identified other stars not in the Zodiac band which rose simultaneously with each sign. These were called *paranatellonta*. At first simply a device to aid the astronomer, they somehow acquired astrological significance in their own right. It was after all reasonable to believe that all the bodies in the heavens, not merely those in the vicinity of the ecliptic, should exercise astrological power and play their part in the cosmic drama. Manilius gives a full list of paranatellonta, for example the Hyades: 'Within the twenty-seventh degree of Aries, the Hyades will rise: those born at this time do not enjoy peace and quiet, but they seek crowds of people and the bustle of affairs'.

Despite the many obscurities of his text, we are fortunate to possess in Manilius's work an extended account of the astrological ideas of this early period. It is strange that he, unlike Vettius Valens, does not analyse any specific horoscopes, or explain exactly how one may be constructed; this suggests either that Manilius was not himself a practising astrologer, or that he was, but he wished to keep this technical knowledge to himself. A feature peculiar to Manilius is that he ascribes the primary influence in all things astrological to the Zodiac signs, whereas in the later astrological tradition it was the planets which were given primacy. This plainly suggest that at this stage astrological thought was in a fluid state, and that alternative theories were in the process of evolution. The dominant picture that emerges from Manilius is of a technical apparatus involving more and more detailed subdivisions of the ecliptic. Quadrants, aspects, houses, decans, lots, dodecatemoria, paranatellonta – all these are dependent on positions measured within the 360° reference system of the ecliptic circle. The principle of cosmic sympathy, the macrocosm-microcosm link, which we encountered in Plato and in the Stoics, is here being formalised and *mathematised* to a very high degree. A system of complex, interrelated, but apparently arbitrary concepts are given a mathematical application, and the process of interpreting individual destiny requires a series of numerical procedures. Was this complexity merely a function of the astrologer's professional self-interest? Was he marking out for himself an arcane territory which no one but the skilled practitioner could possibly master? The source of these numerical concepts and subdivisions is baffling, and we wonder if even Manilius had any knowledge of their origin. If he knew or believed that they derived from celebrated thinkers such as Pythagoras or Plato or Berosus, would he not be anxious to say so, or to give them at least some clear authority from the past? One celebrated doctrine is found set out clearly, but again with

The Aratean cosmos. This cosmic diagram accompanied texts of Aratus's Phaenomena. *The Zodiac surrounds the planetary figures and the earth. The unusual feature is that Mercury and Venus orbit the Sun, which in turn orbits the earth: this system was proposed by Heracleides (fl.350 BC), and it anticipated the theory of Tycho Brahe.*
Bibliotheque Nationale, Paris

✶ Manilius and the Poets ✶

MANILIUS'S verse treatise on astrology – the first comprehensive astrological text to have survived from the ancient world – played a strange part in the lives of two very troubled English poets, widely separated in time: Thomas Creech and A.E.Housman. Creech (1659–1700) was an Oxford scholar who scored a notable success with his translation of Lucretius's poem of Epicurean philosophy, *De natura rerum*. This work was frequently reprinted, and became for a time as widely read as Dryden's translation of Virgil or Pope's Homer. It was natural for Creech to turn his attention to another great didactic Latin poem, which embodied the rival philosophy of Stoicism, and his version of Manilius appeared in 1697. But something had gone wrong with Creech; his colleagues noticed that his behaviour had become erratic, and soon his mind showed signs of collapse. He suffered financial difficulties and an unhappy love affair. Finally he took his own life, under circumstances which became the subject of sensation-seeking pamphlets; it was suggested that he had been driven to suicide by philosophical despair. In fact Creech's translation of Manilius is of interest because it strongly reflected contemporary rationalist thought about the universe and its ordered rule. For Creech, as for Manilius, the movements of the stars and their effects on human beings demonstrated clearly the force of divine intelligence:

> I'll sing how God the world's almighty mind,
> Through all infused and to the all confined,
> Directs the parts and with an equal hand
> Supports the whole, enjoying his command,
> How all agree and how the parts have made
> Strict leagues, subsisting by each other's aid,
> How all by reason move because one soul
> Lives in the parts diffusing through the whole.

This is pure Stoicism, with a strong dash of Newtonian physics thrown in, and its philosophical goal is quietism, resignation before divine providence:

> As we are born we die, our lots are cast,
> And our first hour disposeth of our last.
> Then as the influence of the stars ordains,
> To empires kings are doomed, and slaves to chains.

It is evident from passages like these that Creech was a readable versifier, but no great poet, although allowances must be made for the intractable nature of the material with which he was working. Here is his rendering of the Zodiac Man:

> Now learn what signs the several limbs obey,
> Whose powers they feel and whose obedience pay.
> The Ram defends the neck; the head the Bull;

> The arms bright Twins, are subject to your rule;
> In the shoulders Leo; and the Crab's obeyed
> In the breast; and in the guts the modest Maid;
> In the buttocks Libra; Scorpio warms desires
> In secret parts, and spreads unruly fires;
> The thighs the Centaur; and the Goat commands
> The knees, and binds them up with double bands;
> The parted legs in moist Aquarius meet;
> And Pisces gives protection to the feet.

ship. From 1900 onwards, he devoted thirty years' work to Manilius, not to translating him, but to editing the Latin text. Housman claimed repeatedly that he chose Manilius not for any literary reasons, but purely as a philological challenge. This does not carry conviction, for Housman's own poems are filled with a sense of bitterness and the futility of

The National Portrait Gallery

human ambition, with the sense that 'high heaven and earth ail from the prime foundation'. It is hard not to believe that the Stoic philosophy held a great appeal for Housman, but this time it is the darker aspect of Stoicism, the sense that the universe is ruled by fate, which man may attempt to study but which he cannot alter, and must therefore endure:

> The troubles of our proud and angry dust
> Are from eternity, and shall not fail.
> Bear them we can, and if we can we must.

Housman was certainly no practising astrologer, but the intellectual basis of Manilius's verse undoubtedly attracted him. Compared with the facile optimism of Creech's Augustan couplets, Housman's poems show a neurotic personality finding solace in romantic pessimism, in a grim philosophy of destiny, which he believes destroys all human freedom. Housman did not emulate Creech's suicide, but his poems dwell obsessively on death as the only escape. It is remarkable that a long, obscure, didactic Latin poem should have played so important a part in the lives of these two scholar-poets.

Exactly two centuries after Creech's Manilius was published, A.E.Housman achieved lasting fame with his collection *A Shropshire Lad* (1896). These bittersweet poems are filled with the despair of failed love, friendship broken and intimations of early death – all seen as blows of blind, inexorable fate. Housman was an Oxford-trained scholar, a repressed homosexual who deliberately submerged his emotional life behind a mask of classical scholar-

no indication of its source in earlier literature or in logic: that of the Zodiac Man. Manilius states that each Zodiac sign has special responsibility for the health of a part of the human body, beginning at the head with Aries, and ending at the feet with Pisces. This system must have been devised, although Manilius does not say this, by outspreading the Zodiac band with its signs, and superimposing upon it an image of the human body. In this doctrine the concept of the macrocosm-microcosm link is seen in clearest possible form.

There is however a singular gulf at the heart of Manilius's work, for he never attempts to explain how astrology actually works, what the dynamic behind the whole system is. Is there a power which proceeds from the stars and planets, and if so what is it? Is that power a causal one, or do the heavens function as signs of pre-determined events? These matters of fundamental importance are missing from Manilius. It was the role of one of the greatest mathematical scientists of the classical world, Ptolemy of Alexandria, to offer a coherent theory of how astrology actually worked, and his authority helped to place it on the high intellectual level which it maintained for 1500 years.

THE SCIENTIFIC ASTROLOGY OF CLAUDIUS PTOLEMY

Ptolemy of Alexandria (*fl.*130–170 AD) is one of the towering figures of classical science. His principal work, the *Almagest*, gave a mathematical account of the movements of the heavenly bodies which was to remain the scientific orthodoxy until the era of Copernicus. The geometry of the planetary paths as they were analysed in the *Almagest* underpinned the whole edifice of mathematical astrology. Ptolemy also composed a definitive work on astrology, the *Tetrabiblos*, ('Four Books'), which he opens by arguing that, although the study of pure astronomy is desirable and intellectually rewarding in its own right, there is a further dimension to that study, namely to discover the ways in which changes in the configuration of the heavens produce changes here on earth. It is beyond doubt that the heavenly bodies affect the earth: the tides, the seasons, the climates, the germination of seeds – all these natural cycles are determined by the Sun and the Moon, and if these heavenly bodies exert such an influence, is it not logical to believe that the others, although smaller, must do so too? The philosopher must acknowledge these powerful effects on the earth in general, and Ptolemy goes on to ask:

> Can he not, with respect to an individual man, perceive the general quality of his temperament from the *ambient* at the time of his birth; as for instance that he is such and such in body, and such and such in soul; and predict occasional events by the fact that such and such an ambient is attuned to such and such a temperament and is favourable to prosperity, while another is not so attuned, and is conducive to injury?

The *ambient*, the environment as we should call it, is conceived to impress a certain character or quality upon each individual at the moment of birth. Ptolemy makes the telling point that all seeds of any group, whether man, animal or plant, are generically the same. How comes it then that men and women are found in such an immense diversity of characters and bodily forms, if not through the ambient which prevails at their birth? Among those influences which create this ambient, the stars and planets have a paramount place. It is a fundamental principle that there are physical laws which unite the stars, the earth and humanity, and the discovery and application of these laws is the subject-matter of astrology.

The link between man and the heavens in Ptolemy's thought was the doctrine of the four elements, which were supposed to permeate the whole structure of nature, animate and inanimate, from the dust of the earth to the planets in the sky. We commonly refer to these elements as earth, air, fire and water, but these are really embodiments of something simpler and more fundamental still, namely

Portrait of Ptolemy from a fifteenth-century manuscript. Ptolemy was regarded as the embodiment of astronomy, but was confused with the Ptolemaic kings of Egypt, and was depicted with a crown in scores of pictures.
Biblioteca Marciana, Florence

the four qualities: hot and cold, moist and dry. All the forms of nature, including man, possessed these qualities in varying proportions. Hippocratic and Galenic medicine taught that man's bodily constitution might be analysed in terms of these four qualities, in this context called the humours. There were two humours which were fertile and active – the hot and the moist – while the other two were destructive and passive – the cool and the dry. The link between man and the heavens was this: that the stars and planets too shared these qualities, and spread them through the ether and thus over the earth, in the form of physical rays, in the same way that their light was radiated. The Sun was obviously hot, while the Moon was considered moist; Saturn was cool while Mars was dry and burning; Venus was moist, Jupiter hot and moist; Mercury alone was somehow mutable, sometimes moist and sometimes dry. The rise and fall of the planets in the heavens, and their passage through the key places of the horoscope, magnified or weakened their power in a never-ending cycle.

This is a radically new interpretation of astrological forces, for Ptolemy is presenting the whole subject not in religious or mystical terms, but as a matter of nature, a set of physical laws. Astrology is being *demythologised*: the gods are gone, for it is not Venus or Mars as deities which foster love and war in the world of men, but planets which radiate influence just as they radiate light. This is an attempt to provide a rational, scientific foundation upon which the details of the astrological edifice can be securely based. Ptolemy is well aware that astrology contains much 'superstitious nonsense for which plausible reasons cannot be given', and these he says he will pass over – his word for this is *alogon*, meaning unaccountable, irrational; he will concentrate instead on that which can be explained as physical cause and effect. 'It could easily and very clearly be demonstrated to anyone,' he affirms, 'that a certain power from the outer ether-like and invisible nature, is distributed over and penetrates all the wholly changeable substance round the earth'. Ptolemy did not invent this naturalistic approach to astrology, for it was accepted by Greek thinkers that the stars and planets were not capricious gods, but were superior components in the cosmic order. They were probably animate and intelligent, and probably exercised a subtle but pervasive influence on the world of man. What Ptolemy did however was to give the most thorough and detailed account of astrology on these naturalistic principles, an account which agreed with the best scientific and philosophical tenets of the time.

The fixed stars too share the same qualities as the planets and exercise a similar influence. Ptolemy claims, quite logically, that if the stars of the Zodiac affect the earth, so too must the others, and to all the constellations north and south of the Zodiac he attributes positive or negative powers. These powers are not related in any way to the imagery of the constellations – the bear, the hunter or the eagle – for each constellation is further subdivided into five parts, which are each assigned various qualities. These parts are given the technical name *horia*, boundaries or limits, and they remind us of some of the divisions we encountered in

From a medieval manuscript of Ptolemy's Tetrabiblos: *an astrologer at work with his book and an armillary.*
The British Library
MS.Royal.12.F.vii f.242v

Manilius, the dodecatemoria, the decans and so on. Ptolemy however rejects the first of these as having no rational basis in nature, and he makes no mention of the decans – curiously perhaps, for as an Alexandrian he must have been aware of that Egyptian contribution to astrology. Likewise he rejects the notion that each degree of the ecliptic has its own property of beneficence or malignity. The *horia*, the boundaries, function in the same way as other subdivisions of the signs, that is, they are assigned to each of the planets in turn, so that the qualities of hot or cold, active or passive, beneficent or malignant, are weakened or strengthened in a complex sequence. These subdivisions of the signs became known in Latin as *termini*. If these 'terms' originally signified something real and concrete, then it was soon forgotten, and they became yet another component in the complex chart that was the horoscope. It seems possible for example that they represented a time-division of six days (twelve Zodiac signs, each of five terms makes 60, which divided into 360 days of the year gives six) each of which might have been subject to the lordship of a planet, in the same way that the days of the week were dedicated to the planetary gods.

The bulk of the *Tetrabiblos* is filled with the detailed application of Ptolemy's doctrine of correspondences between earth and heaven. On the level of geography, he catalogues the characteristics of all the nations, and derives them from the Zodiac sign which he considers dominant in the heavens over that nation. For once even Ptolemy does not succeed in giving a rational basis for these links: why Europe should be dominated by the triplicity of signs Aries-Leo-Sagittarius, while Africa is under Cancer-Scorpio-Pisces, he does not explain. However it is clear that these relationships depend more on the planets' rule over the signs than on the signs themselves, for it is a characteristic of Ptolemy that he attributes much greater power to the planets than did Manilius. This is evident again in Ptolemy's discussion of astrological medicine, where he elaborates not the familiar Zodiac Man, which he does mention, but an intriguing Planetary Man:

In the same manuscript an astrologer discusses a child's horoscope with its mother; from their anxious looks, the horoscope must be a bad one.
The British Library
MS.Royal.12.F.vii f.112

> The nature of the planets produces the forms and causes of the symptoms, since of the most important parts of man, Saturn is lord of the right ear, the spleen, the bladder, phlegm and the bones; Jupiter of touch, the lungs, the arteries and the seed; Mars of the left ear, the kidneys, the veins and the genitals; the Sun of sight, the brains, the heart, the nerves and all the right side; Venus of smell, the liver and muscles; Mercury of speech and thought, the tongue, the bile, and the buttocks; and the Moon of taste and of drinking, the mouth, the belly, the womb and all on the left side.

On the level of the individual horoscope, Ptolemy accepts that the moment of conception is of primary importance, but of course it is almost always unknown, and therefore the moment of birth must be used: 'The first might be called the coming-into-being of the human seed, the second the coming-into-being of a man'. He advises that the astrolabe is essential for the exact determination of the moment of birth.

Nowhere in the *Tetrabiblos* does Ptolemy explain the technicalities involved in constructing a horoscope, such as finding the ascendant or calculating planetary positions, for all such matters have been dealt with in his other work, the *Almagest*. Approximately one third of the *Almagest* is devoted to describing in

Right. *Zodiac from a Byzantine manuscript of Ptolemy's* Tetrabiblos. *The central figure is the Sun-god in his chariot, incorrectly, for the earth should be at the centre.*
The Vatican

Below. *A charming Renaissance image of Ptolemy gauging the altitude of a star but pointing to the earth, symbolising the connection between the two realms, which forms the substance of his astrological work* Tetrabiblos.
Private collection

detail the movements of the Sun, Moon and planets, for which Ptolemy presents the mathematical methods for those able to apply them, but also give tables of planetary coordinates. Thus the *Almagest* became the fundamental tool for serious mathematical astrology, enabling celestial positions, past, present and future, to be calculated. It is impossible to exaggerate the importance of this for the practice of serious, mathematical astrology. The astrologer needed to know the positions of the planets, the Zodiac signs, the degree of the ascendant and a number of other points on the ecliptic, for any moment in time. In order to determine these, a mathematical model of their movements was essential, and this is what Ptolemy provided. Very few astrologers of course had the necessary mathematical skills to perform these calculations, so they had recourse to pre-calculated tables. But the mathematical infrastructure was enshrined in the *Almagest*, and over fourteen centuries its parameters would be periodically re-examined and refined, especially by Islamic scholars. The *Almagest* also provided the necessary theory for solving the difficult problem of mundane house division, for Ptolemy accepts the houses as among the most important interpretative devices. Calling them still *topoi* – places – he describes the familiar list involving life, death, friends, family, wealth and so on, and expounds the effects which the presence of each planet has on those areas of human experience. In the matter of aspects, Ptolemy gives a logical explanation for the view that the trine and sextile were harmonious, while the square and opposition were unfortunate: the former two aspects always relate signs which are of the same gender, while the last two bring into conflict signs of the opposite gender.

Among several division-systems found in Ptolemy but not in Manilius is the doctrine that the life of man falls into seven ages, each ruled by one of the planets. The idea of these periods entered western literature, and became famous through Jacques's speech on the seven ages of man in *As You Like It*. This same concern with astrological periods of time is evident in Ptolemy's handling of the complex concept of the prorogator, the point in the horoscope which enabled a subject's length of life to be predicted; understandably enough, this fateful procedure exercised deep fascination for the astrologer's clients. The first step was to determine the subject's *dominus vitae*, the 'lord of life', in other words the planet which is at the most dominant place at the nativity and whose influence was likely to shape the subject's future most strongly. The place is almost invariably the ascendant or the *medium coeli*, although the beginning of the tenth house was also favoured. The birth chart would then need to be progressed, in order to trace the course of the lord of life as it is subject to beneficent or destructive influences. The starting-point was termed the 'aphetic' place – the place from which life was 'unloosed', while the terminal place is the 'anairetic' point – the point of destruction. The number of degrees progressed around the Zodiac must then be converted into time in order to arrive at the fateful moment of death. That moment would be the place when the influences of other planets, signs and points such as the Lots, would combine to overwhelm the subject's lord of life. This procedure clearly did not obey fixed rules, and the astrologer had considerable room for judgement, and perhaps for error; one wonders how many people really desired to know the moment of their own death, and the complexity of the judgements involved must have provided a sense of possible escape from one's fate.

Ptolemy provides a clear philosophical statement of an astrology firmly anchored in the science of his time. That this science is no longer convincing in modern terms should not blind us to Ptolemy's achievement, which became all the more significant in the age of Islam and Christianity, for had the influence of the stars and planets still been attributed to the pagan deities, it is hard to see how astrology could have survived at all in the post-classical world. Only by shifting the ground of astrology so that it was a matter of natural science, could it merit serious consideration by Christian or Islamic thinkers. It is difficult to over-emphasise the gulf that separates this mature, scientific astrology from the Babylonian omen-culture with which we began. In Babylonian thought, the gods sent messages of their intentions via the stars, messages which men could learn to read. In Greek thought, the stars transmitted energies through the ether, which had a physical effect on man, and which he could learn to analyse more or less scientifically. Astrology thus became an important part of a philosophy of nature, and remained so for 1,500 years. Ptolemy's version of astrology however, had enormous implications for the problem which would become dominant in the minds of Christian writers on astrology, that of fate versus free will. If astrology does work through physical laws, through correspondences which are built into the fabric of nature, then it would appear to be strongly fatalistic. The stars would not merely be warning *signs*, as they had been to the Babylonians, but *causes* of earthly events. In this view, the whole of human history would seem to be pre-determined and inescapable, and there was no room for the Babylonian view that the stars or the gods or destiny might be propitiated. However Ptolemy softens this overpowering sense of fatalism by suggesting that, although the nature and influence of the stars are both fixed and determined, the way in which these operate in practice is open or mutable, because of the complexity of the forces involved. The astrologer may also serve an invaluable role in forewarning man so that he may at least modify his fate to some extent:

We should not think of all these things happening to men as if they followed their heavenly cause by some irrevocable divine ordinance... Rather we should think that, while the movement of the heavenly bodies is eternally completed according to a divine and immutable fate, the change of earthly things happens according a natural and mutable fate. And also, while some things happen to men through very general circumstances and not according to the individual's natural endowments – as when because of great and inescapable changes in the heavens men die in great numbers by

Right and facing page:
The constellations Aries and Pisces, from Cicero's Latin translation of Aratus's Phaenomena.
The British Library
Harley MS.647 f.2v and f.3v

fire or plague or flood – other things happen because of small and chance antipathies in the heavens... If what is going to happen to a man is not known, it is bound to follow the sequence dictated by its original nature; whereas if it is foreknown and provided with a remedy, it either does not happen at all or is considerably modified.

Thus Ptolemy upholds the integrity of astrology as based on firm scientific truth, while allowing a degree of flexibility in the way that events actually occur on earth. This problem of the mutability of fate was one which accompanied astrology from its origins, and it is reflected in a famous legend concerning Alexander the Great, which first appeared at about the time of Ptolemy. The legend tells how the Egyptian sage Nectanebus was employed to cast Alexander's birth-horoscope, and how he encouraged the mother, Olympias, to prolong her labour until the moment when the most fortunate aspect of the heavens should appear, thus ensuring a glorious future for the child. The tale is quite unhistorical and was unknown before the second century AD. But it was to be endlessly repeated and debated thereafter: could man influence his destiny in this way, or was such manipulation an illusion, and was everything that happened predetermined by a hidden chain of causes, which man could not escape?

In Manilius and still more in Ptolemy, we have connected, reasoned accounts of astrology from the pens of identifiable individuals. This does not mean that after Ptolemy all astrological beliefs and practices were fixed and agreed, but it does

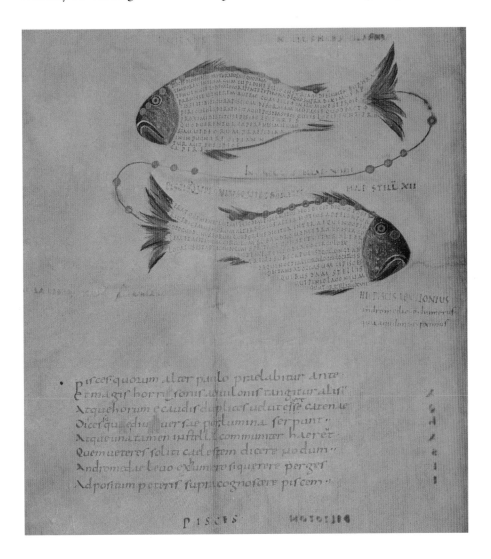

show that astrology was important enough to engage the leading scientific minds of the age, and that it was capable of being forged into a coherent system. There is another group of texts from the Hellenistic period which were equally influential but whose origins are more obscure – the texts now known as the Hermetic writings. These comprise a large number of anonymous works in Greek, many taking the form of Platonic dialogues, dealing with philosophy, astrology, alchemy, magic and medicine. What they had in common was the claim that they were revelations of divine knowledge, given by the god Hermes. The setting of many of these works is Egyptian, for Hermes was identified with the ancient Egyptian deity Thoth, sharing with him patronage of the art of writing, of science and of learning generally. Some of the dialogues are strongly mystical and Platonic, their avowed aim being the ennoblement or spiritual rebirth of man through the revelation of secret knowledge, and to this extent the Hermetic philosophy was akin to contemporary Gnostic religion.

On the scientific level, the works on astrology and alchemy all share the underlying concept that the cosmos is a unified whole whose parts are interrelated, and that the adept should devote himself to learning the laws of sympathy and antipathy by which the universe is regulated. Many of the philosophical Hermetic works have survived complete, while others, especially the astrological works, are known only in fragments. The text which was most esteemed by later astrologers was a dialogue between an mythical Egyptian king, Nechepso, and his high-priest Petosiris. It is now thought to have been composed by an Egyptian Greek in the first century BC, and it contains many of the astrological ideas which we have met in Manilius and Ptolemy – the qualities of the Zodiac signs and planets – but without the many elaborate mathematical subdivisions of the ecliptic. The authority of Nechepso-Petosiris was frequently invoked by classical and medieval astrologers, and Ptolemy himself refers to an aged Egyptian manuscript in his possession which may have been this very work. Other Hermetic texts in which astrology featured included a curious *Brontologion* which analysed different kinds of thunder, explaining them by relating them to the configuration of the heavens at the time of the storm; also a text called *Peri Seismon*, which likewise interpreted earthquakes according to their astrological context. Medicine and the astrological healing power of herbs were discussed in a number of dialogues purporting to be between Hermes and Asclepius, the god of healing who was also considered to have been a historical figure. It was texts of this kind, with their Egyptian setting, which encouraged the mistaken belief that astrology was a science with deep roots in ancient Egypt. Much later, in the European Renaissance, the recovery of many Hermetic writings would give a new and distinctly occult direction to scientific thought.

Ptolemy believed that the Egyptians had 'completely united medicine with astronomical prediction', but that important link was entirely Greek, and depended on the doctrine of the four qualities, which expressed themselves in the human body as the four humours. The Hippocratic school of medicine originated

Planetary deities in their chariots, from De astrorum scientia, *1489, by Leopold of Austria.*
The British Library, IA .6679

from the island of Kos (with its connection with Berosus) in the fourth century BC, and many Hippocratic writings emphasised the place of astrology in both diagnosis and treatment. There were two underlying beliefs: first, that the planets altered the balance of the humours in the body, and second, that the Zodiac signs each governed a part of the human body. The moment of birth determined the relative degree of influence exercised by the heavenly bodies on each individual, and identified the likely causes of sickness:

> Man is called by the wise a world, since he is wholly correspondent with the world's nature. Indeed at the moment of conception there bursts from the seven planets a whole complex of rays that bear on each part of the man, and the same thing happens at the birth-hour according to the position of the twelve signs... If then at the moment of conception or birth one

of the stars finds itself in a bad condition, there is produced an infirmity in
the member corresponding with that star. A man has four main parts –
head, torso, arms and legs. One of these may have become infirm at the
conception-moment or birth by its heavenly patron's having been itself in a
bad position. An eye or ear or tooth may undergo some damage, or speech
may be blurred because the ray of the malevolent planet has come to strike
one of those parts, spoiled and corrupted it.

Therefore the physician would cast horoscopes timed at the subject's birth and
at the onset of the sickness, in order to chart which stars and planets were malevolent. The treatment would often consist in increasing the power of countervailing
signs, through the use of herbal or other natural remedies, for lists were drawn up
in which scores of plants, minerals and animals were said to be associated with
signs or planets. The basis for these associations is unknown, but they were a further consequence of the doctrine of cosmic sympathy, and they became firmly

established, surviving into the era of the modern herbals. This aspect of astrological medicine brings us close to the realm of magic, the use of talismans and
images, which, if made upon an associated stone or gem at an astrologically correct time, might focus the power of the stars, enabling them to be manipulated by
the astrologer-physician. There is more evidence of these practices in the middle
ages, but they were undoubtedly Hellenistic in origin. Medical astrology is one
area where fatalism did not rule, for if a disease was pre-ordained, what purpose
would there be in attempting to treat it?

Medical astrology (sometimes known by the technical term iatromathematics)
was really a special case of the great branch of astrology known as katarchic astrology – that which pertains to sources or beginnings. In these cases, the heavens
were studied to determine the most favourable moment to begin an enterprise, a

*The constellations Leo and
Virgo from a fifteenth-century
manuscript of Ptolemy's*
Almagest.
The British Library
Arundel MS.66 f.40

Ptolemy and the Seven Ages of Man

WHO does not know Jaques's speech from Shakespeare's *As You Like It*, tracing the life of man through seven ages, or seven roles in an extended drama? The infant, the schoolboy, the young lover, the soldier, the magistrate, the man entering old age, and the senile wreck, are all unforgettably sketched in a few lines. By why seven, rather than five, or six or eight? The number seven occurs again and again in literature and legend, but to anyone versed in astronomy, it inevitably suggests the seven classical planets, so that one suspects some ancient and near-forgotten link here. In Ptolemy's great encyclopedia of classical astrology, the *Tetrabiblos*, he does indeed set out the doctrine that there are seven ages in the life of each individual, which are ruled by each of the planets in turn. This scheme begins with the first sphere, that of the Moon, and proceeds outwards through the Ptolemaic spheres to Saturn.

The Moon, Ptolemy says, rules over infancy until the age of four, when Mercury assumes control over childhood for ten years – the schoolboy years of Shakespeare. From the age of fourteen to twenty-two is the age of Venus, of the lover. The longest single period is the age of young, ambitious manhood, ending at forty-two, which is ruled by the Sun; then come fifteen years ruled by Mars and twelve by Jupiter. There is clearly a difference of emphasis here from Shakespeare, where the soldier follows the lover, so that there is no real place for the Sun, while Jupiter, traditionally associated with wisdom and judgement, should govern the years of 'the justice' rather than the aged 'pantaloon'. The schemes merge again in the desolate picture of the last Saturnine age of senility, before death comes to close the sequence.

Ptolemy claims that it is self-evident that the qualities of the planets are reflected in man's progress through these seven life-stages. The Moon, which rules over infancy is changeable, quick in growth (i.e. in waxing and waning); it affects moods and produces instability of personality, and it is a moist body. Mercury's traditional attributes come into play when education forms the soul, intellect and character. The Venus years are those of passion, impetuosity and the unhappiness which springs from love. The Sun shows man's desire for glory and wealth. With Mars, a note of severity or violence enters man's life, for he becomes driven by the desire to achieve fame and power before his declining years set in. Jupiter represents the renunciation of physical labour and the turmoil of ambition, and a movement towards mature judgement, foresight and philosophical detachment. The final years belong to Saturn, the years of cold and silence, of failing strength and intellect.

These periods became traditional among later astrological writers:

The Moon	–	4 years
Mercury	–	10 years
Venus	–	8 years
The Sun	–	19 years
Mars	–	15 years
Jupiter	–	12 years
Saturn	–	variable

But where did these figures come from? They clearly do not coincide with the period of the planets' rotation around the Sun, and no metaphysical justification for them was ever put forward, so some other explanation must be sought. The key appears in those classical texts which refer to the phenomenon of *apokatastasis* – the return to an original position. When applied to the planets, this meant that , in their rather complex paths against the night sky, they will infrequently but periodically be seen against precisely the same background of fixed stars, and it is the periods of these returns which correspond very closely to the periods given by Ptolemy.

This then must be the origin of the seven-ages-of-man image: it has after all a firm astronomical basis, but one which was somehow all-but forgotten, to the extent that it seems to have been unknown even to Ptolemy. The periods of *apokatastasis* give the planetary periods in years, and the characters of the planets explain why the life of man for that period should be under the control of that particular body. This suggests in turn another manifestation of the all-embracing doctrine of correspondence between the macrocosm and the microcosm: these periods of time had been built into the revolutions of the heavenly bodies, and as these shed their influence upon man so his life was imagined to follow the same cycle. In both Ptolemy and Shakespeare, the cycle is described in purely masculine terms, so that the feminine equivalent of the soldier or the magistrate is left completely out of the picture.

Shakespeare was almost certainly unaware of any astrological background to this idea. His contribution was to give the idea its definitive expression, and to raise a slightly obscure astrological doctrine to the level of dramatic poetry, so that the 'Seven Ages of Man' are now irrevocably defined in terms of this speech.

marriage for example, or a coronation, or a journey or military campaign. This practice as later known as 'elections', and it was on matters like these that the astrologer was eagerly consulted, as much as on the central question of the individual's destiny as revealed in his horoscope. It could be – and it was – argued that katarchic astrology was at variance with a strict interpretation of horoscopic astrology, for it seemed to afford the individual opportunities to manipulate his destiny, to outwit the stars. This objection is even stronger in the case of interrogatory astrology, which is based on the interpretation of the heavens at the moment when a question is posed, and which therefore savours more of magical divination than astrology. Ptolemy does not deal with the doctrine of *katarchae*, but many other classical astrologers did write on the subject including Dorotheus of Sidon, who produced an important astrological treatise in the first century AD. Dorotheus claimed to have gathered his knowledge at the fountainheads of ancient wisdom in Babylonia and Egypt, and he expounded *katarchae* to the extent of offering rules for such matters as recovering stolen goods, and even for detecting the thief. There was also the anonymous work already referred to, the *Centiloquium*, consisting of one hundred astrological aphorisms. It was attributed to Ptolemy, but one of the ways in which it differs from him is precisely in its

Zodiac figures from Hyginus's Poeticon Astronomicon, *1482. Hyginus's text was, like that of Aratus, a popular account of the legends behind the constellations.*
The British Library, IA.20540

emphasis on katarchic methods. The practical, mundane, even trivial character of much katarchic astrology was far removed from the philosophical heights of Ptolemy's scientific synthesis between man and the cosmos.

Perhaps the most ambitious expression of the belief in the unity of earth and sky was the concept of the 'Great Year', the idea that when the heavens returned to a certain configuration – usually believed to be that which prevailed when the earth began – then history would either end or re-commence. This sounds like an astrological version of the Stoic doctrines of *ekpyrosis* and *palingenesis*, the series of fiery deaths and rebirths to which the universe was subject, in a never-ending cycle. Plato too in his *Timaeus* mentions the idea of the 'perfect year', which will be reached when all the eight heavenly spheres return to their original positions. It was widely believed that the world had begun when all the planets were in conjunction in the first degree of Aries, the starting-point of the Zodiac and the onset of spring, the season of birth. It seemed logical to imagine that when the planets again reached conjunction in the last degree of Pisces, the end of the Zodiac, the current era of world history would end. This was the source of a truly bizarre vision of eternal recurrence, penned by a fourth-century Neoplatonist, Nemesius;

'The Stoics say that the planets, returning to the same point of longitude and latitude which each occupied when first the universe arose, at fixed periods of time bring about a conflagration and destruction of all things; and they say that the universe reverts anew to the same condition, and that as the stars move again in the same way, everything that took place in the former period is exactly reproduced. Socrates they say, and Plato will again exist, and every single man with the same friends and countrymen; the same things will happen to them, they will meet with the same fortune.

One could hardly imagine a more forceful statement of the doctrine that *everything* on the earth, every material object, every movement, every change, is really dependent on the movements of the stars. A slight variation on this theme was that at the world's birth, each of the planets was in the sign over which it now exercised lordship: the Sun in Leo, the Moon in Cancer, Venus in Libra and so on. Much speculation was devoted to the possible outcome of other great conjunctions of the planets, how they foretold natural cataclysms, the rise and fall of secular powers or the appearance of prophets or philosophers on earth. To chart these great conjunctions was to the macrocosm what the horoscope was to the individual human subject. This form of astrological history – the '*Thema Mundi*' or horoscope of the world – is not found in Manilius or Ptolemy, but was developed by later Hellenistic writers, and it was to exercise a still greater fascination over Islamic, Indian and later western astrologers.

This then was the intellectual level which astrology had reached in the Graeco-Roman world. It was a philosophy of mankind which held enormous appeal because it promised to unfold his character and his future life. Its roots lay in the astral religion which was almost universal at that time. It was entirely consistent with the most advanced scientific thought concerning the mechanism of the universe and the nature of matter. It addressed man's soul and his bodily health. It brought together elements from astronomy, mathematics and philosophy, in a combination which few thinkers could or would ignore. On the other hand its complexities were such that it could never harden into a dogmatic, monolithic system, and it presented intractable, but always enticing, problems concerning freedom, chance and destiny in human life. The Hellenistic era was an age of restless intellectual search, when ideas and beliefs from many different sources met and blended. Astrology was able to co-exist with many other philosophies – Platonism, Stoicism, Gnosticism, Zoroastrianism – all these harmonised perfectly with the principles of astrology, and it in turn was enriched with their deeper levels of philosophical significance.

THE POLITICAL DIMENSION: ASTROLOGY IN ROME

Yet astrology had from the first an appeal beyond the intellectual elite, causing it to spread widely through Graeco-Roman culture. Its impact was felt in the politics, the social life and the literature of Rome, and this despite the fact that much of the important astrological literature was Greek. Astrology arrived in Republican Rome as part of the general importation of religious and philosophical ideas from the east, and from Greece in particular. As early as 290 BC, the Greek cult of Asclepius, the god of healing, was deliberately adopted in Rome in response to an outbreak of plague in the city. There had however been a long period of resistance before some of the more exotic ideas from the east were accepted; the cult of Bacchus for example, with its associated revels, was officially condemned as immoral and likely to undermine social well-being. But edicts and condemnations could not stem the tide of eastern influence, and by the first century BC the first recorded Roman astrologer, the senator Nigidius Figulus, was said to have fore-

told the future greatness of Octavius on the very day of his birth. The scholar Varro was one of the first Roman intellectuals to give serious attention to astrology, and he commissioned a practitioner of the art, Tarutius of Firmium, to cast the horoscope of Romulus and of the city of Rome itself. Another contemporary, the historian Diodorus Siculus, described the origins of astrology in Egypt and Chaldea, and reported that many accurate predictions had been made concerning the rulers of those regions.

The two last great opponents of astrology in Republican Rome were Lucretius and Cicero. Lucretius wrote his great didactic poem *De natura rerum* partly to refute the Stoic doctrine of the periodic death and rebirth of the universe. To Lucretius, all nature was eternal, for it was composed of indestructible atoms, which combine by accident in their random motions to create of the forms in the natural world, including man. In such a view, fatalism was impossible, for there was no design and no divinity in the universe. This atomist philosophy was characteristic of the Epicurean school, which formed the main opposition to Stoicism. In fact astronomy and astral religion were generally destructive of this bleak atomism, for the eternal, unchanging motions of the heavenly bodies seemed to provide the clearest possible evidence for the existence of design and order in the cosmos. Lucretius is reported to have suffered bouts of insanity, and, rather fittingly for the advocate of such a despairing philosophy, to have ended his life by suicide. Cicero, despite his reputation as a Stoic who had studied under the great Posidonius, is said to have assisted in the publication of Lucretius's work, and he was certainly highly critical of fatalism in philosophy. It should be remembered that Republican Rome maintained official augurs, whose task was to interpret various omens, not unlike some of those in ancient Babylonia – omens from animals, from the weather, from ashes and so on, although never apparently from the stars. In the context of a work on divination in general, Cicero attacked the newer doctrines of astrology. His arguments were commonsense rather than philosophical, that inheritance and upbringing must influence a person's life more than the stars, and he asked how a subtle, invisible force from the stars can so impress itself upon the world that it can predetermine events far in the future? He raised the problem of the destiny of twins, which was to become a classical point of attack for astrology's enemies. In the course of his essay, Cicero provides a useful summary of astrology as it was understood by the educated Roman of his time:

> In the starry belt which the Greeks call the Zodiac, there is certain force of such a nature that every part of that belt affects and changes the heavens in a different way, according to the stars that are in this or that locality at a given time. This force is variously affected by those stars called planets. When they have come into that sign of the Zodiac under which some one is born...they form what is called a triangle or square... Now since through the progression and retrogression of the stars the great variety and changes of the seasons take place, and since the power of the Sun produces such results as are before our eyes, they believe that it is not merely probable but certain that, just as the temperature of the air is regulated by this celestial force, so also children at their birth are influenced in soul and body by this force, their minds, manners, disposition, physical condition, career in life and destinies being so determined.

This passage was written around 50 BC, and it is interesting because it puts forward the naturalistic theory of astrology which Ptolemy was to elaborate two centuries later: astrology was believed to work not in obedience to the capricious power of the planetary gods, indeed no divine power is suggested at all, but as a material force pervading the universe, comparable to light or heat or sound. Cicero was sceptical of the existence of such a force, of the complex way in which astrologers claimed to interpret its effects, and above all of the fatalistic view of human life which must accompany it.

Yet even the authority of voices such as Cicero's could not prevent astrology's penetration into Roman life, and it was in the fifty years after this work was written that astrology left the pages of the philosophers' books and became a significant force in the labyrinth of Roman political life. Why did this happen at this time? The obvious connection is with the end of the Republic and the beginnings of monarchical rule. Astrological predictions concerning individual destiny, the character of friends and enemies, the right moment to go to war, the problems of succession – all such matters relate to the personal rule of kings or dictators. It is surely no accident that astrology emerged onto the public stage during the life of the first emperor, Augustus, and that in the century and a half of blood-drenched politics which followed, astrologers became factors if not powers behind the throne.

The historian Suetonius recorded the prophecy given by Nigidius Figulus at the time of Augustus's birth in 63 BC, and he reinforced this with a story dated some twenty years later, when the future ruler was in exile, with a very uncertain future:

> At Apollonia, Augustus and Agrippa together visited the house of Theogenes the astrologer, and climbed upstairs to his observatory; they both wished to consult him about their future careers. Agrippa went first, and

he was prophesied with such almost incredible good fortune that Augustus expected a far less encouraging response, and felt ashamed to disclose the time of his birth. Yet when at last, after a great deal of hesitation, he grudgingly supplied the information for which both were pressing him, Theogenes rose and flung himself at his feet; and this gave Augustus so implicit a faith in his destiny that he even ventured to publish his horoscope, and struck a silver coin stamped with Capricorn, the sign under which he had been born.

Whether one believes the truth of this story, or regards it as typical of the legends which spring up around the life of a powerful ruler, it testifies to the role of astrology both in predicting political events, and in legitimising the position of a ruler. The practice of issuing coins with astrological motifs, usually the birth-sign of the emperor, began here with Augustus. But this imperial use of astrology obviously carried with it its own dangers, for rivals to the throne might also claim

Coin of Augustus, c.20 BC. It was in the reign of Augustus that astrology emerged as a powerful force in Roman politics, and he was the first emperor to issue coins showing his birth-sign.
Department of Coins and Medals
The British Museum

that their horoscopes predicted that greatness awaited them. This was not a matter of absolute truth or falsehood, something that could be proved or disproved, for the casting and still more the interpretation of a horoscope were highly flexible, and many different predictions might be forthcoming. Thus was born both the fascination and the fear which astrology exercised over the Roman emperors of this period. Whether they believed in astrology on a philosophical level or not, it was something which they simply could not afford to ignore, for it could always be used by their rivals to threaten their rule. This explains why the emperors invariably resorted to astrologers themselves, but also issued edicts banning the practice, often under pain of death, as Augustus himself did in 11 AD. These bans sprang not from intellectual scepticism, but from political fear. An ingenious defence against astrological attempts to subvert the emperor's power came with the idea that that the emperor was immune to astrological forces because he himself was divine. An astrologer of the fourth century, Firmicus Maternus, would write:

> Never reply to anyone who asks about the condition of the state or the life of the Roman Emperor: it is both morally wrong and illegal... The Emperor alone is not subject to the course of the stars and in his fate alone the stars have no power of determination. Since he is master of the whole world, his destiny is governed by the judgement of the god most high. Since the whole of the earth's surface is subject to the power of the Emperor, he himself is also considered among those gods whom the supreme power has set up to create and serve all things.

In the reign of Augustus's successor, Tiberius, 14–37 AD, astrology became an instrument of oppression in the hands of a tyrant. Historians of this reign depict the sinister, ageing emperor, withdrawn in his island retreat on Capri, surrounded by a secret police of astrologers commissioned to identify potential rivals, whom he would then murder. Certainly Tiberius employed history's first great court astrologer, Thrasyllus of Alexandria, who was a serious and philosophical practitioner of the art, some of whose writings have survived. Tiberius was in the habit of testing astrologers by inviting them to foretell the time of their own death; he would then take delight in proving them wrong by executing them on the spot. According to Tacitus, he tried this trick on Thrasyllus at their first meeting:

> Thrasyllus, after measuring the positions and distances of the stars, hesitated then showed alarm. The more he looked, the greater his astonishment and fright became. Then he cried that a critical and perhaps fatal emergency was upon him. Tiberius clasped him, commending his divination of his peril, and promised him that he would escape it. Thrasyllus was admitted among his closest friends, and his pronouncements were regarded as oracular.

Just two years after Tiberius's accession came the first trial in which astrology was linked with treason, that of Drusus, who had employed astrologers and necromancers in planning a political coup. According Tacitus, Drusus was ensnared in 'a web of Chaldean promises', and seduced by promises of future glory. A notebook filled with horoscopes and mysterious ciphers was produced in evidence against him. The plot having been discovered, Drusus took his own life, while two of his advisers were executed and further decrees against astrology were enacted. In the fifty years after Tiberius, many variations on the theme of claimed imperial destiny, rebellion and retribution, were played out, notably in the chaotic year 69 AD, the year of four emperors. All the historians of these years – Tacitus, Suetonius, Dio Cassius – agree that astrology was a motive for revolt, and that faith in astrology was now universal. This faith was encouraged by memorable stories, such as that told of Nero's birth, when the astrologer commissioned to cast his horoscope is said to have fainted in terror when he saw it. Similarly the emperor Domitian (r.81–96 AD) discovered that an astrologer named Ascletario had foretold his death. The unfortunate Ascletario was subjected to Tiberius's trick of being invited to predict the manner of his own death:

> Ascletario replied that he would soon be torn to pieces by dogs, whereupon Domitian had him executed on the spot, and gave orders for his funeral rites to be conducted with the greatest care, as a further proof that astrology was a fake. But when the funeral was in progress, a sudden storm scattered the pyre, and dogs mangled the half-burnt corpse.

Of the later emperors, Hadrian and Septimus Severus took a strong personal interest in astrology, the latter decorating the ceilings of his palace with paintings of his own horoscope. Evidence that astrology had thoroughly permeated Roman society by the second century can be seen in the naming of the seven-day week after the planetary gods, and in the many references to astrology by the writers of the time, such as Martial, Juvenal and Lucian. Some of these references are satirical it is true, but it is the superstitions of the vulgar which are being satirised, rather than astrology as an intellectual system. It also became common for emperors to deliberately fulfil astrological prophecies in order to show that the heavens favoured them. The aging Tiberius was worried that Caligula would succeed him on the throne, and consulted Thrasyllus about the problem. Thrasyllus replied that Caligula had as much chance of becoming emperor as he had of driving his chariot across the Bay of Baiae. Caligula heard this story, and, when he did become emperor, he had a pontoon bridge thrown across the bay, and drove over it in triumph, proclaiming himself the equal of Xerxes of Persia.

In the late Empire, certain religious cults flourished which appear to have

The Lion of Commagene

ON THE PEAK of Nimrud Dagh, high in the Taurus Mountains, stands a splendid mausoleum adorned with many statues and reliefs carved in stone. This is the tomb of King Antiochus I of Commagene, a small kingdom comprising part of northern Syria and of present-day Turkey, which broke away from the Seleucid Empire around 160 BC. Commagene reached its zenith under Antiochus, who maintained a skilful balance between Romans and Parthians, and exploited his kingdom's strategic control over the many trade routes through the Taurus Mountains. Among the monuments on Nimrud Dagh, there is a huge stone relief of a lion, its body covered with stars, which attracted the attention of archaeologists in the mid-nineteenth century. Three of the stars stand outside the lion's body, and they are named in Greek as Jupiter, Mercury and Mars, and it was at first believed that this monument was a symbol of royalty, those planetary gods and the lion itself all having royal or warlike associations. However, when the monument was studied by archaeologists versed in astronomy, the possibility emerged that it might be some form of horoscope. Eighteen stars are represented on the body of the lion, and their location is approximately that of the stars in the constellation Leo. The Moon has no symbolic association with royalty, so the presence of a large crescent Moon reinforced the belief that this was indeed a depiction of the heavenly bodies. The puzzle was the absence of the Sun, unless the star within the loop of the tail is the Sun, for it is carved with a larger centre and with nine points, while the other star have eight points.

What date could this monument represent, and was it a birth-horoscope? If the Sun is present, then the mid-summer month of July is clearly suggested, when the Sun is in Leo (and in fact if Mercury is in Leo, then the Sun must be close by). It is possible to compute dates within the era of King Antiochus when Jupiter, Mars and Mercury were in conjunction in Leo. We know from historical records that Antiochus was born in the month of December; fortunately we also know that he was crowned in the mid-summer of 62 BC, and it has been computed that another conjunction of these three planets took place at that time, to be precise on 7 July, and that on this occasion the Moon was also present. Thus it seems certain that this monument represents a horoscope for the time of the coronation of King Antiochus. The combination of the Sun, the Moon and the three most regally-symbolic planets suggests that this date for the coronation was astrologically selected in advance, and then commemorated in stone.

This is in fact the earliest known Greek horoscope with a precise date, pre-dating by several years the oldest surviving papyrus horoscopes. No other such monument embodying a horoscope in stone has ever been found, and this suggests the presence at Antiochus's court of a particularly imaginative astrologer. A further important deduction is possible: the planetary positions which applied at this date relate not directly to the *constellation* but to the *sign* of Leo. At this date the sign of Leo had moved partly into the constellation Cancer due to precessional movement. For symbolic purposes, it was the constellation, the image of Leo, which was required here. It is clear that whoever computed this horoscope was well aware of the phenomenon of precession, and could calculate its effects. This in turn means that Greek astronomical ideas had become familiar in the ancient near east, and could be grafted onto a Babylonian-style regal horoscope, which, despite its generalised appearance, evidently embodied some very precise astronomical calculations. The ruler of this minor and largely-forgotten kingdom therefore left a monument that is in some respects scientifically unique.

possessed an astrological dimension: that of the Sun and that of Mithras. The cult of *Sol Invictus*, the unconquered Sun, was at various times proclaimed the official state religion, first from 218–222 AD, during the reign of Elagabulus, and then more lastingly by Aurelius in 270. Temples were built, while coins, images and texts attempted to reinforce the link between the Sun-god and the emperor. In a sense, this was the culmination of an idea put forward by many Roman

Sol the sun-god, whose cult was promoted by the later Roman emperors.
Staatliches Museum, Berlin

astrologers, that the emperor was beyond the influence of the stars, because he himself was divine. The development of the Sun-cult was only brought to a halt when Constantine abandoned the cult in favour of Christianity. This was a political, public cult, with little religious or philosophical depth, but the same cannot be said of the more intriguing and obscure cult of Mithraism. Because it was private and involved secret rites, no comprehensive written account of the doctrines of Mithraism has survived. It is usually supposed to have shared with the other mystery religions the aim of releasing the spirit of the adept from the bonds of his earthly destiny. The image of Mithras, usually slaying a bull, has been preserved on many sculptured monuments found widely dispersed throughout the Roman Empire. One of the outstanding features of this image is that the god is surrounded by the twelve Zodiac figures: does this mean that Mithraism was in some sense an astrological cult? Because of our ignorance of the doctrines and beliefs of Mithraism, it is impossible to say, but some historians have interpreted this Zodiac as meaning that Mithras was the lord of the world, and therefore the lord of time, and that the Zodiac here functions as no more than a symbol of the cycle of time, with no wider astrological implications. Much that has been written about Mithraism is highly speculative, and there is no positive evidence that it was a cult rooted in astrology

Astrology emerged into the Greek world from twin roots, one in Babylonian astronomy, the other in eastern astral religion. Its fundamental premise was that mankind was organically linked to the universe which surrounded him, an idea which can be traced in many ancient belief-systems. Who the individuals were who mathematised this concept, relating human character and destiny to the measured positions of stars and planets, remains a complete mystery. However the resulting blend of mysticism, mathematics and philosophy proved irresistible to many Greek thinkers. In complete contrast to the Babylonian omen-culture, where the heavens expressed the will of arbitrary deities, Greek scientists, above all Ptolemy, advanced a theory of astrology as an aspect of natural science. The principles of the system were agreed and were relatively clear, but it would be difficult to exaggerate the complexity, indeed the confusion, that reigned in astrological practice. The sub-divisions of the ecliptic, the positions which were considered to be important, the way that influences strengthened or weakened each other as a result of these positions – all these were so numerous as to be

Mithras: images of the late Roman deity Mithras are often shown surrounded by a Zodiac, but this may have been only a symbol that Mithras was the lord of time; the astrological content of Mithraism is uncertain.
University of Newcastle

impossible to reduce to an agreed system, and of any programme of empirical testing or validation, no trace survives. Neither Manilius nor Ptolemy offer a step-by-step guide to casting a horoscope, while those writers who do, such as Dorotheus of Sidon and Firmicus Maternus, differ from each other on many fundamental points. In the naturalistic theory of astrology, the stars and planets were conceived to radiate a myriad of subtle, powerful forces, which were constantly changing, constantly reinforcing or weakening each other from moment to moment, as they moved in a never-ending kaleidoscope of patterns which sprang from the ceaseless rotation of the heavenly spheres: these were the patterns which the astrologer sought to disentangle. By analogy, we might imagine a large orchestra, in which all instruments are sounding together, sometimes harmoniously, sometimes discordantly. Imagine a listener attempting to analyse those sounds by isolating a chosen moment: in that moment he must attribute sounds to each instrument, and say whether they are rising or falling, and whether each component is harmonising with another, or is overpowered by it. This was approximately the task which the astrologer had set himself when he claimed the ability to rationalise the competing celestial influences.

It was Greece which gave astrology its intellectual structure, Rome which gave it a political dimension, an aura of power and danger, and this twofold classical inheritance was to become permanent. Thus over a period of perhaps 200 years, from 100 BC to 100 AD, astrology moved geographically from east to west, and moved intellectually from being a learned pursuit to being a socially powerful force. The subsequent history of astrology in the west was profoundly affected by the rise of Christianity, and by the deepening gulf between the eastern and western sectors of the Roman world. But it had moved eastward too from its Babylonian birthplace, to Sasanian Persia and to India. It was from these eastern sources that astrology would eventually re-enter western intellectual life, through the intermediary of Islamic learning.

CHAPTER THREE

THE MIDDLE AGES:

ECLIPSE AND RE-EMERGENCE

THE POST-CLASSICAL CRISIS

In the year 312 AD the Emperor Constantine embraced the Christian faith, and set in train a process by which Christianity became established as the official religion of the Roman world. Over the next hundred years a series of laws was passed by which pagan beliefs and practices were increasingly circumscribed, and Christianity enthroned. In 358 superstitious pagan practices including magic, divination and astrology became crimes which were theoretically punishable by death. The revival of paganism by Julian the Apostate in 361 found little support, and did not survive the emperor's death a mere two years later. Finally in 407, the very practice of pagan religion was forbidden. By the time of these events, the Roman Empire had been divided into two sectors, west and east. In the eastern, Byzantine sector, the attack on the pagan past was much less ferocious, and astrology was still widely practiced in the fifth century. From this period some treatises on the subject – by Hephaistion of Thebes and Paul of Alexandria for example – and a number of personal and political horoscopes have survived. In 549 however, the Emperor Justinian closed the pagan schools of learning in Athens, an event which symbolises the final end of the classical era, and soon afterwards Byzantine astrology too lapses into silence.

These events formed a great turning-point in the history of western astrology. From its position as a serious intellectual force with roots in Greek philosophy, commanding universal assent and wielding political power, astrology was placed under attack as a heresy and a pagan superstition, incompatible with the spirit of the age. It is not difficult to see why Christian thinkers should be so hostile to astrology. At the core of the new faith was the conviction that, in the battle between good and evil which constitutes human history, both divine grace and human freedom are essential components. If the course of history and the life of every individual are governed by the stars, then both these principles are destroyed. To predict the future must mean that the future is fixed, and a belief in astrology must therefore entail a denial of God's sole power over nature and mankind.

In fact however, the debate over astrology in the early years of the Christian era was not conducted in quite these simple terms – that the universe must be ruled either by God or the stars, but not by both. Had the influence of the stars been seen still in the ancient Babylonian sense, as the power wielded by capricious gods, then the conflict with Christianity would indeed have been straightforward. But the whole tendency of Hellenistic astrology had been to rationalise the influence of the stars, to the extent that Ptolemy had made it a matter of scientific cause and effect. This rationalised astrology was anchored in the Aristotelian

THE great point of contact between astronomy, astrology and religion was always the fact that heaven is both a physical and a spiritual realm: the properties and the mysteries of the heavens may be studied by the scientist and the mystic. This raised obvious questions about the nature of the stars: what actually were they? As physical bodies in the heavens, how did they relate to the divinities who were also supposed to dwell there? The nature of the stars had been a matter of speculation for Mesopotamians, Persians and Greeks, and the conclusion that the stars were divinities, animate and intelligent, fuelled the growth of astrology. But what of the early Christians? How did they explain the paradox that their God dwelled in a physical realm filled with stars, some of which were identified with the pagan gods? The gods might be dismissed, but what of the stars? As a rule, the early Christians were not alive to scientific questions; their overriding concerns were theological and ethical. An exception was Origen in the third century AD, who was, significantly, a native of Alexandria, the city that was the centre of philosophy, gnosticism and classical science. Origen developed many of his views on the natural world in the course of his work *Contra Celsum*, an extended reply to the anti-Christian polemicist Celsus. Celsus had accused Christ of being a sorcerer, who worked his miracles by invoking the demonic powers of earth and heaven. Origen's reply shows a Christian attempting to reconcile religious belief with some of the tenets of pagan science.

Celsus was clearly convinced of the validity of astrology, for he derided the Christians for worshipping heavenly entities, while neglecting the most powerful part of the heavens, namely the stars 'who prophesy clearly to all the world, and who are the true divine heralds'. In reply, Origen explicitly condemned the science of the horoscope as contrary to human freewill. That he should do so is not surprising, but what is surprising is that he went on discuss the nature of the stars and that he repeatedly endorsed the pagan belief that the stars are inhabited by souls or spirits. It was this belief which led him into speculations which actually appear sympathetic to astrology. His starting point was the familiar Greek philosophical principle that movement is proof of will, and that orderly movement is proof of rationality. Origen's position however was not simply an echo of this Platonic tradition, for he cites a number of biblical texts which appeared to show that the stars played a deliberately-planned role in God's government of the universe, such as 'I have commanded all the stars' (Isaiah 45:12) or 'Praise him sun and moon, praise him all you stars and light' (Psalm 148). Origen subscribed to the Platonic idea that all souls are pre-existent, and

have descended from the spiritual realm to the bodily, and that in this process some souls had reached, as it were, the intermediate level of the stars; he even speculated that the stars might be capable of sin.

Origen grants that the stars, as intermediaries between the world of God and that of man, may sometimes function by God's special decree as omens of change of earth. The clearest example of this was the star which announced the birth of Christ, but comets too he certainly regarded as divine omens. In this scheme, the stars are not causes, but are merely signs of great events. Like Plotinus, Origen saw the stars as constituting a form of heavenly writing which only the angels were able to read. But of course the fallen angels could read it too, and Origen shared the Neoplatonic vision of the universe as filled with spirits – good spirits or angels, and demons or fallen angels. He speculated that it was the fallen angels who had revealed the principles of astrology to men, Moreover, he argues, astrology may appear to work sometimes precisely because these demons cunningly correlate their activities with changes in the heavens, in order to seduce men into believing in astrology. For example, Origen suggests that these demons carefully observe the phases of the Moon before they produce the symptoms of epilepsy, so that men will malign the Moon, and will believe that the stars actually cause good and evil. Origen also shared the universal belief in natural astrology, that the stars governed the weather and the natural cycles on earth: that different stars were associated with the four seasons suggested that they were the *causes* of seasonal change, thus producing the fruits of the earth which men enjoy.

Thus, while overtly denying astrology, Origen actually concedes a good deal to it, seeming to admit its validity, indeed its place in the divine scheme of the universe, but then to retreat to the position that it was a forbidden study. His leanings towards Platonism, and specifically to the idea that the stars are spiritual beings, drew him to affirm that God must in some way employ the stars as intermediaries. In other words, there *was* a power in the stars, but it was dependent upon God. This was an attempt to resolve the perceived conflict between God and the stars, but Origen's ideas were too subtle for most other Christians, and he was condemned several times as a heretic in the fourth and fifth centuries. His fate in this respect shows the difficulties of any Christian attempt to appropriate the concepts of pagan science; perhaps the only logical position was that of certain other early Christians who rejected it entirely. Later, in the very different cultural context of the middle ages, Origen's position would become respectable once more.

en une chose qu'il pensst tost
Qd m sai fe meillour ploe

xxvij.

es esteilles
en toe thou
en son al
Om toute
Qml en
et unne
Compter
en treftor
Ana pon

theory of the four qualities, and it was directly related to current medical beliefs about the four humours, so that astrology was tied together with physics and biology in a coherent, scientific whole. Thinkers of the third, fourth and fifth centuries AD, including of course Christian thinkers, had no alternative scientific system to put forward, and no particular reason to dispute this one. Therefore it seemed that there was a level of *natural* astrology which must command universal assent. No one denied that the Sun controlled life, growth and the seasons, or that the Moon affected tides, and perhaps also mental states and female physiology, and the rest of Ptolemy's natural astrology had been presented as a logical extension of these same principles. This idea found its clearest expression in Aristotle's teaching that *all* generation and corruption on the earth were caused by the movements of the heavenly bodies, above all by the Sun's motion along the ecliptic. Astrology's Christian opponents were therefore compelled to identify more closely what aspects of astrology were scientific and acceptable, and which were dangerous and heretical.

Strangely, the terms in which Christian thinkers were to approach this problem for the next thousand years were set out not by a Christian theologian but by a late Greek philosopher, Plotinus, the founder of the Neoplatonic school. Plotinus (205–270 AD) accepted the principles of astrology as a physical system in the Ptolemaic sense, but he set a crucial limit to the power of the heavenly bodies over human life. The soul in Plotinus's thought was a purely spiritual entity, and could not therefore be subject to physical influences, including that of the stars. The human body and the natural environment were certainly subject to that influence, in medical matters for example, or the seasons and the weather. Yet the course of an individual's life, his pursuit of good or evil, his fortune and his destiny, all these were matters for his own intellect and his own choice. This simple and logical principle allowed the retention of Greek scientific ideas, while freeing human life from

The figure of Virgo.
MS Bodl.646 f.19
The Bodleian Library, Oxford

any form of fatalism, and Plotinus's formula was to be echoed by almost all later Christian thinkers who pronounced on astrology.

Plotinus was not a Christian, and several theologians had already considered the problem of astrology and its conflict with their faith. Among the earliest and most severe was Tertullian (*c*.160–220 AD) who classed astrologers uncompromisingly with criminals and heretics. Tertullian was aware of an episode which raised particular difficulty for Christians, namely the star of Bethlehem and the adoration of the magi, both of which seemed to give biblical warrant to the idea that great events were presaged in the stars. Tertullian put forward a curious allegorical interpretation of the three magi, arguing that their gifts of gold, frankincense and myrrh, symbolised pagan learning, including astrology, and that the gifts therefore marked the yielding of paganism to the new lord of this world. Astrology had played a role in the pagan era, but in the new age, Tertullian argued, attempts to predict the future were evil and forbidden, for the future belonged only to God. This approach proved an attractive one – to allow some validity to astrology, but insisting that it was part of the forbidden pagan past. Clement of Alexandria (*c*.150–215) argued that the twelve apostles had replaced the twelve Zodiac signs as governors of human life, but he did not claim that the signs and the planets had never possessed any power, merely that their power was now broken. Tertullian's contemporary, Origen (185–254) employed many Greek philosophical concepts in his version of Christian theology. He subscribed to the Platonic idea of the pre-existence of souls, who descended into their bodies from the stars, and he speculated that the stars were placed in the heavens by God as a kind of divine writing, prefiguring cosmic events. Thus Origen conceded a great deal to astrology, that it is indeed a guide to cosmic events, but he retreated into the position that it was a forbidden study for Christians. Origen implies in fact that God actually employs the stars in some way as *intermediaries* in his governing of the cosmos. In this view, there is a power in the stars which connects them with human life and history, but it is dependent on God. This is an ingenious resolution of the conflict between God and

St Augustine, portrayed by Botticelli. Augustine attacked astrology as a legacy of the pagan past, and his authority weighed heavily against it for centuries.
Uffizi Gallery, Florence

stars, but it is one that is strangely reminiscent of Babylonian astral religion – the stars as the writing of the gods. Perhaps it is not surprising that Origen was denounced as a heretic several times in the fourth and fifth centuries, partly for his speculations on subjects like the pre-existence of souls, or the life of stars.

The idea that the power of the stars was real but was dependent on God, was a compromise fiercely rejected by astrology's most determined Christian critic, St Augustine (354–430). Augustine pointed out that the astrologers attributed both good and evil to the stars; but how can God ever be the author of evil, even through a secondary medium? Some astrologers, he admits, argue that the stars are not causes but signs, but he demonstrates that this is a mere device, which conflicts with all classical accounts of the power of the stars. Augustine made much of the problem of twins and their different fates, although conceived and born together, and he pressed home his attack by demanding to know how the moment of conception or birth could even be measured precisely? This was a profound difficulty for all ancient astrologers; the difference of a few minutes might alter very significantly the configuration of the horoscope, but in the absence of clocks, how could a nativity be timed to the minute, or even the hour? Augustine proclaimed that the pursuit of astrology was no more than a device invented by evil demons to seduce the human mind with promises of power. He ridiculed the pretensions of katarchic astrology, for how, logically, can a man arrange for himself a destiny which he does not have? His arguments were powerful and were repeated over the centuries, his authority serving to reinforce the view that astrology was indeed a pagan heresy which Christians must shun. On the political level, as the Christian church acquired more and more secular power, it was less tolerant of any rival claims to intellectual truth, and all such claims were rejected and branded as heretical.

However the campaign of Christian opposition was not alone responsible for the misfortunes of astrology in the Latin west. Equally important was the decline of classical learning, especially Greek science, which followed the estrangement between Rome and the eastern empire. Astronomical works in Latin were limited to elementary descriptions of the constellations, the most famous being the work by Aratus, which had been translated from Greek by Cicero. Neither Ptolemy's *Almagest*, nor any other treatise on spherical astronomy received a Latin translation, nor did tables of pre-calculated astronomical positions. Without these scientific tools, astrology could not survive, except perhaps on the level of popular superstition. The nativity chart, the horoscope, could not be accurately cast without mathematical astronomy, for textbooks such as that of Manilius explained the language and the concepts of astrology, but not its precise methods. Thus the practice of astrology, as opposed to the general discussion of its validity as a system, all but vanished in the west for almost a thousand years. Many late Latin writers such as Macrobius, Martianus Capella and Boethius speak in philosophical terms about the stars, but there is no astrology in any of their works. Macrobius subscribed to the Platonic notion of the soul's descent through the heavenly spheres to join the body, where it acquires the characteristics of each planetary sphere: intelligence from Saturn, judgement from Jupiter, ardour from Mars, desire from Venus, and articulate speech from Mercury. Boethius, perhaps the most widely-studied medieval author before Aquinas, saw the stars' regular courses as evidence that divine reason ruled the universe, and he certainly seemed to accept natural astrology, while still insisting on the freedom of the human spirit. 'The celestial movements of the stars' he wrote, 'constrain human forces in an indissoluble chain of causes, which, since it starts from the decree of immovable providence, must needs itself also be immutable'. Christian encyclopaedists too, like Isidore of Seville, accepted a good deal of natural astrology – the influence of the Moon on the weather, the role of comets as portents and so on – while always emphasising the freedom of the human spirit, and denying that any fatalistic force emanated from the stars.

ASTROLOGY IN THE ISLAMIC WORLD

While astrology was in decline in the Christian west, it was flourishing in some eastern cultures. It seems to have been transmitted to India by the second century AD, and the first full-length astrological works in Sanskrit date from a century later. Its sources were Hellenistic, but Indian equivalents to the earlier celestial omens of Babylonia have also been found. Clearly there were channels of communication open between India and the Hellenistic world, via Persia. Indian astrology made use of indigenous ideas, such as the transmigration of souls, the five elements (space being added to the usual four) and the caste system. Technically the subdivisions of the zodiac were made even more complex, with each 30° degree sign being divided by 7 and by 9, to create *saptamsas* of $4\frac{2}{7}°$, and *navamsas* of $3\frac{1}{3}°$. The Indians also assigned great importance to the lunar nodes, the points of intersection between the lunar orbit and the ecliptic, making these points equivalent to planets and endowing them with real powers. The one feature of Indian astrology which was transmitted to the west, although it did not entirely take root there, was the system of lunar mansions, the *naksatras*, which were 28

The great Persian astronomer and astrologer al-Tusi instructing pupils at the observatory of Maragha in the mid-thirteenth century.
The British Library
MS.Or.3222 f.105

divisions of the sky where the Moon was located on successive nights. Indian astrology had one important distinguishing feature, namely that it regarded the starting point of the Zodiac as lying always at the first degree of the constellation Aries, and not at the point where that degree crossed the ecliptic, which is a moving point. Thus the Indian Zodiac signs are fixed to their parent constellations, and avoid the problem of precession, which stems from the western tropical Zodiac. Ptolemaic astronomy took deep root in India by the eighth century AD, and in the period when mathematical astrology was unknown in the west, the practice of horoscope-casting in India was on a thoroughly scientific footing.

Hellenistic astrology flourished also in Sasanian Persia from the third century onwards, where it was particularly drawn to the idea of the 'Great Year'. The aim here was to draw up schemes of astrological history, in which cycles of time marked by astronomical events, almost always planetary conjunctions, were related to earthly events – to the lives of kings, the rise and fall of empires, the appearance of prophets, great natural disasters such as plagues, and so on. Special mention should be made of the Sasanian city of Harran, in north-western Mesopotamia, which remained for many centuries a highly influential centre of Hermetic philosophy and astrology. The scholars of Harran seem to have been the last custodians of the Mandaean cult, a pre-Islamic religion of the middle east, which among other things involved star-worship. They resisted both Christianity and enforced conversion to Islam until the eleventh century, and adopted Hermes as their prophet, identifying him with Enoch in the Bible and with Idris in the Koran. The Harranians fulfilled an important role in the history of Hermetism and Neoplatonism, which they transmitted to Islam through scholars such as Thabit Ibn Qurrah, who carried these ideas to the House of Wisdom in Baghdad.

The culture which embraced astrology most fervently, which studied its classical origins, and developed it most fully as a cosmic philosophy, was that of Islam. Since Islam was also a revealed religion, as Christianity was, and even more severe and uncompromising than Christianity, it is perhaps surprising that astrology – a pagan philosophy of nature – should have held such an appeal for some of its leading thinkers. The answer appears to lie in the Islamic doctrine of *tawhid*, the one-ness of God, from which in its turn followed the wholeness of wisdom. The role of the philosopher was to gather all wisdom, from whatever source, into an intellectual synthesis which should complement the religious revelation. For Islamic thinkers, at the heart of astrology lay the rediscovery of mankind's cosmic nature, the links between man and the heavens which God had built into his creation. Islamic thinkers turned to sources in Greece, Persia and India in their quest for the details of astrological practice and its philosophical foundations. As within Christianity, there was indeed conflict with Islam concerning this highly intellectualised approach to faith and its use of pagan science. But for various reasons, this conflict emerged only at a late stage, notably in the thirteenth century AD, and for a long period from the eighth to the twelfth century Islamic scholars produced a series of astrological works which built on classical foundations, and which went on to shape the future of western astrology. Astronomy was one of the central interest of Islamic scientists, and if religious justification was needed for this study, it could be found in passages in the Koran such as: 'He it is who hath set for you the stars, that ye may guide your course by them amid the darkness of the land and the sea.'

Islamic mastery of astronomy is exemplified by two devices, which their scholars may not have invented, but which they developed to a high degree: the astrolabe and the *zij*. The astrolabe was the instrument which became the visible symbol of the astronomer's skill. Partly an observational instrument and partly a calculating device, it was essentially an analogue model of the heavens, enabling its user to determine the time from the Sun or the stars, and which degree of the ecliptic was in the ascendant at any give moment, which was the starting-point in casting any horoscope. The *zij* was a compendium of mathematical astronomy, which gave the data and the formulae for calculating celestial positions, as well for

An exquisite Persian horoscope, datable to 1384, the nativity of Sultan Iskandar, who was a grandson of Tamerlane. Unusually, the ascendant is at the top of the picture. Venus is in the third house playing a lute; the Sun is in the fifth house, while in the sixth house are gathered the Moon, Jupiter, Saturn and Mercury.
The Wellcome Institute

related subjects such as chronology, trigonometry and geography. Much of the material in the *zij* was derived from Ptolemy, but it continued to be revised as Islamic astronomers built up their own corpus of observations and improved calculating techniques. Manuscript *zijes* circulated in their hundreds through centres such as Baghdad, Alexandria, Isfahan, and Granada. This rigorous tradition of mathematical astronomy, exemplified in the astrolabe and the *zij*, underlay the Islamic practice of astrology from the eighth century onwards, and this continuation of Greek scientific methods contrasts strongly with the extinction of classical astrology in the Latin west. Under princely patronage, Islamic scientists also undertook a programme of observation of the heavens that was far in advance of anything in the Latin west. Persian observatories in particular succeeded in improving the parameters of mathematical astronomy, by painstaking measurement of stellar and planetary positions.

The 'first Arab philosopher' – first in time and first in eminence – was al-Kindi (*c*.801–866) whose self-appointed task was to introduce the concepts and the language of Hellenic philosophy into Islamic thought. Al-Kindi justified this enterprise by the classic argument that reason and revelation were twin pathways to the same truth. He was a leading figure in the 'House of Wisdom' in Baghdad, where the writings of Plato, Aristotle, Euclid and Ptolemy were translated into Arabic. Al-Kindi was sympathetic to astrology, and was especially drawn to historical astrology, the use of the heavens to discern patterns of secular events here on earth. One of the most relevant of al-Kindi's works to astrology was his *De Radiis* ('On Rays') in which he sets out a philosophical basis for various kinds of magic, including that which uses the influence of the stars. The rays of the title are rays of cosmic sympathy which permit objects to affect one another, and the astrological power of the stars is a classic example of this effect. 'The diversity of things in the world of the elements apparent at any time' argues al-Kindi, 'proceeds from two causes, namely the diversity of their matter, and the changing operation of the stellar rays'. This concept of rays which are diverse because they proceed from different elements, became in al-Kindi's hands an all-powerful principle of science:

> If it were given to anyone to comprehend the whole condition of the celestial harmony, he would know fully the world of the elements, with all that is contained therein at any place and any time, as knowing the caused from the cause…and whoever has acquired the knowledge of the whole condition of the celestial harmony, will know the past, the present and the future.

It would be difficult to imagine a more grandiose claim for astrology than this: the whole cosmic process is seen as determinist, but the determinism is firmly based in science and may, theoretically, be mastered. The idea of planetary conjunctions as a periodic focussing of powerful stellar emanations followed naturally from al-Kindi's doctrine of rays.

In this field, al-Kindi had been preceded by a slightly earlier authority, Masha'Allah (*fl*.762–816), a Jewish native of Basra who went to work in Baghdad, indeed his astrological advice was influential in the decision to found the city on 30 July 762. He is the first Jewish astrologer known to us by name, and he signals the Jewish acceptance of astrology after the long centuries of opposition recorded in the Old Testament. In the Jewish tradition, various figures such as Abraham and Enoch would be claimed as founders and teachers of astrological wisdom, while Zodiacs seem to have become an acceptable element in the decoration of synagogues from the third century AD onwards. The Jewish contribution to astrological mysticism would become important to medieval and Renaissance scholars. Masha'Allah drew on the three living traditions – the Greek, the Sasanian and the Indian. He devised a scheme of world history in which significant events were marked by conjunctions of the planets Saturn and Jupiter; the biblical flood, the birth of Christ and the birth of Muhammad are distinguished in this

Facing page.
Top: *Arab astrologers at work with reference books and an astrolabe, from a picture depicting the birth of Tamerlane.*
The Art Archive

Bottom left. *The astrolabe, the two-dimensional model of the heavens perfected by Islamic scientists.*
Department of Oriental Antiquities, The British Museum

Bottom right. *A Persian plate, dated 1563 AD and decorated with elegant Zodiac figures.*
Staatliches Museum, Berlin

way as great turning-points, with many lesser events also connected to such conjunctions. The work of both Masha'Allah and al-Kindi on conjunctions served to prepare the way for the most influential of all Islamic astrologers, Abu-Mashar (787–886), who became known and revered in the west as Albumasar. A native of Balkh in central Asia, a frontier city of the former Sasanian empire, where intellectual cross-currents met from Greece, Persia, India and China, Abu-Mashar too

Right. *Portrait of Abu Mashar, the founder of Islamic astrology, whose theories concerning the power of planetary conjunctions were immensely influential in east and west.*
Bibliotheque Nationale, Paris

Facing page. *The moon in the constellation Cancer from an Islamic manuscript of the fourteenth century. The three subsidiary figures are the decans, the ten-degree subdivisions of the signs, which came to be seen as personified powers.*
MS.Or.113 f7v
The Bodleian Library, Oxford

migrated to Baghdad and became active in the House of Wisdom. He was able to advance an eclectic philosophy within the Islamic faith by urging that all wisdom is one and emanates from the same divine revelation. In his *Great Introduction to the Science of Astrology*, Abu-Mashar created a subtle and powerful intellectual foundation for astrology, which was indebted to the cosmology of Aristotle.

He posited that there existed three levels of being, which may be thought of as three concentric spheres. The outermost is the divine sphere, the sphere of light; at the centre is the ethereal sphere, containing the stars and planets; the lowest sphere is the sub-lunar, earthly sphere, where the four elements meet in constant motion and change. Abu-Mashar accepted the Platonic doctrine that man's soul has descended from the sphere of light to the earthly sphere, and must now strive

to return to its origin. In order to achieve this he must first pass through the celestial spheres, and therefore both science and religion urge us to study the movements and qualities of the stars and planets. Astronomy and astrology thus acquire a central place in human destiny. The task of astrology is to codify the interaction between the earthly and ethereal spheres, the potential of the former to be influenced by the latter, and the ways in which these influences wax and wane with the cycles of the heavens. Abu-Mashar followed the Hermetic tradition in asserting that knowledge of astrology, and of the three levels of being, came from the revelation of Hermes and of other prophetic figure of various nations. These multiple revelations explain the diffusion of astrological wisdom through Egypt, Persia, India and Greece.

Upon this foundation, Abu-Mashar built his most characteristic doctrine, that of the planetary conjunctions as turning-points of history. The rarer the conjunction – clearly those which involve the slower-moving outer planets – the greater would be its likely effects. Jupiter and Saturn were the largest and most distant of the planets, and mythologically they were also the most powerful of the ancient gods; for this reason their conjunctions were associated with the fortunes of great religious cultures. Roughly speaking, such events occur every twenty years, and at intervals of 120° around the ecliptic. This means that successive conjunctions are evenly spaced and fall in every fourth sign of the Zodiac. The three signs in which successive conjunctions fall was called a 'triplicity', and each triplicity was considered to be governed by one of the four elements – earth, air, fire or water. Now the periods of rotation of Jupiter and Saturn are such that the point of conjunction is not fixed against the background of Zodiac stars. Instead, each successive conjunction takes place some $2\frac{1}{2}°$ further forward along the ecliptic than the previous one. The result is that four conjunctions can take place in each sign, and twelve in each triplicity. After 260 years ($12 \times 20 + 20$), the thirteenth conjunction will move into a new triplicity, and after 960 years, the cycle will be complete and the conjunction will return to its original triplicity. Thus for those like Abu-Mashar who wished to finds patterns in history, three periods were available of 20, 260 and 960 years. These were called respectively a great conjunction, a major conjunction and a maximal conjunction. The second two were claimed to be especially fraught with significance for earthly affairs, for example it was a shift from an airy to a watery triplicity which marked the biblical flood, and the same shift almost 4,000 years later marked the birth of Islam itself. The aspect of Mars and of the Sun were very influential in modifying the effects of these conjunctions, while Abu-Mashar also wrote an entire treatise on the malignant effects of conjunctions between Mars and Saturn in the sign of Cancer.

If we ask what the source could be for this elaborate edifice, it must surely lie in the mathematical inheritance from Pythagoras and Plato, the belief that numerical symmetry was proof of some deep-lying pattern in nature. The formation by successive conjunctions of an equilateral triangle, which was itself slowing rotating about the earth, irresistibly suggested the periodic focussing of celestial powers upon mankind. In Abu-Mashar's hands, this system became a powerful, unorthodox tool of historical interpretation. It assumed that all human institutions were impermanent, including the Abbasid caliphate, and ultimately even Islam itself. This is once again testimony to the diverse, international character of Islamic learning, which was united by Arabic as a *lingua franca*, but not at this stage by exclusive religious orthodoxy. In ninth-century Baghdad, there was in fact great concern about the strength and future duration of the Abbasid caliphate in the face of unrest among non-Arab subject peoples. Philosophers such as al-Kindi and Abu-Mashar considered this problem carefully, the latter predicting the end of the Abbasid era a little more than three centuries hence. In this prediction he was not far from the truth, for the dynasty came to an end when Baghdad was sacked by the Mongols in 1258.

Abu-Mashar's authority and influence among later Islamic astrologers was immense. This was due partly to the philosophical depth which he brought to astrology, and the profound claims which he made for it. But he also wrote in detail on practical matters, and produced his own *zij*. His planetary model was evidently Ptolemaic, although he claimed that his data was drawn from a manuscript buried at Isfahan before the Flood. He wrote extensively on katarchic and electional astrology. He increased still further the complexity of astrological practice by adding to the number of Lots which should be calculated, and he treated

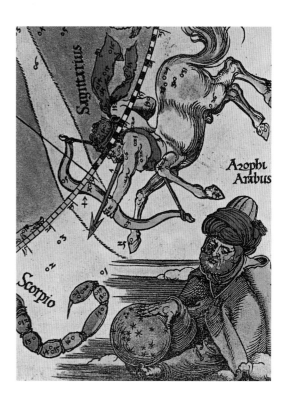

Al-Sufi, as imagined by Albrecht Dürer.
Private collection

Left. *The constellation Leo from the star-catalogue of the Persian astronomer al-Sufi; the constellation is shown in double-aspect, as seen from the earth, and reversed as on a star-globe.*
The British Library
Ms.Or.5323.f45

the lunar nodes as equivalent to planets. The nodes are the two points when the Moon's orbit crosses the ecliptic; one is therefore the ascending node, the other the descending. For reasons that have never been explained, these points were known as the Head and Tail of the Dragon – *Caput* and *Cauda Draconis*. If there was behind this some ancient, mythological dragon of the sky, no record of it has survived, although a connection with the constellation Serpens seems plausible. The northern node was usually regarded as a favourable place, the southern node as a place of danger (in Shakespeare's *King Lear*, Edmund, the arch-villain, says 'My father compounded with my mother under the dragon's tail and my nativity was under *Ursa Major*, so that it follows I am rough and lecherous'). The treatment of *caput* and *cauda* as planets, as physical bodies with their own points of higher and lower influence, was really at odds with the Ptolemaic theory of natural

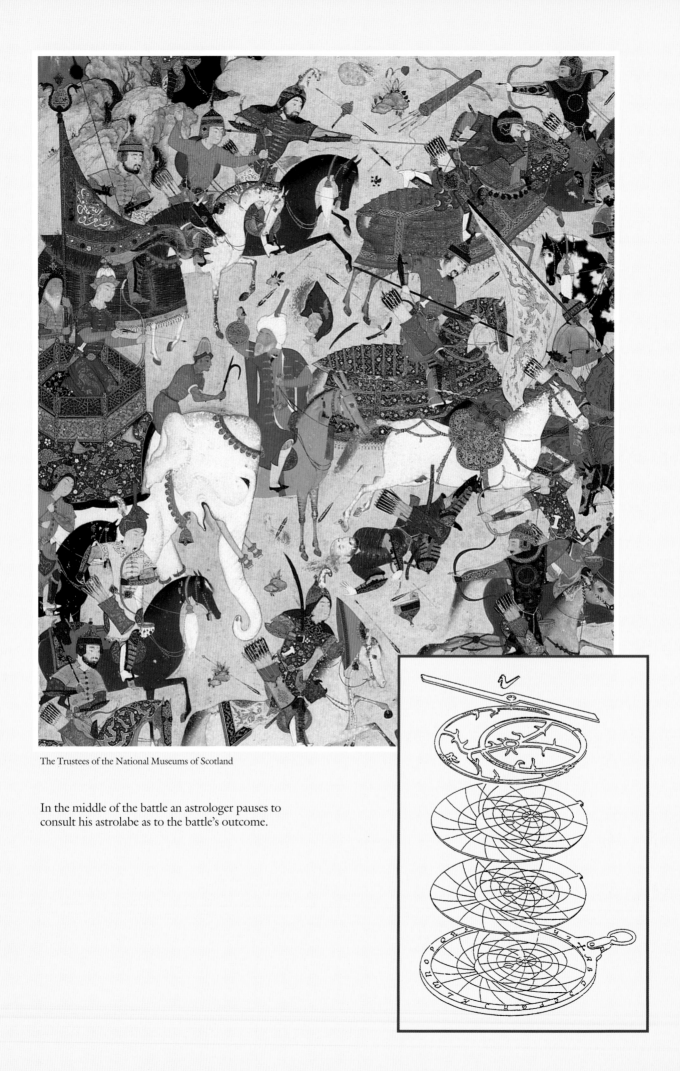

In the middle of the battle an astrologer pauses to
consult his astrolabe as to the battle's outcome.

THE visual symbol of Islamic astronomical skill was the astrolabe, shown in innumerable medieval pictures in the hands of astronomers and astrologers. The astrolabe was a two-dimensional model or analogue of the heavens which had many functions, but for the astrologer its primary role was to determine, for any required date, the position of the stars and the Sun, and to determine which Zodiac sign was in the ascendant. It was also invaluable for telling the time during the hours of darkness. The astrolabe could not help however with the motions of the planets, for these were too complex to be built into its structure, and for these mathematical tables had to be used.

The astrolabe consisted fundamentally of two disc-shaped metal parts, both constructed according to mathematical principles, the one designed to be placed over the other. The top part was the 'rete' (meaning 'net') which took the form of an open fretted disc, and which was actually a map showing the positions of several dozen stars. The map was plotted on the polar stereographic projection, in which the stars on the celestial sphere were spread out onto a flat plane having the north celestial pole at its centre, and continuing as far south as the Tropic of Capricorn, which formed the circumference and the edge of the map. On the metal fretwork of the rete, sharp pointers marked the positions of the chosen stars. A smaller inner circle, eccentric to the polar point and tangent to both tropics, represented the ecliptic. Of course the astrolabe was not being used at the pole, and the map had to be converted by adding a coordinate system relevant to a local horizon, and this was the function of the lower plate, or climate. On this plate, lines of equal celestial latitude and longitude were plotted to appear as a mesh of curved lines. When the rete was placed over the climate plate, and when a chosen star was correctly located in celestial latitude and azimuth, the astrolabe became an accurate map of the heavens valid for that latitude on earth. Both the climate and the rete were pinned into a framing disc called the mater, upon which were inscribed the 360 degrees of the circle, and other data including the hours. The final component was the alidade, a straight rule which crossed the diameter of the astrolabe, and which was used as a sighting device for taking the altitudes of stars. Different climate plates could be used to correspond with the latitude at which the instrument was being used.

How was the astrolabe actually used by the astrologer? Assuming a birth had occurred on 14 January at 10 a.m., the first step towards erecting a horoscope is to find the Sun's position on the ecliptic at that date. On the reverse of the mater was engraved a Zodiac calendar, which gave the Sun's position in the twelve zodiacal constellations through the year. In this case, on 14 January the Sun is at 4 degrees of Aquarius. The rule is then set to mark the tenth hour on the rim, and the rete is turned until the fourth degree of Aquarius touches the rule. The astrolabe is now set: it offers a map of the heavens for 10 a.m. for the 14 January, and it will therefore tell the astrologer at a glance which sign of the Zodiac was crossing the eastern horizon – the ascendant; it will naturally also give the midheaven and the descendant . Corrections for precession could be made for a birth many years in the past or future. To find the current time, this process is reversed: the Sun by day or a chosen star by night is sighted with the rule and its altitude read from the scale of degrees, say 10 degrees. The rete is then turned until the pointer for the Sun or the star is over the latitude-line for 10 degrees. The edge of the rule is then aligned with that point, and the hour can be read from the rim of the astrolabe.

The astrolabe was evidently of enormous value to the astrologer, saving him many hours' calculation of celestial positions. Where did this ingenious device originate? An apocryphal story was told by Islamic astronomers claiming that it was Ptolemy who invented the astrolabe by accident: he was out riding one day carrying a small celestial globe made of brass, which he dropped; his horse then trampled it flat, thus producing the first astrolabe. The attribution to Ptolemy at least is correct, for the theory by which the celestial sphere could be projected onto a plane surface was well known to him. However there is no clear evidence that planispheric instruments of this kind were ever made by Hellenistic astronomers. The first description of the astrolabe as such was composed in Alexandria in the sixth century AD; Arabic treatises were being written late in the eighth century, while the oldest surviving instrument dates from a little after 850. Western knowledge of the astrolabe entered Europe, probably through Spain, in the eleventh century, and the first Latin treatise on the subject may have been written by Gerbert of Aurilliac, the future Pope Sylvester II. The oldest surviving western instrument is dated from around the year 1200. One of the best-known texts on the astrolabe was traditionally ascribed to Masha'Allah, and it was this which formed the basis of the first treatise in English, written in 1392 by Geoffrey Chaucer, as an instruction manual for his son Lewis, who sadly did not survive into manhood. Securely based in mathematical astronomy, beautifully crafted in metal, and conceptually satisfying as a model of the heavens, the astrolabe was a visible symbol, as the *zij* was an abstract one, of the process by which classical science was preserved and developed by Islamic scholars, and then transmitted to the Latin west.

astrology, since they were not bodies, but merely mathematical points, and could not therefore exercise an influence that could be explained within any physical theory. The same is true of another group of places emphasised by Abu-Mashar, the transits. These are the points on the Zodiac in a progressed chart where a planet passes through a point previously occupied by another planet. These transit points were considered to be of great significance, for the second planet would either intensify or negate the power of the first, and the skilled astrologer could not afford to neglect these counter-influences.

It is clear that Islamic astrology enjoyed a rather short period of intellectual development, the years 760 to 880 embracing the careers of Masha'Allah, al-Kindi and Abu-Mashar. The works of these three authorities, especially Abu-Mashar,

Cosmic diagram c.1080 AD. The Arabic formula la ilahah illa'llah –there is no God but Allah – has four words, seven syllables and twelve letters. The Ismaili philosopher Nasir Khusraw considered that these corresponded to the structure of the cosmos: four elements, seven planets and twelve Zodiac signs.

Facing page. *An Islamic cosmos: the planets, the Zodiac signs, the lunar mansions, and the decans constitute a vast sphere turned by heavenly angels.*
The Art Archive

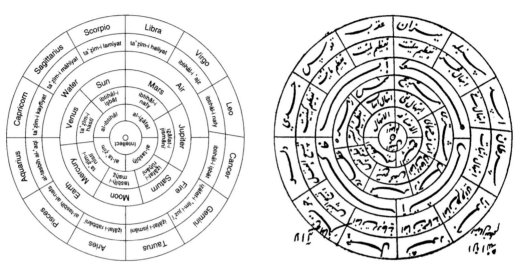

formed an effective Bible of the science. It is easy to see why astrological history in particular exercised such a strong appeal. Islam was a new and aggressive force upon the stage of world history; it claimed divine authority, and it had opposed and conquered the established secular powers in Arabia, Persia, Asia Minor and Egypt. Yet it still faced a great cultural and religious enemy in Christianity, and therefore its role in the divine plan for the world, its possible dominance or decline in the future, were matters of intense interest. Although it did not development significantly, astrology remained intellectually and socially powerful in Islam for some three centuries after Abu-Mashar. It represented one aspect of the international science and philosophy gathered by scholars of the new religion. Its philosophical foundation was largely Greek, drawn from Plato and Aristotle, and it utilised the theory of the four elements and the astronomy of Ptolemy. This eclectic intellectual legacy was integrated within the religious demands of Islam by the doctrine of the one-ness of wisdom. Astrology as an aspect of Hellenic science flourished first in Abbasid Baghdad because the caliphs of the ninth century were sympathetic to the movement known as *Mu'tazilah*, which upheld the primacy of reason. It was already long-established in the eastern sections of the Islamic world, but it took root also in the west, in Moslem Spain. But, as in Christianity, there was opposition to what was seen as an invasion of religion by pagan or rationalist thought. Most of this opposition sprang from religious motifs, exemplified in the work of the eleventh-century mystic al-Ghazali, whose *Destruction of the Philosophers* was a classic refutation of secular philosophy and science, including astrology. But not all opposition arose from religious motifs, and some of the great philosopher-scientists, such as al-Biruni, Ibn Sina (Avicenna) and Ibn Rushd (Averroës) were critical of astrology on intellectual grounds. By the thirteenth century, Islamic astrology had become moribund, and, under attack from religious and philosophical opponents, it declined considerably in importance. Curiously, this decline occurred at precisely the time when translations of

ودنحی غز راسلك دولت قنادی وازدز به بری مغرببنه وبری مشرقن وبری جهانبلروك اخرنده وربیه نحوارضك تحتنده یه وبوعز راسل یلم لوحفوظ
نظر ایدوب جمله مخلوقاتی کی کوزرابرنك کوزیرنك اکاوکنده رده یه هیچ برکسه ك دوحن قبض ایله رالا اجلی کلوب وعمری تمام اولوب مزرقی اخراولینیجه تنوبنلرك
روحطیر ن صاغ البله قبض ایدوب علینه رفع ایلز یه وکارلروك جانلرن صولن البله قبض ایدوب بجخنه ایصال ایلز یه ودنخی انس ابن مالك رضی
عنهما اسند صحیح ایله رسولحضرتعلیه السلامدن روایت ایدوبایدرکه ادم علیه الصلوة والسلام اشبو اولکی کوکدزره یه ودنخی بنلوقرانی کوکدن

صورة الأفلاك

اقرلواوالله اعلم وبینم کوزره ك فلك یه قمرۀ درفلك یه الحکماشاء اهل رصد شوبله زعم امتشلرکه اشبواولکی انکوك قات وله راوکی فلك قمر
منسوبدرقمر سعد دنطبیعت عنده خاكی فایبدر ی مراجله سردی وتردردیه کیفیتنی دنشوی شبیدزدی ولودن ك کوکده یه ایتمشلرکه بوفلك قمر ایله ارضك اینی یوز
یکرمی محالی انی بیك دورتیوزقرق میلبندره یه وبوفلك الکلی یوزاون سکرنبك البش النی میلابدره یه ودنخی بوفلك جرمی اوتوزطقوز ارضك جرمی قدریه
وربع جرمی قدریه ودنخی اینلدلر بوفلك قمرانی اعلسی ما اسدزفلك عطارده واذهامی ما اسدکی عنان یه وبوفلك جرمی دوفلك یکری یك کوین

Islamic astrological works into Latin were sparking the great revival of astrology in the west, after centuries of neglect.

THE REVIVAL OF ASTROLOGY IN THE LATIN WEST

In the year 1184, the English chronicler, Roger of Hoveden, noted that the 'all the world's prognosticators, Spanish and Sicilian, Greek and Latin' were turning their attention to the conjunction of all the planets which was to due to take place in the constellation Libra in 1186. Predictions of disasters to befall Saracens or Christians poured from the west and the east respectively; storms, plagues and other natural disasters were prophesied; new prophets were confidently awaited; seers experienced trances, and even died with enigmatic prophecies on their lips. In due course the conjunction occurred, with no earth-shattering consequences that we know of. Yet historically this conjunction, or rather the feverish anticipation of it, is of great interest as marking definitively the re-awakening of the west to the long forgotten science of astrology. Had this conjunction occurred a century earlier, it would undoubtedly have passed unnoticed in western Europe: what had changed in the twelfth century to explain the impact of this astrological event?

Astrology returned to the west from Islamic sources, and it came as part of the general revival of classical learning, which saw the foundation of the first universities and which resulted in a new synthesis between religion and philosophy. It came from Arabic sources because Islamic scholars alone had preserved and extended the heritage of Greek literature. The major works of Greek science in particular had never appeared in Latin translations, and had therefore long been unknown in the west. The most important point of contact with Islamic learning was in the Spain of the *Reconquista*, when Islam's cultural centres came under Christian control, together with the scholars who were able to translate from Arabic into Latin. It has been said that the fall of Toledo in 1085 placed the richest philosophical library in Europe at the disposal of western scholars, and the work of translation began soon afterwards, co-ordinated by scholars from Italy, Germany and Britain, but dependant on the expertise of Spanish Arabs and Jews.

Western interest in Islamic learning had been stirred somewhat earlier, when Gerbert of Aurillac, who reigned as Pope Sylvester II from 999 to 1003, had travelled to Spain to study mathematics and astronomy. Gerbert became one of only a handful of western scholars familiar with spherical geometry, with the astrolabe and with the Arabic numbering system; indeed his learning so impressed his contemporaries that legends circulated attributing his wisdom to the devil's coaching. Gerbert's early death in 1003 may have slightly delayed the transmission of Arabic science to the west. At the beginning of the twelfth century, a French historian of the First Crusade would write 'The knowledge of the stars is as poor and rare in the west as it is flourishing through constant practice in the east, where indeed it originated'. The influential encyclopaedic writers of this period – William of Conches, Hugh of St Victor, Bernard Sylvester – all discuss astrology in terms which suggest only a general awareness of what it involved. This is all that Hugh of St Victor, writing around the year 1130, had to say upon the subject:

> The difference between astronomy and astrology is that astronomy is so called from the laws of the stars: *nomos* means law and *logos* means discourse. So it seems that astronomy deals with the laws of the stars and the turning of the heavens, the positions and circles, the courses and risings and settings of the constellations, and why each is called what it is. Astrology considers the stars with relation to the observation of birth and death and all sorts of other events, and is partly natural and partly superstitious. The natural part deals with corporeal things and their make-up, things which vary with the constitution of the heavens, such as health and sick-

Portrait of Gerbert of Aurillac, who became Pope Sylvester II in the year 999, and who spread knowledge of Islamic science to the European centres of learning.
Aachen Cathedral

ness, storms and calm weather, fertility and barrenness. The superstitious part is concerned with contingent events, and those falling under free will, and this part the astrologers deal with.

This preserves the clear distinction which we have already noticed between the natural powers of the stars, which affect bodily health, meteorology and so on, and their alleged power to determine the course of human life. Such brief accounts of astrology often appeared alongside discussions of other semi-occult science, such as alchemy, herbalism, geomancy or numerology. That these magi-

God placing the Sun in Aries
- an astronomical version of
the creation, for the universe
was supposed to have begun
with the Sun and planets in
conjunction in the first degree
of Aries, the starting-point of
the Zodiac. From Giruoto's
Pontificale, *1520.*
The British Library, 471 f.2.

cal sciences did actually work in some way was accepted as beyond question, but there were two possible views as to why they worked. Either they all succeeded in tapping hidden energies in nature, or they only worked because demons were manipulating the natural phenomena. In either view, the question whether it was permissible or not to study those sciences was a highly controversial question. What would now emerge in the twelfth and thirteenth centuries was the view that sciences like astrology worked because they were natural mechanisms devised by God to govern his creation. The stars might thus be seen, as Plotinus had first argued, as intermediaries through which life and events on earth were regulated. Bernard Sylvester spoke of the stars and planets as 'gods who serve God in person, who receive from God the secrets of the future, which they impose upon the lower species of the universe.' This daring idea had been put forward by Origen, and echoed by Boethius, but rejected by St Augustine. In one of his works, Bernard made the symbolic figure of *Nous*, the mind of the universe, explain to Nature: 'I would have you behold the sky, inscribed with a multiform variety of images, which like a book with open pages containing the future in cryptic letters, I have revealed to the eyes of the more learned.' Medieval astrologers would often put this more simply by asking why, if the stars performed no function, God should have created them? Bernard taught that God had written in the sky a 'fatal law', a series of events latent in the stars which time would unfold, even the birth of Christ being foretold there. To Bernard, astrology was highly spiritualised and numinous, and he did not expound the mechanics of horoscopes, conjunctions and so on. How precise and how extensive the influence of the stars might be was highly uncertain, but at least this was a philosophical formula which permitted, or even encouraged, further study. In this view astrology was but one aspect of the vision of nature as an autonomous entity, which God had created and had caused to function in a rational way. Thus the stage was set for astrology to emerge not as a demonic

God painting the Zodiac signs: astrology was integrated within Christianity by the theory that God used the stars and planets as intermediaries to govern his creation, and therefore that he created the Zodiac and gave the signs their various qualities.
The Vatican

art but as a science reconcilable with Christianity. One of the results of this new approach to natural science would be the recovery of the Platonic concept of the macrocosm-microcosm link; to give just one example, Adelard of Bath, one of the leading translators from the Arabic, argued that the existence of music was one of the strongest proofs that the soul of man had descended from the stars, for earthly music was but a recollection of the music of the spheres.

By the time that Hugh of St Victor was writing his rather detached definition of astrology, the work of translating fundamental texts from Arabic was under way. Adelard of Bath translated the astronomical tables of al-Khwarizmi, and some of the works of Abu-Mashar. Plato of Tivoli produced the first Latin version of Ptolemy's *Tetrabiblos*, while the all-important *Almagest* followed soon afterwards from the pen of Gerard of Cremona, the most prolific of the translators. Treatises on the astrolabe, simplified commentaries on Ptolemy, and planetary tables completed the apparatus of astronomy which was now offered to the Latin west for the first time. The manufacture of astrolabes spread widely in the west from the thirteenth century, and many treatises were written to explain its use, including one by Geoffrey Chaucer. Mastery of the astrolabe was of enormous help in determining time, and in an age before clocks, the importance of this problem is hard to exaggerate. Hours, days and months were not – as they are to us – a series of figures to be found on clocks or calendars. Time was measurable only by visible events in the sky, and to calculate the regular succession of those took considerable effort and study. This was the medieval art of *computus*, and it applied both to the hours of the day and to the longer-term problem of constructing a calendar. One of the fundamental texts of computus was Bede's *De temporum ratione*, in which the all-important method for determining the date of Easter was set out. The controversy about the date of Easter, and the stimulus which it gave to the art of computus, was one area in which exact science had remained alive in the Latin west. The problem of time-measurement had enormous implications for astrology: the whole configuration of the heavens is con-

Great men and their guiding stars: a strange assortment of famous men are shown in this manuscript – Seneca, Ismail, Theodosius – each influenced by a certain planet.
Nationalbibliothek, Vienna

stantly changing, and small errors in time might result in crucial differences in the positions of stars and planets, and therefore in their influence. Nowhere was this more true than in the theory of conjunctions. Abu-Mashar's *Great Introduction to the Science of Astrology*, and his *Book of Conjunctions*, in the version by John of Seville, were soon among the most studied of astrological texts. When the great planetary conjunction of 1186 occurred, scholars throughout western Europe were aware of what it was, how it had been predicted, and why it might be so important.

These scholars were of course all Christians and all churchmen: how therefore did they reconcile themselves to their task of introducing to the Christian world an occult practice with its twofold inheritance from pagan science and Islamic learning? What had changed in the eight centuries since the church fathers had condemned astrology as a pagan heresy? The obvious difference was that Christians were no longer a minority group in an alien culture, for society itself was

The Zodiac of San Miniato, Florence. In late medieval Europe, astrology was so widely accepted that it was considered a suitable subject to decorate the floor of a church; this design appears to show Islamic influence.
San Miniato, Florence/Scala

now Christian. Paganism had vanished into the mists of history: the church itself was now established as the custodian of culture, and it was secure. Astrology could now be safely treated as an aspect of science or learning, part of a classical tradition on the same level as the philosophy of Aristotle or the poetry of Virgil, which the church could absorb without danger. Moreover the twelfth century saw the first stirrings of a new approach to natural philosophy. That the universe was God's creation was clear from the book of Genesis; but what were the actual structures and mechanism employed by the creator to sustain it, and were they open to rational analysis? The classical legacy, preserved and developed by Arabic commentators, provided an intellectual framework with which to explore these questions, and the acceptance of this challenge was a key component in the twelfth-century renaissance. This legacy merely happened to be clothed in the Arabic language, and it was not Islamic in essence, therefore no treachery was involved in translating it. John of Seville wrote at the end of one of his versions of Abu-Mashar; 'Finished, with praise to God for his help, and a curse on Mahomet and his followers.'

Thus the revival of astrology must be seen as part of the recovery of classical science and philosophy, with no grave suspicion that this was an irreligious art. The simultaneous revival of Aristotelian rationalism had, arguably, more disturbing consequences for Christian thought, for a new theology developed which emphasised the primacy of reason. According to this school of thought, there *is* a natural knowledge of God independent of revelation, and the intellect of man can analyse the laws which govern the natural world, and so deduce the character of its creator. In this intellectual revolution, the western understanding of astrology gained a new depth. Aristotle had proposed firstly that the stars moved in response to some form of divine direction, and secondly that these movements were implicated in generation and change upon earth. When the theologians set out to Christianise Aristotle's unnamed prime mover, in other words to identify it with God, fresh attention was directed to the study of the stars as a means of understanding the divine workings of the universe.

GOD OR DESTINY: THE DEBATE ABOUT THE LIMITS OF ASTROLOGY

As Christian scholars absorbed this new learning and sought to integrate it with their religious principles, the great challenge was to preserve the freedom of the human will and its relationship to God. Man's physical make-up, and the world he lived in, might be subject to the influences of the stars, but the claims of astrology to foretell the future, and to read character as something fixed and pre-determined, could still arouse the hostility of the church. We do not know how far the practice of astrology had spread in the social sense during the thirteenth century; probably not very far, and probably it still remained more a subject for intellectual debate than for actual practice. No personal horoscopes survive from this time, and there are very few records as yet of the type of court astrologer who would later become a familiar figure. Nevertheless it became obligatory for theologians and encyclopaedists to discuss astrology, and to try to set some dividing-line between the natural and the judicial branches of the art. Leading thinkers, such as Robert Grosseteste, Albertus Magnus, Roger Bacon and Thomas Aquinas, all accepted that certain changes in the sublunary world were caused by the movements of the heavenly bodies: disease was linked through the doctrine of the humours to the influence of cold or hot stars; generation and decay in the plant and animal world followed the cycle of the Sun; the weather and natural forces such as tides, floods and earthquakes were all believed to be celestial in origin, with the Moon as the prime influence here. In the emerging science of alchemy too, it was thought that metals and minerals had affinities with the stars which it was essential for the practitioner to understand before he could make any progress in his art. All this was not superstition, but good contemporary science. Grosseteste, Bishop of Lincoln and Chancellor of Oxford University, wrote:

> Natural philosophy needs the assistance of astronomia more than of the rest of the sciences, for there are no, or few, works of ours or of nature, as for example the propagation of plants, the transmutation of minerals, the curing of sickness, which can be removed from the sway of astronomia. For nature below effects nothing unless celestial power moves it and directs it from potency into act.

This is as clear as a statement as one could ask for of the principle of natural astrology. But the wider issue of human destiny, the moral, spiritual and social dimensions of our lives, are not to be analysed so clearly. Even if we conceded that the stars might influence a person's character and will, Grosseteste argues that the astrologer could never achieve sufficient accuracy of time-measurement to be certain of his predictions. Moreover the will and the soul are not physical entities, and therefore they cannot be subject to the influences of the stars, and those who claim that they are have been misled by demons. This was spelled out more fully by Grosseteste's contemporary, Berthold of Regensburg:

> As God gave their powers to stones and to herbs and to words, so also he gave power to the stars, that they have power over all things, except over

THAT Geoffrey Chaucer had a special interest in astronomy and astrology has long been known. He composed the first English treatise on the astrolabe, in the use of which he was evidently an expert, and his poetry is littered with references to the stars and planets. At first sight these allusions might appear to be simply rhetorical devices, as for example when the Wife of Bath boasts that her passionate nature stems from the power of Mars and Venus at her nativity. However modern scholarship has made it clear that Chaucer's use of astrology is at a more profound and deliberate level than this, and that he will frequently build into his entire narrative a hidden level of astrological meaning. Typically, his human characters would represent stars and planets, and their encounters and interactions would mirror precisely the movements of the heavenly bodies. When this is understood, apparently passing references to the heavens, which might be seen as merely giving colour to the narrative, become central features in an astronomical allegory. This is true both of *The Canterbury Tales* and of Chaucer's other works.

On the surface, 'The Nun's Priest's Tale' is an unsophisticated, almost childish farmyard story of a vain cockerel who is caught by a fox, but who narrowly escapes with his life. The characters of the animals are drawn in humorous, quasi-human colours, and the reader might well suspect some element of fable, except that no particular moral seems to suggest itself, beyond the obvious one that it can often be safer to hold one's tongue than to chatter. However Chaucer has given a clue to his deeper meaning by specifying, with an odd precision, the date on which the story takes place – 3 May, when the Sun was in Taurus. Why should such a story require an exact date? It is when the cockerel announces the break of day to his *seven* hens, that the allegory begins to emerge. The cockerel represents the Sun, and the hens are the Pleiades, the seven stars in the constellation Taurus. Calculations for the 1390s – the years when Chaucer was at work composing 'The Canterbury Tales' – reveal that on 3 May 1392, Saturn entered the sign of Taurus and approached conjunction with the Sun: Saturn is clearly the fox which threatened the cockerel. The timely arrival of the widow (owner of the farmyard) and her two daughters, corresponds to the rising of the Moon and the twin scales of Libra. Horoscopes cast for various times during that day confirm the allegory in many points of detail, for example at the precise moment when Saturn rises above the horizon, it is in conjunction with *cauda draconis*, the dragon's tail, a place of evil scheming, greed and treachery. As if to point towards the hidden meaning in this apparently jejune tale, the narrator concludes:

If you think my story is absurd,
A foolish trifle of a beast and bird,
A fable of a fox, a cock or hen,
Take hold upon the moral gentlemen.

The astrological dimension of this story is underlined by a discussion of the central problem of astrology – the conflict between predestination and freewill – a discussion which one would otherwise be very surprised to find in a farmyard fable.

Elsewhere in *The Canterbury Tales* it is possible to decode further allegories. 'The Franklin's Tale' concerns the apparent submersion beneath the sea of a rocky stretch of the Brittany coast. Here again, the precise date which Chaucer gives enable us to say that on 25 December 1387, exceptionally high tides occurred which explain the miracle, and to infer that the magician whose power lay behind it was actually an astrologer who was able to calculate the Moon's tidal effects far into the future. In 'The Squire's Tale' the characters at the opening feast, and the arriving and departing guests, correspond precisely to movements among the heavenly bodies. Here too the miraculous 'horse of brass' which is able to transport man or woman through time and space, is of course the astrolabe itself. The 'horse' was the familiar name for the central pin which

held the parts of the astrolabe in place; we are told that the touching of the pin, in other words the re-setting of the astrolabe, would bring the user back home. Outside *The Canterbury Tales*, the short poem 'The Complaint of Mars' (illustrated on the left) creates a transparent allegory, where the deities of Mars, Venus and Phoebus act in a way which mirrors their planetary counterparts. It seems possible that when Chaucer had finished reading his poems aloud to his courtly audiences, as we know he did from contemporary illustrations, he may have demonstrated these coded meanings by use of the astrolabe.

The question remains why the poet laboured to embed these intricate hidden meanings within narratives which were already long and complex? Was it simply a delight in learning, in artifice and allegory for its own sake? This is certainly possible, but it seems likely that Chaucer had a deeper and more philosophic purpose, namely to show, in the setting of worldly narratives, that unity of man and the cosmos which lay at the heart of all astrological belief. We do not know where Chaucer's own beliefs about astrology lay, for his poems yield conflicting statements, but his Man of Law is made to claim that:

The death of every man is there to see,
Patterned in stars clearer than in a glass,
Could one but read how all will come to pass.

That Chaucer, the secular story-teller and bawdy humorist, was truly concerned with philosophy is evident from the end of 'Troilus and Criseyde' where he praises spiritual above worldly love, and from the famous retraction which concludes *The Canterbury Tales*, in which he prays for forgiveness for his works of worldly vanity, and commends the reader to his translation of the philosophy of Boethius. His allegories of the stars and planets show a writer saturated in medieval astrology, making a skilled and deliberate use of that science, but keeping his ultimate motives and beliefs hidden.

Jenach sagt es Etliche nüczliche
vnderschayde von dem firmament vnd

one thing. They have power over trees and over vines, over leaves and grasses, over vegetables and herbs, over corn and all such things; over the birds in the air, over the animals in the forests, and over the fishes in the water, and over the worms in the earth; over all such things that are under heaven, over them our Lord gave power to the stars, except over one thing. Over that thing, no man has any power, not any might, neither have stars nor herbs nor words nor stones nor angel nor devil nor any man, but God alone: it is man's free will.

This is a forceful statement of the classic Christian position, a position consistent with the dominant natural philosophy of the day, and also theologically safe. Yet as we re-read Berthold's list, the outstanding thing about it is the enormous power granted to the stars to govern every aspect of the creation, so that they undoubtedly enjoy the status of intermediaries between God and the universe. It is true to say that in this period *no one* questioned or denied the validity of natural astrology. But natural astrology alone did not satisfy the more adventurous spirits, such as Roger Bacon (*c.*1219–1292) whose tastes were for what he called 'the secret books' of science and magic. Bacon accepted completely Aristotle's principle that the celestial bodies are the cause of generation and corruption in all inferior things. But he was inclined to a more occult view of the influences of the stars than his contemporaries: he did not accept that they influenced man because they shared with him the four qualities of heat, cold, moistness and dryness; rather they have the power to cause these effects through their mysterious powers, which we cannot as yet understand. Bacon had no doubt of the power of talismans, amulets and images 'if they are engraved in accordance with the aspect of the sky at the correct times, then can all injuries be repelled and all useful undertakings be promoted'. In this view astrology was one of the many scientific means of drawing down and harnessing the real but little-understood forces of nature. Bacon was deeply impressed by Abu-Mashar's astrological approach to world history. He claimed that the great events chronicled in the Bible could be shown to coincide with astrological conjunctions. Even the birth of Christ had, he calculated, occurred at a conjunction of Jupiter and Saturn, and was a natural event and therefore subject to the influences of the stars which were predominant at that moment. He devised a scheme to prove that each conjunction of Jupiter with the other planets signified the law and character of a new religion. An earlier conjunction with Saturn had signified the birth of Judaism, the faith that was the oldest in time. The conjunction with Mars signified the law of the Chaldees; that with the Sun the law of the Egyptians; that with Venus the Islamic law; and Christianity is associated with Mercury because 'the law of Mercury is more difficult to believe than the others, and presents more difficulties to the human intellect.' This rather tortuous argument probably refers to the motion of the planet Mercury, which, in Ptolemy's scheme, is the most complex of all and thus

Left. *The claims of astrology: in this symbolic picture, blind fortune on the left appears to raise and cast down men at random, while the clear-sighted figure of astrology on the right is studying the mirror of true wisdom.*
Private collection

Right. *The Wheel of Fortune: this familiar concept is here linked to the seven planets, each enjoying their moment of ascendancy. From the top clockwise: Mars, Jupiter, Saturn, Moon, Mercury, Venus, Sun. The wheel is turned by an angel, for the whole system is under divine direction.*
Alinari

fittingly represents the mysteries of the true faith. In Bacon's system, the Moon's malign force was associated with Antichrist, with corruption, lying and necro-mancy; but the Moon's rapid motion shows that this influence will not endure long. Bacon urged the church not to reject astrology, but to make use of its extraordinary resources to out-manoeuvre its Islamic enemies and the Antichrist. He pointed to the all-conquering forces of Tartary and Islam, and attributed their success to their skill in astrology.

Bacon occupies an important place as a theorist of astrology, but there is no evidence that he practised the casting of horoscopes. He advanced its claims as an intellectual system, but the interesting thing about Bacon is that he combined his theories with an experimental approach to science which was unique in its time. His reported researches into fields such as optics, gunpowder, manned flight, mapmaking and so on, have made him more famous than any other medieval scientist, and he clearly believed that the influences of the stars might be as concrete and practical in their results as these, if man could learn to analyse them correctly. He claimed that recent destructive European wars might have been avoided if astrology had been scientifically applied; 'Oh how great a profit to the church of God might have been procured if the disposition of the sky for those times had been foreseen by the wise, and known to the prelates and princes, and restricted by zeal for peace! Then there would not have been such slaughter of Christians, nor so many souls sent below.' Bacon believed, indeed he urged this view upon the Pope himself, that a closer and more experimental knowledge of nature could not fail to confirm the Christian faith, and in this plan astrology played a considerable role. He dreamed of establishing astrology as a science among other sciences in the universities of Europe, but the death of the sympathetic Pope Clement IV dashed these ambitions. Bacon was deeply unpopular with some of

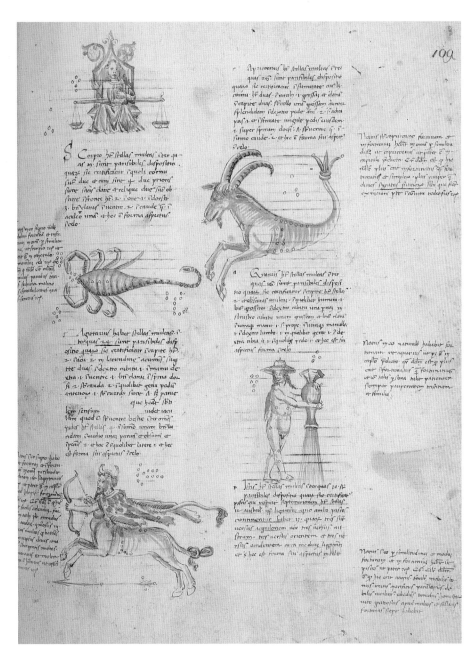

Five Zodiac figures from a fourteenth-century manuscript of the works of Michael Scot.
MS.Bodl.266 f.109
The Bodleian Library, Oxford

his fellow Franciscans, and was eventually imprisoned for the novelty of his teachings. Bacon was not a practising astrologer, nor even very lucid in his theories, but he does show how astrology was taking a profound hold on the thinkers of the thirteenth century.

The first practising astrologers of the middle ages known to us by name begin to appear at this time, figures such as Guido Bonatti and Michael Scot, both of whose works survive, and who are named as astrologers or soothsayers by Dante, and placed by him in the eighth circle of hell, their heads twisted round upon their bodies as punishment for their attempts to see into the future. Bonatti was the author of a lengthy *Liber Astronomicus*, written on a fairly popular level, which was widely copied and read, and which was being printed in English translation as late as the seventeenth century; Dante's grim description of his fate did not seem to inflict any grave damage on his reputation. Michael Scot had a Europe-wide reputation as a wizard of awesome powers. Typical of the stories told about him was that of the banquet at which Scot's guests sat down to an empty table, to which Scot then summoned marvellous dishes, carried in by his demons, while he explained that one dish came from the table of the King of France, another from the King of Hungary, and so on. Yet Scot had studied at Toledo and had translated astronomical works from the Arabic, before entering the service of the Emperor Frederick II, and becoming astrologer at his court in Sicily. In 1235 Frederick married Isabella, sister of Henry III of England, and a contemporary chronicler tells us that he 'refused to know her carnally until the fitting hour should be told him by his astrologer' – presumably this was Scot himself. Scot wrote a voluminous 'Introduction to Astrology' in which he listed some of his astrological sources as Ptolemy, Euclid, Aristotle and the Islamic masters, and it is clear that Scot embraced astrology as part of the intellectual legacy of philosophy and science descended from the Greeks through the medium of Arabic scholarship. Although Scot condemns the place of magic and necromancy in astrology, he cannot conceal his own fascination with the occult side of the science. He lists twenty-eight varieties of divination, such as augury by dreams, by birdsong, by examination of corpses, and so on, and he asserts that all of them are true, but that some of them are forbidden to the good Christian. In this work too, Scot repeats a wild and fanciful history of astrology which was generally current in the medieval west: that it was revealed to the patriarchs, whose descendants carried it to Egypt, and that the giant Atlas took it from North Africa to Spain, where Gilbertus (Gerbert) learned it from the Arabs and introduced it into Europe. Scot gave a highly occult version of the dynamics of astrology, asserting that certain transcendent spirits dwelled in the signs of the Zodiac, giving them their individual characters, and furthermore that these spirits might be conjured by the uses of images and incantations. The planets too had each its ruling spirit who exercised their power over the earth through metals, gems and plants associated with them. Unlike theorists such as Grosseteste and Bacon, Scot deals with the technicalities of astrology, with aspects, elections, conjunctions and so on, but he is strangely silent on the crucial subject of horoscopes, so that one is forced to wonder how far he had mastered the precise techniques involved.

A weightier and more respectable figure than the colourful Scot, was Albertus Magnus, a leading thinker of thirteenth-century Christendom, and one who accepted natural astrology as an integral part of his world-view. Translations of Ptolemy's *Tetrabiblos* and of the works of Abu-Mashar are listed by Albertus among his recommended basic texts for the study of astronomy and astrology. He shared the belief that the stars were instruments of the Prime Mover of the universe, and act as intermediaries between God the first cause of all things, and matter itself. He gave explicit scientific form to this concept by arguing that the four elements, from which everything in the earthly realm is composed, were generated by the motions of the heavenly bodies. The stars' influence may be seen in such fields as meteorology, mineralogy, medicine, herbalism and so on, but as always, any fatalistic power over human life is denied. This, Albertus explains, is because 'The essence of the soul is wholly and solely from the First Cause', that is the soul is not composed of the four elements, nor is it ruled by intermediaries, but stands in a direct relationship to God. He addresses the delicate question whether Christ in his human nature was subject to stars, and answers that he was not, on the principle that 'the lawgiver is not subject to the law'. Yet so great is Albertus's faith in natural astrology that he concedes that Christ's greatness must indeed have been shown in the configuration of the skies at his birth, although not caused by it, and that God used the stars as signs of his intentions.

Albertus's pupil, whose influence far exceeded that of his master, was Thomas

Albertus Magnus, the scholar-scientist of the medieval church, who gave considerable weight to astrology in his system of nature.
Alinari

Aquinas, author of the synthesis of philosophy, faith and science which forms the crown of medieval learning. Aquinas accepted completely the Aristotelian theory that the oblique motion of the Sun and stars around the ecliptic was responsible for change, growth and decay on earth; this was a matter of nature and of physics. In his *Summa Theologica*, he then posed the direct question 'Whether the heavenly

bodies are the cause of human acts?' He pointed to the ways in which the stars do indeed affect man's bodily nature, as was universally believed by medieval physicians. But clearly they also affect the 'organs of the soul' such as the eyes, and therefore they must be considered to affect the soul and the intellect to some extent. Thomas went on to give a very original explanation of the immunity of the soul and intellect from astral influence, while still allowing some place for judicial astrology. His argument was that all the physical effects of natural astrology work upon man's body, upon his appetites and passions. These are of course closely linked with character and behaviour, and therefore it is true to say that some aspects of peoples' lives may be determined by the stars. This is not quite as simple as saying that the stars rule the body but not the mind, for Aquinas has recognised that the personality has in part a physical basis. Rather he is saying that there are individuals who are wise enough to overcome their passionate natures, and live spiritual and intellectual lives, and that these people may rise above stellar influences, whose reality he does not attempt to deny:

A printed edition of Naturalia *by Albertus Magnus, showing plants which embodied planetary influences: on the left the lily and Saturn, on the right chicory and the Sun.*
The British Library, 716.e.32

Very many men follow their passions, which are motions of the sensitive appetite, alongside which passions the heavenly bodies can work. Few men are wise enough to resist passions of this kind. And therefore astrologers, as in many things, can make true predictions, especially in general; not however in particular, for nothing stops any man from resisting his passions by his free will. Therefore the astrologers themselves say that 'the wise man is master of the stars, inasmuch as he is master of his passions.

This interesting phrase *homo dominatur astris*, 'the wise man is master of the stars', became a key formula in the medieval debate about astrology and fatalism. The expression was not coined by Aquinas, but his use of it lent it additional weight. Aquinas was thoroughly classical in his views about the links between man and the heavenly bodies, and astrology for him was but one component in a larger scientific system which involved astronomy, physics and human biology.

The impact of Aristotelianism and rationalism on theology, so evident in the thought of Albertus and Aquinas, thoroughly alarmed many in the church, who saw in it the invasion of religion by secular philosophy. This feeling came to a head in 1277, when Bishop Stephen Tempier of Paris issued a famous attack on the influence which contemporary philosophy was exerting on theological teaching. In this attack, Greek and Islamic philosophers, among them Aristotle, Avicenna and Averroes, were condemned, along with those such as Aquinas who accepted their system of thought. As part of this rationalist movement, judicial astrology was singled out for severe criticism, while even some tenets of natural astrology were treated with great caution. Some of the condemned propositions which were claimed to be found in the new rationalist teaching included the following:

> That by different signs in the heavens there are signified different conditions in men, both of their spiritual gifts and their temporal affairs.
> That our will is subject to the power of the heavenly bodies.
> That fate, which is a universal disposition, proceeds from the divine providence not immediately, but by mediation of the movement of the heavenly bodies.
> That anyone attribute health and sickness, life and death, to the position of the stars and the aspect of Fortune, saying that if Fortune is well-aspected to him he will live, and if not he will die.
> That in the hour of the begetting of a man in his body and consequently in his soul, which follows the body, by the ordering of the causes superior and inferior, there is in a man a disposition inclining him to such and such actions and events. This is an error, unless it is understood to mean 'natural events' and 'by way of a disposition.

The disquiet which astrology had aroused among some churchmen may be judged from the strength of this statement. The third proposition here is a denial of the almost universally-accepted theory that God made use of the stars as intermediaries to govern many aspects of the temporal realm. The fourth proposition might be read as contradicting the fundamental tenet of medieval medicine, namely that the systems of the human body respond by natural laws to the influences of the planets. This edict of condemnation was not a universal statement of doctrine binding on the entire church, for its real aim was to control the content of teaching at the theological school in Paris, and a similar condemnation was issued in Oxford very soon afterwards. However, Paris was the acknowledged centre of contemporary learning, hence the importance of this statement, directed at the heart of theological teaching in Europe. But the progress of astrology was irresistible, and in truth this condemnation seems to have had no lasting force. By 1323 Aquinas had been canonised, and given the additional title of honour 'Doctor of the Church', and the arguments which he had drawn out concerning the validity and the limits of astrology commanded almost universal assent.

The music of the spheres. The idea that each planet emitted its own notes and that together they formed a harmony in the heavens dates back to Pythagoras; authorities disagreed however as to the order of the notes.
Bayerisches Staatsbibliothek, Munich

*T*HE *great mortality appeared at Avignon in June 1348 when I was in the service of Pope Clement VI. It produced fever, the spitting of blood, with tumours in the external parts, chiefly in the armpits and the groin, and people died in three days. It was so contagious that not only by staying together, but even by looking at one another, people caught it. Men died without attendants and were buried without priests. Charity was dead and hope was crushed. I call it great because it covered the whole world, for it began in the east, and passed through our region towards the west. It was so great that it left scarcely a fourth part of the people... Many were in doubt about the cause of this mortality. In some places they thought the Jews had poisoned the world, so they killed them. In others that it was the poor deformed, and they drove them out. Many believed that it came from the stars as God's punishment.*

This graphic picture of the Black Death was penned by Guy de Chauliac, a celebrated physician who personally survived the plague. It is an eloquent testimony to the horror which the event aroused in the consciousness of Europe, the conviction that this was an event of cosmic proportions which threatened to destroy humanity. Such an event must have a cause, and the explanations put forward by contemporaries give a valuable insight into medieval science. From 1348 onwards, tracts describing the plague began to circulate, most of them offering advice on how to avoid the infection, and speaking in a general way of 'a corruption of the air'. The most significant pronouncement was the one which brought astrology into the picture. It was dated October 1348 and came from the medical faculty of the University of Paris, which had been commanded by King Philip VI to consider the origin of the plague. Their judgement was that on 28 March 1345, a triple conjunction of Mars, Jupiter and Saturn had taken place in the constellation Aquarius, and that this was the direct cause of the 'pernicious corruption of the surrounding air, as well as other signs of mortality, famine and other catastrophes.' Aristotle and other unnamed sources were cited to support this theory, and the sequence of events was explained in the following way: Jupiter is a warm, humid planet which draws up evil vapours from the earth and its oceans; Mars being excessively hot and dry, set fire to those vapours, whence there were in the air, flashes of lightning, pestilential vapours and fires, especially since Mars, a malevolent planet generating choler and wars, was from October 1347 until May 1348 in Leo with the Head of the Dragon. Not only did all of them, being warm, attract many vapours, but Mars on the wane was in evil aspect with Jupiter, engendering a disposition hostile to humanity. From this were generated strong winds, which Jupiter has the power of raising, from the south, giving rise to great heat and dampness.

This novel explanation, citing a conjunction which had occurred three years before the outbreak, clearly exercised a persuasive influence on all later writers on the plague, for the theory that the stars were the direct cause had not been mentioned before. A contemporary Italian tract claimed to be a translation of the Paris judgement, but gave a different and more dramatic explanation of the astrology involved. In India, it was stated, the Sun and the constellations struggled violently with the waters of the Great Sea, the greater part of which was drawn up in vapours which corrupted the air. These spread through India, Arabia and the Mediterranean, and none could survive them as long as the Sun remained in Leo. But the Sun and the constellations were 'striving by their divine might to aid the human race', to break through the mist and change it into rain which would purify the air. From this rain people should protect themselves, and after it should build great fires in the open and in their houses. Further tracts all agreed that nature had indeed shown ominous signs before the plague arrived, with reports of yellow skies, violent winds from the south, fish dying in the sea, the appearance of multitudes of reptiles, and fruit rotting on the trees.

That the air had, in general terms, become corrupted, seemed beyond doubt, and in medieval science the air was not divided from the realm of the stars and planets – instead they formed a continuum. The strength or weakness of the four elemental qualities – heat, cold, dryness, and moistness – was continuously affected by the planets, most obviously in the field of human health in the balance of the humours. The concept of corrupt air was thus an exact, large-scale parallel to the sickness of the individual. But there were a number of difficulties with the astrological theory. Why did the plague strike some towns and spare others nearby? Some astrologers answered by invoking the doctrine of the aspects: the rays of the malevolent planets struck only those towns which were badly positioned. But this was confusing, for it seems to run counter to the notion that the air become universally corrupt. Why did the plague not cease when the conjunction ceased, and why had previous conjunctions never produced such dire results? Some astrologers, such as Geoffrey of Meaux in France and John Ashenden in England, claimed that the total lunar eclipse of 18 March 1345 was the really significant celestial event, rather than the conjunction alone. A few tracts opposed the dominant astrological theory and proposed instead that the earthquake which struck Germany, Austria and Hungary in 1347 had allowed corrupting vapours to escape from the bowels of the earth, and that this was the true cause.

These astrologers were of course rationalising after the event. Ashenden liked to claim that he had predicted the plague before it occurred, but he had actually foretold that the usual threefold curses of war, famine and disease would follow the eclipse. Of course there was too an empirical understanding of infection – that the clothes of the dead must be burned, and so on – but infection had no attraction as the ultimate cause. The ultimate cause of this disaster, as of all other events on earth, was the will of God; but the means which God employed to express divine displeasure was the natural mechanism of astrological forces. The role of the stars as intermediaries through which God governed the universe was perfectly displayed in the case of this great conjunction followed by a catastrophic plague. The theory of the elements, and the interdependence of man and the universe provided a clear, scientific framework within which the great plague might be understood. The reconciliation of astrology and the Christian religion could not be more evident. The episode of the Black Death, and the link which the Paris doctors made with the planetary conjunction three years earlier, had the effect of raising the prestige of astrology, and confirming its place within the scheme of medieval science.

ASTROLOGY AND MEDIEVAL SCIENCE

Astrology was part of the system of medieval sciences, and as such it interacted with other fields of learning. For example astro-meteorology proceeded from the conviction that the stars and planets radiated physical effects such as heat or moisture, which were conveyed through the ether to cause on the earth storms or floods or droughts. Comets – rarer and more dramatic in their appearances – had always been seen as portents of great events on earth. Strangely perhaps, Ptolemy had had nothing to say about them, but the literature on comets grew considerably during the middle ages. Geoffrey of Meaux, a scholar who worked at Paris and Oxford between 1315 and 1350, discussed two theories as to the origin of comets. One was that they were deliberate creations of the divine will to give warning of future calamities; Geoffrey however preferred the second theory, that they were engendered naturally in the sky as the result of conjunctions or aspects of the planets, and that they served to greatly reinforce the significance of those events. Their effects were sometimes believed to be physical in that they exuded vapours, hot or cold, moist or dry, which affected the air and produced strange, perhaps poisonous effects. Geoffrey composed treatises on the comets which appeared in 1315 and 1337, in which he predicted that the toxic effects would give rise to physical disease and political unrest. Many medieval authors attempted to classify comets according to types, and to allocate them to various planets whose natures they shared. In medieval thought there was of course no awareness of the nature and extent of the earth's atmosphere, and consequently no distinction was made between atmospheric and astronomical phenomena. The link between astronomy and meteorology had ancient roots, going back to the earliest omens of Babylonia, and the link was preserved in the popular mind for centuries through the weather predictions given in the yearly almanacs.

The science which provided the essential infrastructure of astrology was of course mathematics. The absence of astronomical data in Latin had been one of the principal causes of the near-extinction of astrology in the west from the late Roman period onwards. When the western astrological revival began in the twelfth century, it was essential that not only theoretical and philosophical works were translated from the Arabic, but also the mathematical tools with which celestial positions could be determined. The fundamental work on planetary motion, Ptolemy's *Almagest*, had never been available in Latin during the thousand years following its composition, until the Latin translation by Gerard of Cremona was completed around the year 1175. The mathematical tools in question took the form of texts which analysed the motions of each planet in such a way that their positions at any given moment could be computed – in astrological terms the planets could be placed within the horoscope. Such texts began with a radix, the position of each planet at the epoch from which the whole work was dated. Then followed data on the mean speed of the planets, parameters of their movements in latitude and longitude, periods of retrogradation and invisibility, and all the data necessary for the astronomer to chart celestial movements. Added to the mathematical formulae would be tables in which the actual positions of each planet through a certain future period would be given. For the astrologer these would be the vital part of the text, unless he himself was a skilled mathematician. The most important medieval texts of this kind were the Toledan Tables and the Alfonsine Tables. The first were produced by a group of Islamic astronomers working in Toledo in the second half of the eleventh century; one hundred years later Latin versions had been produced which were circulating in France and in England, with the necessary corrections for the different latitude. The Toledan tables enshrined the mathematics of Ptolemy, and they provided the basic framework of all mathematical astronomy for two centuries. They were generally replaced by the Alfonsine tables, which were produced, again at Toledo, under the patronage of King Alfonso the Wise. Dated to the epoch 1252, they were the work of Jewish, Muslim and Christian scholars, and they contained much additional material concerning the astrolabe, precession, computus, and so on, forming virtually an encyclopedia of astronomy. The diffusion of first the Toledan and then the Alfonsine Tables was a necessary precondition for the emergence of practical astrology in Europe. While a few astrologers were also skilled

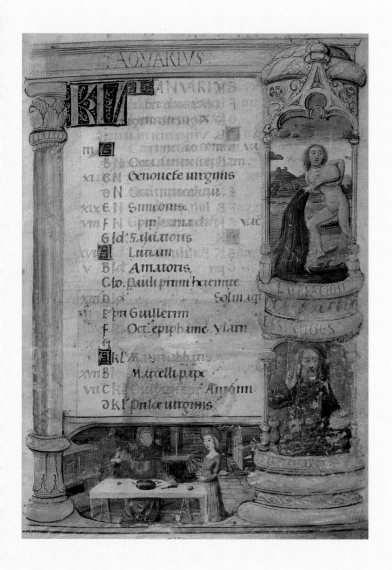

mathematicians, able to make detailed calculations for themselves, a growing number would inevitably rely on pre-calculated tables, and it was essential that they understood the corrections which should be made for different latitudes or different epochs. The leading mathematician, Adelard of Bath, was a great admirer of Islamic science and a translator of several important works from Arabic into Latin, and he may have been the only man in twelfth-century England qualified to cast a genuine horoscope. Yet several of his horoscopes survive which contain serious technical errors, for example making no corrections for latitude from the Arabic tables which he employed . If Adelard was typical of twelfth-century practice, then some little time would evidently be needed before the

The Zodiac signs were familiar images in medieval calendars, but they functioned here as symbols of time, with little or no astrological significance.
The British Library
Add.MS.35315 f.1.
and Add.MS.11866 f.1

ONE OF THE best-known and most evocative images in the history of astrology is the Zodiac Man, the human figure with the twelve Zodiac signs drawn on his body. This image appeared in hundreds of medieval manuscripts, it made the transition into printed works of astrology, and it survived in popular almanacs down to the nineteenth century. Its general significance has always been well understood, namely that each Zodiac signs governed the health of one part of the body, beginning in the head with Aries and progressing downwards to Pisces and the feet. The first full textual description of this system is to be found in the Latin poet Manilius's *Astronomicon*, dated around 15–20 AD. Curiously, neither Manilius nor any other classical writer offers any rationalisation for the scheme by which the signs and the bodily parts were related, but one may easily be inferred: if the Zodiac circle is outspread in a plane and a human figure is imposed on it, it will be seen that the signs fall on the parts of the body assigned to them by this astrological teaching. This image of the Zodiac Man can thus be seen as embodying in the clearest possible way the concept of the macrocosm-microcosm link, the mysterious correspondence between man and the heavens. The image must have acquired additional resonance in classical times from its resemblance to images of deities within a circular or oval frame surrounded by the Zodiac signs: both Mithras and Sol, the Sun-god, were shown in this way, and later even Christian artists adopted the image.

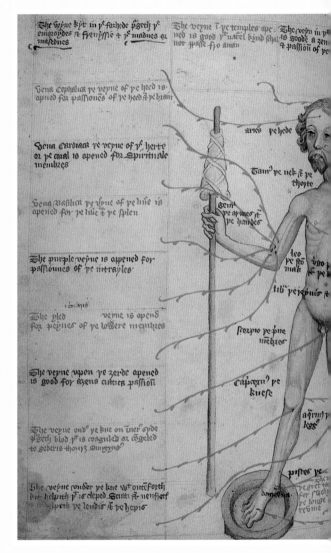

Aside from the symbolic value however, the Zodiac Man acquired a more specific significance in medieval science, a science in which astrology played an essential role. The fundamental tenet of astrological medicine was that man's physical nature depended on the balance of the four primary qualities of heat, cold, moistness and dryness – called in the human body the humours – and that the dominant influence on this balance came from the heavens. The planets shared these qualities directly, and the power of the planets was strengthened or weakened according to their place in the different Zodiac signs. Above all, the Moon was believed to exercise the greatest influence on the humoral fluids, just as it did on terrestrial fluids through its power over tides. If all sickness was considered to result from an imbalance of the humoral fluids, then the accepted method of restoring that balance was to bleed the patient. Phlebotomy – bleeding – was the indispensable technique of the physician from the middle ages to the eighteenth century, but it must be carried out scientifically or further disturbance of the fluids would result. It became a classic maxim that neither bleeding nor any other form of treatment of a part of the body must be attempted if the Moon stood in

the Zodiac sign which governed that part. For example, if the Moon were in Gemini, it could be dangerous or even fatal to bleed the arms, shoulders or hands. Thus the Zodiac Man functioned as visual mnemonic for use in phlebotomy, and it would be supplemented by tables giving the position of the Moon and other relevant astronomical data, or by instruments such as calendar-wheels, by which those positions might be found from the date. This connection between the Zodiac Man and the practice of bleeding was made explicit in a related image – the 'Vein Man', in which the principal veins of the body which were suitable for bleeding

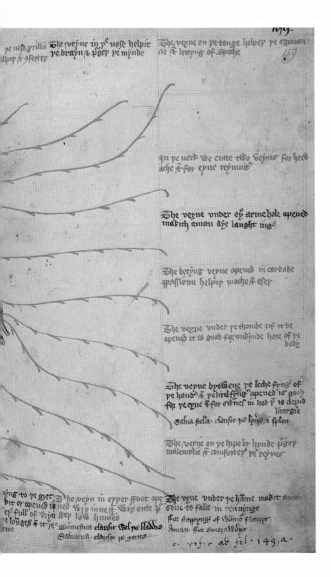

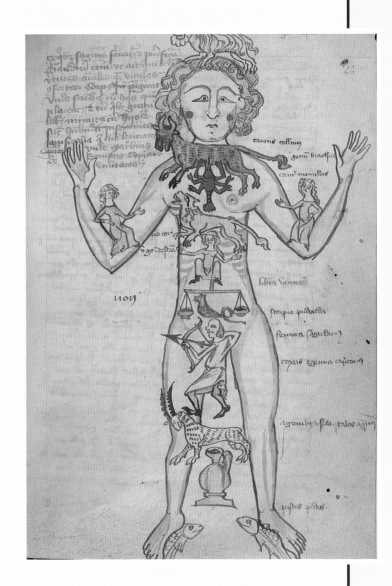

were shown and labelled under the nearest Zodiac sign.

However, astrological medicine resembled all other aspects of astrology, in that, while its main principles were clear, its detailed practice was fiendishly complicated. The governing of the human body by the twelve Zodiac signs was one such principle; but the planets had all, from classical times, been given specific powers over parts of the body too, and in fact a 'Planet Man' image was developed, although it is found more rarely. Then the positions of the planets at the onset of sickness, the 'decumbiture', as well as at the patient's nativity, had also to be considered. The result was that all these competing forces formed a web of interlocking influences which the physician must struggle to disentangle. In this, as in the casting of horoscopes, the professional astrologer marked out for himself an arcane territory to which he alone possessed the key. The potential confusions of theory and practice were mildly satirised by Shakespeare in *Twelfth Night*, when Sir Andrew Aguecheek exclaims 'Taurus! That's sides and heart,' and Sir Toby Belch corrects him, 'No sir, it is legs and thighs.' Both were wrong of course, for it was neck and throat, and no doubt the knowledgeable audience, perfectly familiar with their Zodiac Man, laughed at their foolishness.

mathematical basis of astrology was correctly applied by European astrologers. By contrast, by the late fourteenth century spherical astronomy had taken its place in the university curriculum, and scholars such as Richard of Wallingford in England and Nicole Oresme in France had thoroughly mastered the theory of planetary motion.

The emerging science of alchemy was one of the most exciting and controversial of medieval studies, and it was one which was wrapped in a far darker cloak of arcane philosophy than astrology itself. There was one special aspect of alchemy which linked it closely to astrology, namely that the metals corresponded in some way with the planets and shared their natures. This doctrine had been taught from the earliest origins of the science in Alexandrian Egypt; clearly it is easy to associate gold with Sun, and silver with the Moon. The other less obvious correspondences were Mars and iron, copper and Venus, quicksilver and Mercury, Jupiter and tin, lead and Saturn. Some alchemical writers seem to have believed that these metals actually arrived on earth from their respective planets, in cosmic storms perhaps. Behind the physical operations of the alchemist lay the belief that it was not matter alone which was being manipulated, but the transcendent powers of the planets, working through their earthly vessels, and all alchemists studied astrology in order to find the most propitious moment to carry out their experiments. From the idea of correspondences flowed the doctrine of talismans, the belief that the powers of the Zodiac signs or the planets might be harnessed in their images, incised on gems or metals, if they were made at the astrologically correct moment. This was veering very close to magic, and from a strictly religious viewpoint was suspect, and the effects of talismans could easily be attributed to the work of demons. Yet this practice was repeatedly discussed and certainly dismissed by authorities such as Grosseteste and Albertus Magnus. The

Above. *Medieval astrologers and surveyors at work, in a fifteenth-century manuscript. The men are said to be Egyptians, repeating the classical and medieval belief that the mathematical sciences, including astrology, were discovered by the Egyptians.*
The British Library
Royal MS.20.B.XX f.3

Facing page. *Horoscopes and alchemy: alchemists believed that their experiments must be conducted at astrologically favourable times because the earthly elements which they were manipulating were in fact embodiments of planetary qualities.*
The British Library
Add.MS.10302 f.67v

principle of correspondences also lay behind the use of herbs in medicine, the belief that plants shared the qualities of the celestial bodies, and that this fact could be systematically used to strengthen or weaken the influence of the planets over the human body. The Sun was linked to the heliotrope, the Moon to the peony; Saturn to sempervivum and Jupiter to agrimony; fennel was Mars's plant,

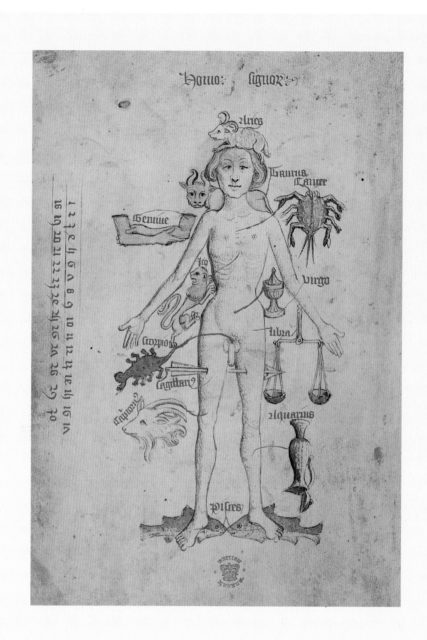

Right and facing page.
Astrological medicine: these illustrations from a fifteenth-century surgeon's manual show the familiar Zodiac Man and an adjustable horoscope-dial to set the position of the sun.
The British Library
Egerton MS.2572 ff.50r-51

while Verbena belonged to Mercury. These were some of the most common, but all astrologers had their lists and their favourites.

One of the original applications of omens in ancient Babylon had been to predict the course of disease, and the science most closely linked to astrology throughout the middle ages was always medicine, which was of more universal interest than alchemy. Without exception, all the medical authorities of the middle ages and the Renaissance accepted that astrological learning was essential to the practice of medicine, since, as one of them put it, 'All things here below, air, water, the complexions, sickness and so on, suffer change in accordance with the motions of the planets'. The principles of medical astrology had scarcely changed since the classical era when the foundations had been laid by Hippocrates and Galen. First the four elements or qualities manifested themselves in the human body as the four humours, respectively blood, black bile, phlegm and yellow bile,

also known as choler. These humours in turn are responsible for the four temperaments – sanguine, melancholic, phlegmatic and choleric. Every individual was a blend of these four humours, but when their balance was disturbed, sickness resulted. The greatest single cause of such an imbalance was the movements of the planets, for their physical natures shared these qualities. The predominance of a hot planet like Jupiter or a cool one like Saturn, would cause the relevant humour to ebb or flow like a tide within the body. Broadly speaking, the qualities of the planets were usually believed to be related to the humours in this way:

The Sun	–	Hot and Dry	–	Choleric
Mars	–	Hot and Dry	–	Choleric
Jupiter	–	Hot and Moist	–	Sanguine
Saturn	–	Cold and Dry	–	Melancholic
The Moon	–	Cold and Moist	–	Phlegmatic
Venus	–	Cold and Moist	–	Phlegmatic
Mercury	–	Variable	–	Variable

The second great principle of diagnosis and treatment was that the parts of the human body are all under the special influence of one of the Zodiac signs, from Aries at the head to Pisces at the feet. This scheme was arrived at by outspreading the image of the human figure upon the Zodiac circle, the most forceful expression of the supposed correspondence between man and the cosmos. The physician therefore must consult a patient's horoscope, first to determine his humour, then at the time of the onset of the disease, and again to find a propitious moment for treatment. This type of medicine relied heavily on the theory of critical moments, when the sickness would either culminate in death, or disappear. Chaucer's doctor could;

> ...guess the ascending of the star
> Wherein his patient's fortunes settled were.
> He knew the course of every malady,
> Whether it were of cold or heat or moist or dry.

Medicine on these principles was taught in the universities of Europe from the thirteenth century onwards, where it took its place beside philosophy and the other sciences like mathematics and astronomy, all drawn from the same classical and Islamic authorities. It was in this period that astrological terms became part of the English language: the temperaments inspired by the planets are obvious – Martial, Mercurial, Jovial and so on., and the 'lunatic' who is under the sway of the Moon. But there are also 'disaster' – something descended from the stars; 'consider' – something judged by the stars; good or bad 'aspects' to a question; somewhat later, 'venereal' disease and 'influenza' would show the extent to which astrology still dominated medical thought.

In 1184, a great conjunction of the planets had passed off without disastrous results; but a century and a half later, a similar conjunction of Saturn, Jupiter and Mars in the sign of Aquarius was identified by contemporaries as the cause of a truly cataclysmic event. In 1347 the Black Death – bubonic plague – arrived in the west and swept through Europe, killing perhaps one third of the entire population in two years. Physicians and scholars all speculated on the cause of this catastrophe, and the medical faculty of the University of Paris, commissioned to report on the crisis, attributed it to a 'corruption of the air' caused by the conjunction. John of Ashendon, an Oxford astrologer active at this time, made a special study of conjunction theory, and turned his attention to the next one, which was due in 1365, in which the planets Jupiter and Saturn would pass from the triplicity of air in to that of water in the sign of Scorpio. He considered that this conjunction heralded great religious events, possibly the destruction of the Saracens, who would however be replaced by a new sect equally false and cruel. This idea that impending catastrophe faced the Islamic faith was widespread at this time, stemming from Abu-Mashar's prediction that Islam would survive for 693 years. To our eyes, there is of course not the slightest evidence of a link between a planetary conjunction and a crisis such as the Black Death, but as with most medieval science, such connections would be described in a theoretical or conceptual way. There was not, and could not be, any precise explanation of how these connections operated. The theory of the qualities and the principle of correspondences together provided a conceptual framework which was coherent and plausible, but whose detailed workings could never be demonstrated.

Clearly astrology had now taken its place at the centre of European intellectual life, and it had done this by developing the vital distinction between natural and judicial astrology. That this distinction was all-important is shown by the fate of Cecco d'Ascoli, the only medieval astrologer that we know of to be burned at the stake for his writings. Cecco had been lecturing at Bologna on both medicine and astronomy, when he was found guilty in 1324 of offences against the faith, and was ordered to cease teaching. In 1326 in he was in Florence as a court astrologer, but apparently his offence was repeated, and he was executed in the following year. We have no clear, contemporary evidence about what exactly Cecco said or

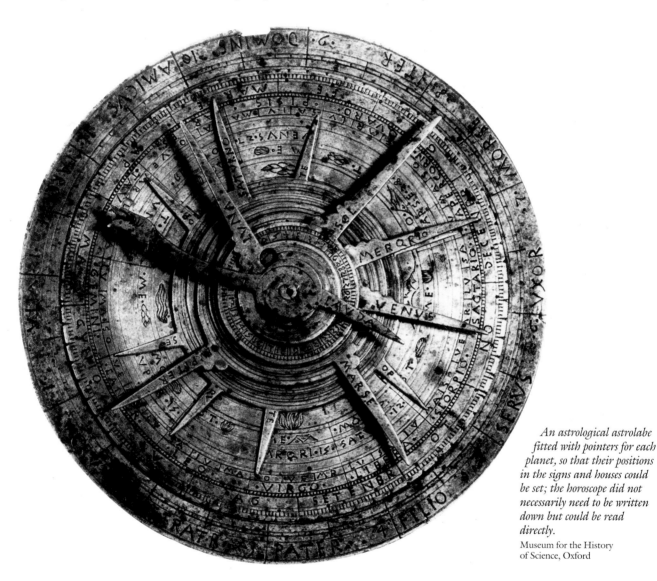

An astrological astrolabe fitted with pointers for each planet, so that their positions in the signs and houses could be set; the horoscope did not necessarily need to be written down but could be read directly.

Museum for the History of Science, Oxford

wrote that was so controversial. His surviving writings seem conventional enough, although it is possible that their texts were later tampered with, to make them theologically safer. Commentators some time afterwards reported that he applied astrology to the life of Christ, and cast Christ's horoscope, maintaining that his birth in human form must have placed him under the rule of the stars. If this is true, then it suggests that Cecco transgressed the general ban on judicial astrology, and that he chose to discuss the most provocative example of it that he could find. However Cecco's punishment did not signal a general attack upon astrologers, and this suggest that there may have been some very special circumstances surrounding his case. This episode is a reminder of the reasons why, one

thousand years earlier, astrology had been rejected as having no place within the Christian world-view. Astrology had returned as part of the new form of natural philosophy which emerged during the twelfth century, rediscovered from classical and Islamic sources. Christian churchmen now found this natural philosophy intellectually convincing, but certain limits had still to be enforced over the scope of astrology: the claim that human destiny was subject to the stars was still controversial, while speculations about God's freedom to act were totally unacceptable.

Above. *Man as the microcosm, the focus of the natural forces of the universe, including the four elements and the seven planets.*
The figure is unmistakably Christ-like, and shows the microcosm doctrine entirely integrated within medieval Christianity.
Bayerisches Staatsbibliothek, Munich

Facing page. *Man as the centre of the universe, from the works of the mystic, St Hildegard of Bingen. Here man replaces the earth at the centre of the cosmos, and becomes the focus of celestial forces – the basic tenet of astrology.*
Scala

CHAPTER FOUR

THE RENAISSANCE:

TRIUMPH AND DOWNFALL

ASTROLOGY AND POWER POLITICS IN ENGLAND AND FRANCE

In the autumn of 1441, London was electrified by revelations which emerged during a sensational criminal trial involving astrology, witchcraft and treason. Eleanor Cobham, Duchess of Gloucester, wife of the Lord Protector of the realm, was accused of plotting against the life of King Henry VI, aided by two astrologers, Richard Bolingbroke and Thomas Southwell, and by a woman known as 'The Witch of Eye', whose name was Margery Jourdemayne (Eye is a village in Suffolk). The Duchess admitted that she had consulted Bolingbroke and Southwell for astrological help in conceiving a child. These two men were reputable physicians and senior Oxford scholars, and the former was the author of a treatise on judicial astrology. Together, for reasons which were never satisfactorily explained away, these people cast a horoscope of the king, which predicted that he would soon die a violent death. This whole episode was dramatised in Part Two of *King Henry VI*, where Shakespeare shows the prophecy being produced by necromancy, by spirits conjured from hell. But the prediction was undoubtedly astrological, for the original horoscope still survives. It is uncertain whether Eleanor was in fact intriguing against the king, or whether she had fallen into a trap set by her enemies at court to destroy her and her husband. Shakespeare suggests that it was both, that she was ambitious, but that her ambitions were known and used by her enemies. Bolingbroke and Southwell were paid to question the stars about the king's fate, and they gave the answer which they thought was expected to such a question. Unfortunately their actions were exposed, they found themselves on the losing side in a court intrigue, and they paid the price. All four were found guilty; Bolingbroke was hung, drawn and quartered at Smithfield, while Southwell only escaped the same fate by dying in prison. Margery Jourdemayne was burned, and Eleanor Cobham was exiled for life. The king commissioned two astrologers to produce an alternative interpretation of the horoscope. Ironically of course, the first prediction – the treasonable one – was correct, and Henry was to die a violent death; but that was much later, and a keen observer of English politics at the time might perhaps have predicted that without the help of astrology.

The 1441 case demonstrates forcefully that astrology had ceased to be a subject of interest only to the intellectual elite. It had emerged from the scholar's study and had become a powerful force in the political and social life of the fifteenth century. There is a clear parallel here with astrology's position in Rome during the reign of Tiberius. Monarchs and their enemies could both employ astrologers whose self-interest lay in telling their patrons what they wished to hear, especially

The horoscope of King Henry VI cast by Roger Bolingbroke and Thomas Southwell in 1448. Its prediction of the king's violent death led to the death of the two distinguished astrologers.
Cambridge University Library

160

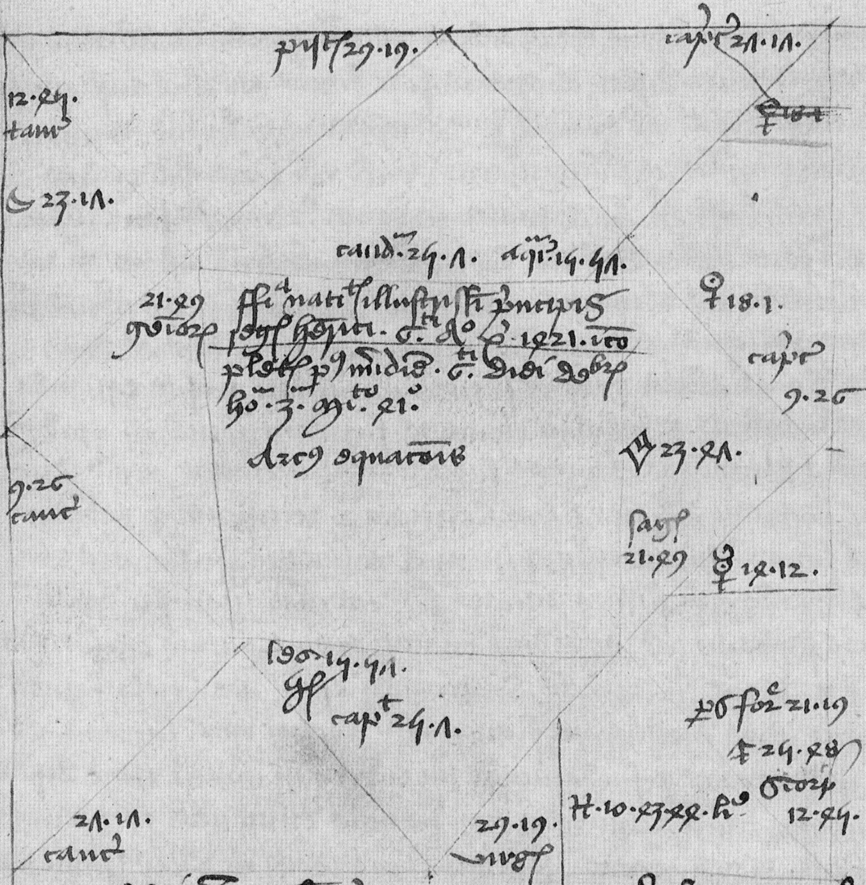

Primum capitulum prime partis in corrigendo figuram radicis

Hec figura rectificata est per Aminodar medij celi ad instans Iouis diei
et abmixtas coniunctionis precedentis ista natiuitatem cuius locus erat
13 gradibus Sagittarij. Hec autem figura et equatio domorum calculata est
in gradibus et minutis secundum tabulam ascensionis signorum Magistri
Johannis de Lineriis eleuatas super latitudinem 51 graduum quam est
nostro proposterior pro loco natiuitatis et matris accedentem ad veram latitudinem eiusdem loci latitudo enim loci illius scilicet Wyndesour minor est
latitudine London quia mater accedit ad meridiem etsi non directe cuius
latitudo tamen parum excedat latitudinem. In gradibus quia solitudo per
22 in sequitur igitur quod latitudo Wyndesour minus habet in 4 per tantum
minus in 4 quantus est minus miliarios quo Wyndesour excedat London
versus meridiem et ratio est quia ad minimum cuilibet miliario a
linea in austrum correspondet vnum minutum latitudinis et vltra quia sicut

27. Iouis

Wyndesour. 51. 0
latitudo London 51. 24

quod non sit verum indicat situs
plane inter oriente et occidentem.
ut tot minutis differet etiam ad
meridie tederet windesour
cum absit londinio tria 20000 pas.

on the key question of the likely timing of a ruler's death. By the time of the Cobham case, astrology was no longer just an intellectual pursuit, but had resumed its role as a 'Royal Art', a role it had enjoyed in Babylon, Rome and in the Islamic world – with dangerous political and personal consequences. Astrology had acquired a broader social relevance, but had not yet become a popular art: instead, its claimed ability to foretell the future had made an appeal to those wielding power of any kind. In the medieval context, only those wielding power needed to know the future, for what did the future matter to the common man, whose life was obscure, unchanging and monotonous? The king however could not afford to ignore auguries, and he would be wise to cultivate the various arts of divination in his role as a shaper of destiny. This theme of astrology as a Royal Art is one which left its traces on medieval literature; Geoffrey of Monmouth for example, describes King Arthur's court as sustaining a school of two hundred philosophers 'learned in astronomy and the other arts, who diligently observed the movements of the stars, and foretold to King Arthur by accurate calculations the coming of any remarkable thing.' It has been suggested that such descriptions embody rumours of the Muslim court of Toledo, brought to the west by the Christian scholars who studied Islamic science in Spain.

Above. *Horoscope of King Edward III, born 13 November 1312. This horoscope was set down a century or more after the event, and is so full of omens of future glory that it seems contrived: the Sun is in the Ascendant, Mars in his own domicile of Scorpio, while Juipter is in conjunction with the Lot of Fortune.*
The British Library
Royal MS.12.F.XVII f.153v

Facing page. *King Edward III's copy of* Secreta Secretorum, *a treatise on divination supposedly written by Aristotle for Alexander the Great. Here we see the king surrounded by his astrologers.*
The British Library
Add.MS.47680 f.53v

The rise of astrology to a central and powerful position in court circles occurred throughout Europe from around the year 1300 onwards, and it forms a clear intellectual link between the middle ages and the Renaissance. In fact as far as astrology is concerned, the true Renaissance occurred late in the twelfth century, with the recovery of the science from Islamic sources. Thereafter, its doctrines and techniques spread irresistibly through the universities and courts of Europe. The literary and artistic Renaissance of the fifteenth century added a new philosophical dimension to astrology, but its rebirth as an intellectual force was by then an established fact. The long centuries of Christian hostility to astrology had finally been in vain, and astrology became of intense and universal interest to philosophers, churchmen, rulers and courtiers. Astrology had survived all the attacks directed at it, and had proved impossible to stop or to ignore. This was especially true for kings and those around them, for any prediction of misfortune or death could become a rallying-point for one's enemies, and demanded an alternative prediction to refute it. The rivalries and uncertainties of political life produced a feverish desire to foretell, and therefore perhaps control, the future, and astrology's claim to fulfil this need explains its irresistible appeal. This appeal was all the greater because astrology was not merely a system of divination, but had widened into a system of beliefs about cosmology, natural events, health and disease, destiny and death. To the obvious question how this system could co-exist with nominal Christianity, the answer is that it was made to complement Christianity. Orthodox religion avowed the *fact* that God governed the world; astrology

explained *how* he did so – through the mechanism of the stars, through the complex, all-powerful influences which they rained down upon the earth. Astrology fulfilled the role of a science, and a science which could be shown to be part of the divine plan of the universe.

In the case of England and France, the period of the Hundred Years' War, from 1337 to 1453, is rich in records of astrology's political importance. From contemporary chronicles, it appears that both the English and the French combatants frequently sought astrological advice about the best moment to engage in battle, often by studying horoscopes of the military leaders. John Ashendon, the leading Oxford astrologer who had made a special study of astrology and world history, predicted in the early 1340s that the king of England would gain great victories overseas. Personal horoscopes had been rare in the west during the twelfth and thirteenth centuries, but horoscopes for the English and French kings of the fourteenth century do survive, although they are not necessarily contemporary with their subjects. Edward III was a pious monarch, who seems to have resisted the rise of astrology, so that a horoscope cast for him which is rich in auspicious omens was probably the later work of an admiring subject. In this horoscope, the Sun is in the house of the ascendant, Mars is in its own house of Scorpio and is in conjunction with Venus, while Jupiter is in conjunction with Lot of Fortune. This was an astonishingly propitious chart, and fitting for the warlike ruler who lead England into the long conflict with France, and who was the victor at the Battle of Crècy. Ironically therefore, it was in a victory sermon preached after that battle that King Edward listened to an attack on astrology by the future Archbishop of Canterbury, Thomas Bradwardine, who asked:

> 'What astrologer could predict this? What astrologer could judge that this would happen? What astrologer could foresee such a thing? Indeed, beloved, here is one prediction which will never be proved false: whatever God wishes to happen or to be done, that is done; whoever God wishes to be victorious, he is victorious, and whoever God wishes to reign, he will reign. Although therefore the heavens and the earth, and all things under the heavens should be against you, if God is for you, what can harm you?'

Bradwardine was eloquently voicing here the traditional Christian hostility to astrology, to man's futile attempts to pry into the future; and indeed within three years, Bradwardine himself would be dead of the plague, while Edward III would experience no further military triumphs in his reign. King Edward's only direct link with astrology is that he is known to have possessed a fine manuscript copy of the *Secreta Secretorum*, a widely-studied work of the middle ages, supposedly written by Aristotle to his pupil Alexander the Great, but probably composed by an Islamic author in eleventh-century Spain. Roger Bacon had made a version of the *Secreta* sometime before 1250, and it was translated into most of the European vernacular languages, copies being owned by the royal families of France, Italy, Poland, Hungary and Bohemia. The text deals with alchemy and various forms of divination, including astrology, and its purpose is to urge the propriety of these studies to any king. The author of this manual of occult science urges that the wise ruler 'Will neither rise up nor sit down nor eat nor drink nor do anything without the advice of men learned in the art of astrology'. King Edward's manuscript shows a number of images of a king surrounded by his astrological advisers. Many versions of this work, including Bacon's, are at pains to show that these arts of divination are entirely consistent with the training of a Christian ruler, and that he might do great good to his subjects and to the church and to the whole world by acquiring the keys to nature's secrets.

If Edward III was cool towards astrology, the more cultured and exotic tastes of his successor, King Richard II, seem to have drawn him closer to divination, prophecy and the occult. His troubled reign suggests the natural conclusion that this interest in the supernatural tended to flourish as a result of the tension and unrest of the times. This interest could then spread as a matter of fashion, just as

Renaissance princes could be drawn by fashion to art, literature or architecture. An interesting interrogatory horoscope survives relating to King Richard, namely a judicial question dated 5 July 1376, to determine 'Whether Richard of Burgundy would possess the throne of England'. This came just weeks after the death of the

Another illustration from the Secreta Secretorum; *the king, above, consults with his astrologers about the horoscope of the child born to the queen, below.*
The British Library
Add MS.47680 f.31v

heir to the throne, Edward the Black Prince, when the aged king Edward III had less than a year to live. The signs were undoubtedly auspicious for Richard, with Jupiter in the ascendant and Venus and Mercury in the midheaven; a note on the horoscope declares that events followed the course predicted. The chroniclers of Richard II's reign, such as Thomas Walsingham, all agree that the young king soon showed his unstable character by associating with sorcerers and astrologers, and that his reign was characterised by disturbing political prophecies. Walsingham was undoubtedly hostile to Richard, and interpreted the appearance of a comet in 1382 as presaging war and bloodshed. Still more significant was the conjunction of Jupiter and Saturn in May 1385, for this was followed by 'a great confusion in the kingdom, for earthly events are affected by the heavens, like a pen writing upon paper'. King Richard's own personal interest in astrology is attested by his ownership of a magnificent encyclopedia of divination, describing the sciences of astrology, physiognomy, the unravelling of dreams, and geomancy. Geomancy was the interpretation of patterns in sand or small stones; it was a system that had been much cultivated by Islamic practitioners, and it was seen as an easier alternative to the difficult science of astrology. King Richard's book contains in tabular form, 3,000 geomantic answers to twenty-five basic problems, such as the outcome of an illness, the wisdom of undertaking a journey, whether to engage in armed conflict, and so on. That King Richard II should resort to such devices confirms the view of him as a troubled and unstable monarch. Further testimony to the growing currency of astrology in court circles comes in the poetry of Chaucer, whose work is not only saturated with astrological references,

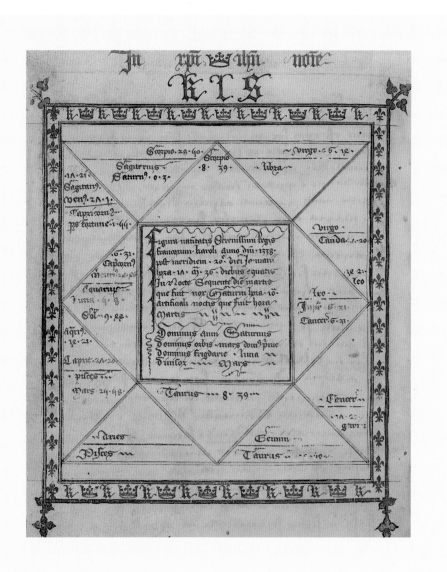

The horoscope of king Charles V of France: an unusual royal horoscope, for while the Sun is in the ascendant, the disposition of the other planets is quite ambiguous.
St John's College, Oxford

but who frequently built allegories of stellar and planetary movements into the narrative structure of his poems.

Undoubtedly a more scholarly monarch than Richard was his French counterpart, King Charles V, in whose vast (for its time) personal library there were more than one hundred works on astrology and other forms of occult science. He founded – with Papal approval – a college of astrology within the University of Paris, endowing it with a library and the necessary astronomical instruments. Charles was known as Charles the Wise, and he surrounded himself with scholars, artists and intellectuals of all kinds. It was to Charles that Nicole Oresme, churchman, mathematician and author of the first French translations of Aristotle, addressed several influential treatises warning of the dangers and false claims of astrology. Oresme did not dispute the legitimate scientific aspects of astrology –

the role of the stars in medicine, in meteorology or in the cycles of world history –
but he revived the traditional Christian arguments against any attempt to predict
the future or read the fate of individuals.

At the outset of his argument, Oresme raised the interesting problem as to
whether we can be certain that the movements of the heavenly bodies are truly
commensurable, that is that their paths and velocities maintain constant proportion and ratio to each other. If they are not truly commensurable, then Oresme

*Charles V, the
scholar-king of
France, using an
armillary sphere.*
St John's College,
Oxford

doubted that there could exist any basis at all for making forecasts from them, for
incommensurability would undermine the harmony of the heavens, and render
impossible any precise knowledge of the stars' effects. Oresme then built up a catalogue of rational, commonsense objections to judicial astrology. In defending
the freedom of the individual from the decrees of the stars, he emphasised that
natural or secondary causes weigh at least as heavily as the power of the stars.
Thus one cannot ignore the disposition of parents when predicting a child's
future, and look only at the configuration of the heavens. Although a great commentator on Aristotle, Oresme denied that the heavenly motions are the cause of
all processes here on earth, and he believed that generation and corruption would
continue even if the heavens ceased to move. He denied that any occult force
emanated from the stars, and asserted that light, heat and the four primary

qualities are all that reach the earth from the sky. The doctrine of houses – that the stars exert their influence in different areas of life depending on their position in an arbitrary plan of the sky – he found utterly without logic; likewise he rejected the idea that each planet can dominate a certain day of the week or hour of the day. On interrogations and elections he was particularly severe, finding no possible rationale in science for them. Horoscopes he allowed might have some slight value in indicating a person's natural inclinations, but human life could never been seen as fixed and pre-determined. The denial of occult influences, and the denial of our ability to map such influences even if they exist, is the central thrust of Oresme's case, and it stands apart from his religious objections to the infringement of human freewill. He did not deny that historical events could be forecast in a general way – events such as wars, plagues, revolutions and the like – but he did not believe that they could be assigned to precise times or places. For example, he had no doubt that comets and other natural phenomena were portents of change on earth, but where their effects would fall was, he felt, beyond human knowledge.

Oresme represents a continuing tradition of resistance to the claims of judicial astrology, but his scepticism seems to have been shared by only a minority of French thinkers of the time, and some very powerful church figures rejected Oresme's arguments. Pierre D'Ailly, the great conciliarist, Cardinal of the church, and author of the influential scientific work *L'Image du Monde*, maintained that God had indeed established astrology as part of the divine rule of the universe, and that it was not in conflict with theology. While it was true that men could not infallibly explain all the effects of the stars, this was no grounds for abandoning astrology, for neither could men understand all the mysteries of theology or natural science, yet they did not abandon these pursuits because of their difficulties. The study of astrology, D'Ailly thought, was an aspect of natural theology, and he allowed very wide powers to the stars to determine events in the natural and human world. His defence of astrology is all the more significant when we remember how powerful a figure D'Ailly was in the church, and that no work of his was ever criticised or condemned as dangerous. Oresme died in 1382, during the long interval in the Hundred Years' War, but in 1407, civil war broke out in France, while in 1413 Henry V of England renewed hostilities. Significantly, a large French collection of horoscopes survives which were cast during the troubled period 1407–37, and whose purpose is to explain the rise and fall of certain individuals and families who played leading roles in these events: Philip, Duke of Burgundy, Henry IV and Henry V of England, Charles VII of France, John, Duke of Bedford, and several others. The existence of such horoscopes demonstrates the simple fact that polemics such Oresme's against astrology never had the slightest effect in lessening interest in the subject.

Some years after these events, in 1494, the astrologer Symon de Phares came into conflict with the theology faculty in Paris, and was forbidden to practise his art. As in the earlier case of Cecco d'Ascoli, the exact offence for which Symon was singled out is not known. Symon had been consulted by the young king, Charles VIII, so he can hardly have been a totally disreputable figure. The sequel to this condemnation was important, for Symon set out to vindicate himself and to secure the return of his confiscated books by writing a history of astrology. His *Receuil des plus célèbres astrologues* sought to show that astrology was a noble and religious practice, which had originated with the patriarchs of the Old Testament and had been cultivated by philosophers and kings in Babylonia, Greece and Rome. When Symon deals with the more recent past, he offers numerous anecdotes of the use of astrology during the period of the Hundred Years War. Many of Symon's stories, and the astrologers he names, appear in no other sources, and we have no means of knowing how much of his work may be invention or exaggeration. He seems to have assumed a high level of credulity in his king, to whom the work is addressed, and in his accusers, whom he hoped to win over. Typical of Symon's claims for the military impact of astrology during the war was his account of an astrologer named Yves de Saint Branchier, who caused the defeat of an English army under John de Montfort and the Duke of Lancaster, by casting horoscopes of the English leaders, and picking a day for battle when their stars were deeply inauspicious. Symon declares that many French astrologers had foretold the disastrous outcome of the Battle of Crècy and of Poitiers. He seems to have been sympathetic to King Richard II, and names a number of astrologers who had forewarned him that he would be deposed or even killed. Symon's pur

A star shining into a birth-chamber, shedding its influence on the new-born child.
The British Library
Arundel MS.66 f.148

pose was to persuade his king, Charles VIII, that astrologers should not be persecuted but protected and rewarded, and few of his stories can be verified or treated seriously. But he was undoubtedly drawing on a large body of anecdote, recollection and gossip, some written and some unwritten and now lost, which had gathered around the subject of astrology in fifteenth-century France, and whose existence shows once again the enormous interest in astrology outside the scholar's study.

A further development particularly evident in the fifteenth century was the linking of astrology with sorcery in treason trials. There was no astrological element in the case of Joan of Arc, but it was irresistible to Joan's enemies to brand her as a sorceress. In England the case of Eleanor Cobham was not the sole example. In 1419 Friar John Randolph, an Oxford divine who was patronised by Humphrey Duke of Gloucester and who was the author of a work on astronomy, was implicated in the conspiracy by Queen Joan of Navarre, widow of King Henry IV, against her stepson, Henry V. Joan was accused of having used sorcery to destroy the king 'en le plus haute et horrible manere'. Fearing for his life, Friar Randolph fled the country, but was recaptured and imprisoned in the Tower of London. The matter never came to open trial, and we know few details of the conspiracy, but it must have involved sorcery and astrological prediction. Joan was held in confinement for three years but released in 1422, on the death of Henry V, while Randolph languished in the Tower, where he died in 1429. A third such case occurred in 1477 during the reign of Edward IV, when two Oxford scholars, John Stacey and Thomas Blake, were tried for treason, having calculated the nativities of the King and of Edward, Prince of Wales, and having predicted when the King would die. 'In order to carry their traitorous intentions into effect', claimed their accusers, 'they worked and calculated by art, magic, necromancy and astronomy, the death and final destruction of the King and Prince.' Stacey and Blake had been commissioned in their parts by Thomas Burdett, an agent of the Duke of Clarence, who was both brother and enemy to the King. Clarence attempted to defend his agent, Burdett, but was himself arrested and later executed for treason, while the lesser men perished as victims of Clarence's downfall.

It is worth pausing to ask why astrology should have been associated in cases like these, and in some of the polemical attacks on it, with sorcery and magic? Had not astrology been developed alongside astronomy and mathematics as an academic science, which was considered to work , according to the classical doctrine, through strictly physical laws? Shakespeare's depiction in *Henry VI* of Bolingbroke and Southwell raising a demon before Eleanor Cobham was clearly more dramatic than showing them calculating a horoscope, but was there really any necessary connection between astrology and demon-ology? The answer seems to be that a view of the nature of astrological influence had grown up which was very different from the classical doctrine. In this alternative view, the universe was full of spirits, intelligences or demons, each associated with the planets and the Zodiac signs, and it was these spirits which caused astrological effects. Astrology veered into magic when it claimed that the adept could conjure these spirits and compel them to reveal the future. This tradition of astrological necromancy was present in the writings of certain figures such as Michael Scot, and later Antonius de Monte Ulmi. Antonius was active in Bologna in the 1380s, and claimed to have been consulted by the Emperor, Charles IV. He composed a book on conventional astrology, which was later praised by no less a figure than the astronomer Regiomontanus, and which was printed in Nurnberg in 1540. But he also wrote an exposition of necromancy, usually referred to as *Liber Intelligentiarium* which was decidedly unorthodox. In this work, Antonius explains that when a child is born, the chief intelligence of the relevant Zodiac sign appoints subordinate spirits to direct that individual's life, and that the planetary spirits also vie for influence over him. These spirits may be conjured

Facing page. *Fortune with a wheel, elevating men to worldly power around the king, then casting them down once more. The belief in Fortune as a real force in human life was an important stimulus to astrology, which offered the chance to rationalise Fortune's power*
The British Library
Royal MS.18.D.II f.30v

Below. *Magician raising a demon from within a magic circle, as prescribed by Antonius de Monte Ulmi. Some astrologers suggested that the powers of the signs and planets were in reality personal, demonic spirits which could be invoked by the adept. This picture is from the title-page of Marlowe's play* Doctor Faustus.
The British Library, c34.d.27

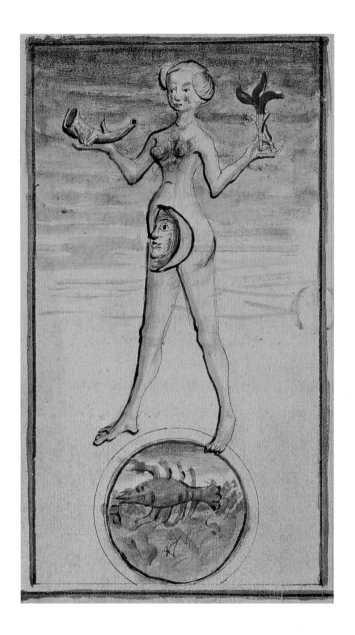

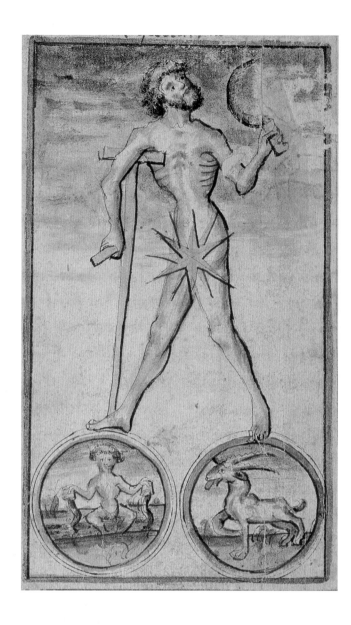

by incantations, by burning herbs or by focussing light through gems. They can be made to appear in mirrors or water, and they can even be imprisoned in bottles. When conjuring such spirits, the practitioner should operate from within a magic circle, traced with consecrated words and symbols. This form of magic seems to preserve a substratum of pagan, animistic beliefs which had little to do with the scientific astrology of the classical tradition, but they were in a sense easier to understand because they personalised astrological forces, and they were certainly easier to condemn. The figure of Faust was really the Renaissance culmination of this ancient fascination with forbidden powers.

All the astrologers in these sorcery trials had been trained at Oxford, some especially at Merton College, where there was a very strong tradition of mathematics and astronomy. But Cambridge too had developed a school of astrologers, and some of them became embroiled in politics. Lewis of Caerleon was physician and astrologer to several noble families, and to Henry, Earl of Richmond, later King Henry VII. When Richmond joined a rebellion against King Richard III, Lewis was imprisoned in the Tower as his associate. He was spared execution however, and employed his time in calculating astronomical tables. When Richmond seized the throne, Lewis was restored to favour as the new King's physician and

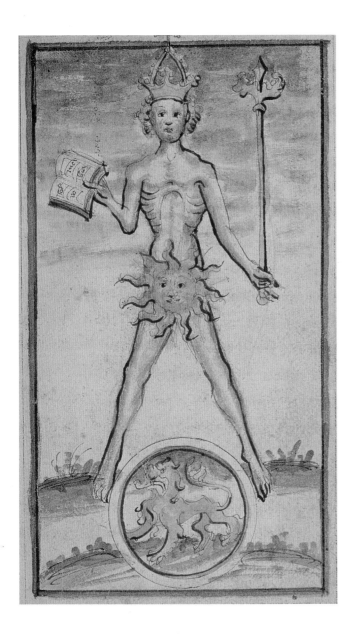

astrologer. He was succeeded by another Cambridge scholar, John Argentine, Provost of King's College from 1501 to 1508. Argentine had studied medicine and astrology in Italy, where the two disciplines were inextricably linked at universities such as Padua and Bologna. He had court contact before the accession of Henry VII, and was in fact the last physician to attend the Princes in the Tower. Argentine's position during the reign of Henry VII was officially that of physician, and it was somewhat later, around 1550, that royal accounts begin to show payments made to 'astronomers' alongside those made to physicians and apothecaries. Argentine compiled his own manuscript of astrological theory and practice, drawn from leading authorities, among whom was the executed Roger Bolingbroke. Argentine's papers also contain an intriguing proof of the ever-widening popularity of astrology: a manuscript of instructions for an astrological board game, in which the pieces are the seven planets which move against the background of the Zodiac stars. The connection in the fifteenth and sixteenth centuries between university scholarship and astrology had one very interesting result, namely the preservation of a large number of medieval astrological manuscripts. Many works in private, monastic or college libraries would undoubtedly have perished had not scholars such as Dee, Ashmole, Digby and Savile been

keenly interested in astrology and collected copies of the works of authors rang-
ing from Ptolemy and Abu-Mashar to Roger Bacon, John Ashendon and even
Roger Bolingbroke.

In spite of the evident dangers of the profession to those whose work took
them into court circles, it is clear that more and more scholars were now practis-

Right and facing page.
*Spheres of planetary influence.
A favourite motif among
medieval and Renaissance
illustrators were the areas of
life thought to be under the
special control of each planet.
Here we see Mercury presiding
over the activities of artists,
scholars and technicians;
Venus of course ruled love and
pleasure. These pictures were
sometimes known as
'Mercury's Children', 'The
Children of Venus' and so on.*
The British Library, L.R. 408.l.4.

ing as consultant astrologers, and that their clients were coming from an ever-
widening social base. From the mid-fifteenth century, the first accounts survive of
astrologer-physicians maintaining private consulting practices. John Crophill,
who lived and worked in rural Essex from 1430 to 1480, kept notes of his practice
as a doctor, describing the problems which his patients brought to him and his
advice and treatment. A similar notebook was kept by Richard Trewythian who

practised in London from 1442 to 1458, and who also combined medicine and astrology. Neither Crophill nor Trewythian were university scholars in the mould of Bolingbroke or Argentine., and their clients were certainly not aristocratic.

There can be no doubt that the arrival of printing was a powerful factor in spreading astrology downwards through the social classes. In continental Europe,

annual prognostications had appeared as broadsheets or pamphlets from the 1460s, giving general predictions about the weather, visitations of plague, natural disasters, poor harvests and so on. At universities such as Padua, a salaried doctor of astrology was required to compose these yearly forecasts, which would later become metamorphosed into the popular almanacs. In England the practice arrived somewhat later, but by 1497 William Parron, an Italian-born astrologer

William Parron: the inglorious career of England's first Royal Astrologer

LATE fifteenth-century England was a promising place for an astrologer to market his skills. The instability of the Wars of the Roses had created an appetite for prophecy, and print had arrived to widen the appeal of astrology, which had formerly been an elite and royal art. Yet the dangerous legacy of the fifteenth century, the perceived link between prophecy and treason, made it essential for a practising astrol-oger to gain secure royal patronage, and having gained it, he would take pains to ensure that his predictions glorified his master's political career.

Gulielmus Parronus (his Italian name is unknown) was a native of Piacenza who arrived in England around 1487, and in his fifteen years' residence, he combined private astrological work for his court patrons with published predictions for the popular market. He was in fact the first to issue in England, shortly before the year 1500, printed almanacs of the kind which had been current in Europe for almost fifty years. Parron succeeded in establishing himself in the court of King Henry VII, and by the autumn of 1499, he was engaged in two very different works, one for his royal patron and the other for the public at large. The latter work was his *Anni MD Prognosticon*, general predictions for the year 1500, comprising such familiar topics as the weather, harvest, general sickness, civil unrest and so on. The other, more interesting work was not published, but remained in manuscript for presentation to the king. This was the treatise *De astrorum vi fatali*, which was a brief, traditional argument for the fatal power wielded by the stars. Parron judiciously illustrated this power by reference to the horoscopes of certain of Henry VII's enemies – Richard III, and the rebels Perkin Warbeck and the Earl of Warwick, whose stars all foretold a violent end after vainly resisting the true king.

The great sadness of King Henry's reign was the death in 1502 of the crown prince Arthur, on whom many hopes had rested. Parron responded to this event late in the same year by offering to the king another private treatise, *Liber de optima fata Henrici Eboraci ducis et optimorum ipsus parentum* – 'A book concerning the high good fortune awaiting Henry, Duke of York and likewise his parents'. Rarely can an astrologer have laid his reputation so openly on the line, and rarely can he have been proved so disastrously wrong. The purpose of the text was simply to comfort the king and queen for the loss of their cherished elder son by predicting for his successor – the future King Henry VIII – and for themselves, length of life and a glorious reign. This manuscript is illuminated with a unique astrological image – a world map enclosed within the framework of a horoscope, clearly intended to show the world-dominating role of the future king. Where then did Parron go wrong? For Henry VIII he predicted a devout life as an outstanding servant of the church; he would also enjoy a blissful married life, and leave a large number of sons to secure the future of the realm. All this, with hindsight, is merely laughable, but at least Henry's break with Rome and his tangled marriages were thirty years in the future, so that Parron was on safe enough ground. Far worse for Parron was his prediction that the Queen, Elizabeth of York, would live to be 80 at least: she died just months later, in February 1503 at the age of 37. At a stroke, all Parron's work was undone, his treatises on the inevitability of the decrees written in the stars were rubbished, and he himself hastily vanished, both from the court and England, never to return. Shrewd, suspicious, hard and unforgiving, Henry VII was not the man to overlook such a blunder, which must have served in his eyes to reduce astrologers to time-serving flatterers.

Sir Thomas More composed a 'Rueful Lamentation of the Death of Queen Elizabeth' which pours scorn on the obsequious astrologer:

> Yet was I late promised otherwise,
> This year to live in wealth and delice;
> Lo, whereto cometh thy blandishing promise,
> O false astrology devinatrice,
> Of God's secrets making thyself so wise?
> How true is for this year thy prophecy?
> The year yet lasteth, and lo now here I lye.

Parron was never heard of again. Yet he has his place in history, for his prognostications – the yearly printed almanac – were soon imitated by other astrologers, and took root in England, and flourished for more than three centuries.

employed by King Henry VII, had written the first general prognostications to be printed in England. Just as royal horoscopes had answered questions about the future of dynasties, the almanacs would satisfy the popular desire to see into the future in mundane matters such as the weather and the harvest, and they would flourish and survive all changes in intellectual taste over the next five centuries. From being a learned science debated by university scholars, astrology had moved in the course of two centuries to become a royal art, where questions about destiny and the future were fraught with suspicions of treason and the threat of death; finally it had become a fashion for probing the future in which the masses could share by consulting a local expert, or by buying a penny almanac. All the warnings of the theologians and the philosophers about the dangers and the limitations of astrology had been in vain, and its consequent progress through society and into the popular consciousness had proved irresistible. The underlying reason for its apparent invincibility was surely this: that even its opponents had always admitted the validity of natural astrology as part of the cosmic scheme. Consequently the limits of astrology, and the extent to which celestial influence might work upon mankind could never finally be decided, and would always remain a subject of doubt and dispute. Not until this scientific consensus – that astrology was part of the cosmic scheme – began to crumble, would personal astrology finally lose its credibility.

PHILOSOPHICAL RENEWAL FROM ITALY

The diffusion of astrology beyond the world of the scholars during the period 1250–1450 occurred because the conviction grew that astrology was part of the cosmic order, and that its laws influenced all aspects of man's natural and social life. This conviction spread through all levels of society until it became the common currency of the time, the language of the streets. The doctrines involved, the network of beliefs which linked astronomy, medicine and the physical sciences, were essentially those of the Hellenistic age, with little that would have been unrecognisable to Ptolemy. The difference was that astrology was now taking root in a Christian culture, and therefore medieval astrologers devoted enormous energy to proving that these beliefs were not inconsistent with God's rule over the universe.

But astrology was to reach the height of its influence, when, from Renaissance Italy there emerged in the years 1450–1500 a new philosophical movement in which the interrelation of man, nature and the universe on the astrological level was a basic principle. This movement sprang from the revived Platonism and Hermetic philosophy which was centred in Florence, around the work of Marsilio Ficino (1433–1499). In 1459 Ficino began working under the patronage of Cosimo de Medici translating and elucidating the works of Plato, many of which would now become available to educated Europeans for the first time. Ficino was a physician, well-versed in astrology, and he was also a priest, but he was able to justify his veneration for the pagan past by expounding his doctrine of the 'perennial philosophy', an ancient wisdom which was pre-Christian, which expressed truths inspired by the one universal soul, but which might be revealed through philosophers and prophets of many different times and cultures; with great daring, Ficino praised the teaching of Socrates, for example, as prefiguring that of Christ himself. The pagan gods could be understood as symbols or embodiments of universal forces such as love, conflict, time or intellect. This to Ficino was all a matter of nature: nature was permeated with energies and sympathies which linked the earthly realm with the heavenly. From this central principle sprang an elaborate system of natural magic, through which the adept could learn to focus these energies. Chief among these were the qualities of the stars, which might be gathered and re-directed by the use of astral talismans – one of Ficino's chief works on this subject was entitled 'On Capturing the Life of the Stars'.

The figure of Hermes portrayed in a pavement mosaic in Siena Cathedral, dated around 1485; the inscription praises Hermes as a prophet of Christ.
Siena Cathedral/Scala

Much of this was probably evolving in Ficino's thought at an early stage, but it was given a powerful new emphasis by the rediscovery of the so-called Hermetic writings, which had long been known in the west by reputation only. These documents were brought to Florence from Greece and acquired by Cosimo de Medici around 1460. He commissioned Ficino to translate them, and by 1471 the text and a brief commentary were published. These writings took the form of dialogues purporting to be the words of the Egyptian deity Thoth to his disciples, and they were believed to be of immense antiquity, pre-dating the revelation of the biblical law to Moses. Thoth was the god of the intellect, and of language, the inventor of writing, and even, in some accounts, the creator of the world through his voicing of magical formulae. Greek awareness of Thoth dates from the time of Herodotus, and he was identified with his Greek counterpart, Hermes, and given the appellation Trismegistus, or thrice-great, signifying that he combined the functions of king, philosopher and priest. Ficino explained fully what he believed to be Hermes's place in the hierarchy of wisdom:

> As Plato writes, it was a custom among the Egyptians to choose priests from among philosophers, and kings from among the company of priests... Being thus the first among philosophers, he (Thoth-Hermes) progressed from natural philosophy and mathematics to the contemplation of the gods, and was the first to discourse most learnedly concerning the majesty of God, the orders of daemons and the transmigration of souls. He is therefore called the first inventor of theology, and Orpheus following him, attained to portions of the divine wisdom. Pythagoras succeeded him in philosophy, then Zoroaster, and Philolaus, teacher of our divine Plato, followed him. In this way a system of primitive theology was formulated by a wonderful series of six philosophers, taking its beginnings from Hermes and completed finally by Plato. Hermes however wrote many books having to do with the knowledge of divine things, in which lie revealed mysteries as arcane as his oracles are amazing. Nor very often does he speak as a philosopher, so much as a prophet, and sings events that are to come. Here he foresaw the ruin of antique religion, there the future judgement, the resurrection of the world, the glory of the blessed and the punishment of sins.

Here we see Ficino's belief in a perennial philosophy apparently vindicated by these texts from ancient Egypt, and we see that one of their chief sources of authority was their supposed anticipation of Christian doctrine. The Hermetic writings speak of God as a father, and of the creative power in the universe as the Son of God. The early church fathers, including St Augustine, knew the Hermetic writings and accepted their antiquity, but Augustine had argued that their prophecy of Christ could only have been achieved with the aid of demons. Hermes was known by name and repute in the middle ages, and was especially associated with magical astrology and the use of talismans, and as such was condemned by Albertus Magnus, although lauded by Roger Bacon. Hermetic philosophy in the Renaissance was to give a huge impetus to astrological magic – the attempt to draw down and direct the powers of the stars. This was to some extent a departure from classical astrology, for pure astrology was a mathematical discipline which enabled men to read fortune, character or destiny from the stars. The manipulation of celestial energies through magic was a very different ambition, although of course it presupposed an astrological framework.

It was in the early seventeenth century that the scholar Isaac Casaubon demonstrated that the language and the thought of the Hermetic texts proved them to date from the second century AD, a view now universally accepted. But Ficino and his contemporaries saw a succession of ancient and classical teachers who had each acquired wisdom from their predecessor. The link thus formed between Greek thought and much older religious traditions is interesting in view of the near-certainty of influences from eastern religions upon Plato and his successors, including the founders of astrology. It should be recalled that in the middle ages and the Renaissance, novelty of philosophy or religion was not a prized quality, indeed there was no higher recommendation of an idea than to show that it had been believed by ancient and famous authorities. Philosophical argument was largely conducted by calling upon the great names of the past and making them serve as forces in intellectual battle – Plato, Aristotle, Cicero, Boethius, Aquinas, and so on. Before the age of Columbus and Copernicus, the authority of the past was paramount, and novelty was no virtue. The central inspiration of Renaissance thinkers was their belief that they were reaching back beyond the era of medieval Christendom to a nobler classical past which had possessed a profound philosophical tradition of its own. Ficino had no doubt that Hermes was a historical figure, from whom the great philosophical tradition of Greece had descended; indeed so great was Ficino's veneration for Hermes that he even wondered if Hermes *was* Moses, presenting divine wisdom in another form and through another persona.

Since we now know that the Hermetic writings originated in second-century Egypt and preserve a form of Hellenistic gnosticism, it is not at all surprising that astrology forms an essential part of their system. Throughout the Hermetic writings, events in this world are considered to be ruled by the stars and planets. The magical practices described here presuppose that nature is saturated with divine

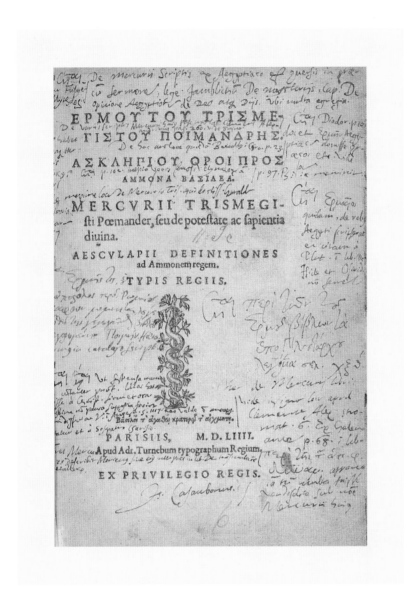

The copy of the Hermetic texts owned and annotated by the seventeenth-century scholar Isaac Casaubon. It was Casaubon whose researches demonstrated that these texts were not the product of ancient Egypt, but of the second century AD.
The British Library, 491.d.14.

influences which rain down from the stars, and which the magus can learn to control. One of the Hermetic texts describes the Egyptian rituals for drawing down cosmic power from the stars to animate the statues of their gods. Another text parallels in astrological language the biblical account of the creation of the world. The Platonic demiurge is said to have made seven governors – the planets – which encircle and rule the earth, and their rule was called destiny; the movements of these seven spheres was the cause of all processes of life and death below. In another text, the thirty-six decans are said to stand outside the spheres of the universe, each ruling ten degrees of the heavens and shaping the affairs of men, both social and individual. The signs of the Zodiac too radiate astrological influences upon the earth, and the signs are not impersonal physical forces, but intelligences or 'demons' – spirits, without the evil connotation which the word demon now has. It is characteristic of the Hermetic universe that it is thronged with demons,

who control our lives from the moment of our birth, for each astrological moment is ruled by its own demon, apparently sub-creations of the demons who rule the stars and planets. As in Hinduism, divinities and demons are everywhere, in a confusing contradiction of the basic monotheism of the Platonic ideal. In Hermetic as in Christian thought however, man's reason and soul are not enslaved to these astral forces, and through the training of the intellect he can rise above nature. At death it was possible for the soul to ascend through the spheres, casting off the imperfections of each, and achieving the Platonic ideal of oneness with God; indeed, as with the ancient mystery religions, part of the allure of this philosophy was that this ideal might be achievable before death. It cannot be said that the Hermetic writings offered a logical or coherent system of philosophy; instead they promised direct knowledge and experience of the divine, and as a prelude to this knowledge, an understanding of astrological forces was considered essential.

Whatever the dispassionate critic may make of the curious labyrinth of Hermetic beliefs, it exercised an enormous fascination between the years 1450 and 1600, and it helped to foster the taste for the occult so evident in the writers, artists and indeed the scientists of the Renaissance. Natural science was still pre-empirical, and was unable to address the problem of cause and effect in a quantitative way. In this vacuum, a belief that occult forces were present in the earth and the heavens was eagerly accepted. Truth, certain truth, did not reside in facts or in data or in the physical world, for the simple reason that so little was known about the way the physical world worked. Truth was transcendent, metaphysical, hidden until revealed, and the revelation of Hermes was regarded as being almost as important as the biblical revelation. The magical, demonic view of nature persisted until sufficient empirical data was accumulated late in the seventeenth century to destroy it. It is a striking fact that most of the leading scientists – or 'natural philosophers' – of the sixteenth and seventeenth centuries maintained a strong interest in occult forces at the same time that they were shaping a new rationalist approach to nature. From Paracelsus to Newton, major innovative thinkers like Bacon, Tycho, Kepler, Gilbert, Napier, van Helmont and many others never abandoned their belief that the 'secrets of nature' were of an occult kind. Astrology was without doubt the best-understood of these occult forces, the most systematic and the one made most familiar by the classical authorities. Ficino set out a whole philosophy of talismans, in which flowers, animals, minerals and music partake of the nature of one of the planets, so that, for example, the melancholy effects of Saturn may be warded off by surrounding oneself with flowers which are related to Venus or the Sun. As a supreme talisman, he recommended a model (or perhaps a painting like the ceiling paintings of sixteenth-century palaces) of the entire cosmic system, which could be used to draw down a whole range of celestial powers, and which in turn would draw the mind up to the contemplation of the heavens. The reversion to a pagan, animistic belief in a world populated by spirits is not easy to understand, but that it happened is witnessed by the poets and artists of this period, for it was precisely in the 1470s that the pagan gods began to re-appear as subjects in western art after an absence of a thousand years. In literature too, scholars began the eager collection and re-interpretation of classical poetry, drama and philosophy, much of which was of course saturated with references to the pagan gods. The identity and the character of the planets and constellations were clearly mythological, and this formed a further link between astrology and the aesthetic interest of the Renaissance. The art and literature of the sixteenth century teem with mythological motifs, and from this fashionable aesthetic interest in the pagan gods it followed naturally that astrology, as the science of the influence on mankind of the gods and planets, should be studied even more eagerly than in the past. The courts which patronised the new classical learning – Florence, Milan, Naples or Venice – were the same courts where astrology became such a prevalent pursuit.

No doubt there was in all this an element of pure fashion, the excitement of new and challenging ideas, and the desire of writers, artists and their patrons to participate in the latest vogue. The astrological theme in art had in one sense survived throughout the middle ages through the many illustrations of Zodiac figures and planetary gods, and it emerged in a more dynamic form after 1470, for example in the astrological frescoes at Ferrara, painted by Francesco del Cossa. But for many serious thinkers the matter went deeper than mere fashion, and the Hermetic philosophy almost achieved the status of a new religion. Its association with Egypt and its 'prophecies' of Christianity gave it an authority and respectability which enchanted even the Catholic church. In Siena around the year 1485, an image of Hermes was set into the cathedral pavement, with an inscription calling him the contemporary of Moses and the prophet of Christ. Hermes was cited by professors, churchmen and politicians as well as by astrologers. Lazarelli saluted Hermes as 'father of theologians, magicians and alchemists', and argued that he far pre-dated Moses, indeed that much of the

Mosaic theology was this same ancient wisdom in a different guise. No less a scientist than Copernicus studied the Hermetic philosophy when he visited Italy, and he quoted Hermes's phrase that the Sun is 'a visible god', leading to some speculation that this mystical attention to the Sun may have been an important starting-point for the Copernican theory. Kepler studied the Hermetic writings very carefully, and quoted them in his work on the harmony of the universe. Hermetism even inspired its own pseudo-Messiah in the person of Giovanni Mercurio de Corregio, who appeared in Rome on Palm Sunday 1484, clothed in winged sandals, and wearing a crown of thorns topped by a crescent Moon, and proclaimed himself to be Hermes, an angel of wisdom, the highest manifestation of

Right. *The Sun, Moon and stars are all shining together outside this astrologer's study as he works with his client.*
The British Library, L.32/65

Facing page. *Astrologers interpreting an eclipse, by Antoine Caron. This French painting of c.1580 captures the feverish atmosphere of Renaissance court astrology.*
Bridgeman Art Library

Jesus Christ. Corregio's end is unknown, but he re-appeared several times in Florence, and later in France, and was impressive enough to secure the protection of Lorenzo de Medici, and to gain many adherents. Hermetic thought flourished in France too, where leading churchmen wrote works of Hermetic-Christian synthesis. Some even saw Hermetism as a possible new religion, a way out of the Protestant-Catholic wars which were plaguing Europe. The same idealistic vision was carried in 1591 to the Pope himself by Francesco Patrizi, who dedicated his work *The New Universal Philosophy* to Gregory XIV, urging him to establish the Hermetic doctrines, with their astrological framework, as being on the same level as the Bible and the Christian Fathers. Under their luminous influence, Patrizi suggested, all the doctrinal problems of the church, and even the schism between Rome and the Protestants, might be healed. Sadly for Patrizi, Gregory's successor, Clement VIII, did not see things exactly in this light, and the work was condemned by the Inquisition, although Patrizi's retraction saved him from punishment. In all this, the supposed antiquity of the Hermetic works was crucial in establishing their authority, and it did indeed seem to many that a new book of Genesis had been discovered.

The appeal of Hermetism and the encouragement it gave to astrology continued

The month of March by Francesco de Cossa, one of the cycle of astrological frescoes painted for the Duke of Este in the 1470s. Above is an idealised scene of courtly life, while below are the astrological powers which direct human affairs. The three figures above Aries are the decans, the Egyptian entities governing each ten-degree division of the Zodiac sign.
Scala

to broaden during the sixteenth century, and innovative mystical thinkers such as Bruno and Campanella were steeped in Hermetic, astrological ideas. The Renaissance magus of fact or fiction – Cornelius Agrippa, Bruno, Paracelsus, Faust – strove to break out of the sterile world of orthodox religious thought into a more personal and powerful understanding of nature. In this context, astrology was seen as a central part of a philosophy of nature, impressive in its scientific structure, and enticing in its promise of power. This exalted philosophy complemented the Humanism of the late fifteenth century, which centred on a revaluation of man. Man was seen as the centre of the universe, occupying a special place between earth and heaven, and it was within the power of the sciences to elucidate complex relations between man and the cosmos. The long tradition of Christian opposition to the occult sciences and to certain aspects of astrology, was now weakened by the Renaissance cult of Humanism. The career and writing of Tomasso Campanella (1569–1639) provide one of the most original intellectual uses of astrology, together with an attempt to harmonise occult science with Christianity. The story of Campanella's life – his Dominican training, his heresies, his part in a political revolt and his terrible punishments – is well-known. His long years of imprisonment did not prevent his becoming a prolific author of theological, scientific and mystical works, but his most accessible and striking work is the *Citta del Sole*, 'The City of the Sun', a utopian vision of an ideal city supposedly discovered by a traveller in the New World. The city was divided into seven circular parts, named after the seven planets. In the centre stood a temple of the

Sun, containing a huge depiction of the earth and the heavens, with descriptions of the power which each star exercised over the earth; in this temple, seven lamps symbolised the planets. The life of the city was founded on astrological principles, for it was governed by Magi who understood how to draw down, through astral magic, the beneficent influences of the heavens. The walls of the city were decorated with portraits of the great founders of science and philosophy – Moses, Hermes, Osiris, Mahomet and Christ. As with all utopias the breeding of children was carefully planned, and the best astrological moments for conception and birth were ascertained. The central idea behind the life of the city was that it should be governed in accordance with natural magic, principally that of the heavens. It was Christian to the extent that, in Campanella's system, Christ was a great magus and legislator, whose teachings could be made to harmonise with the other components of his mystical science. The ideals of 'The City of the Sun' were those which had inspired Campanella in his political activity, and he never abandoned the hope that some great ruler would initiate a magically-based reform of religious and civil life.

After his eventual release from prison, Campanella had an opportunity to demonstrate his astrological magic before Pope Urban VIII himself. The pope, the aristocratic and learned Maffeo Barberini, had a strong interest in astrology, and had conceived a special fear of an eclipse, which his enemies had prophesied would cause his death. In a sealed room, lamps symbolising the planets and the Zodiac signs were lit, while plants, gems and music were employed in a ceremony which aimed at constructing a substitute and favourable heaven, to defeat the threats from the real heaven outside. Urban was to live for a further sixteen years, but whether he thanked Campanella for this seems doubtful, for he was later to change his views and issue severe condemnations of astrology. Campanella tried to persuade the pope and then other leaders that such astrological magic, in the hands of a skilled Hermetic priesthood, could preserve a state from evil celestial influences. Campanella spent his last years in France in the 1630s, well-received at court where he cast horoscopes for the great, but scorned by the leaders of the new philosophy, Mersenne and Descartes, to whom his system and his dreams were absurd.

Giordano Bruno too proposed a reform of intellectual and religious life, and in one of his works *The Overthrow of the Triumphal Beast*, he declared symbolically that this process must begin with the reform of the heavens. The vices associated with the bestial constellations are to be driven out as a necessary prelude to the reform of a degenerate world, a reform led by the planetary gods. 'If we thus reform our heaven', says Jupiter, 'the constellations and influences shall be new, for all things depend upon the upper world.' Bruno acknowledged the influence of one of the most celebrated of Renaissance magicians, Cornelius Agrippa (1486–1535), whose book *De occulta philosophia* of 1533 was one of the most frequently quoted occult works. Agrippa acquired a lurid reputation for casting spells, keeping familiars, bringing the dead to life, and many other things, and he has been identified as a possible model for the figure of Faust. The basis of Agrippa's magic was the doctrine of the three-level universe: the elemental world, the celestial world and the intellectual world. Each world is directed by forces from the world above it, so that the power of the supreme creator descends through the angels in the intellectual world, to the stars in the celestial world, which in turn control events in the elemental world, the world of man. The magus believes that we can draw down powers from the upper world by astrological

The dragon of the Zodiac whose head and tail – caput and cauda – acquired the status of planets in classical astrology. These points were in fact the lunar nodes, the two places where the Moon's path crossed the ecliptic each month. The origin of the dragon image is unknown. The dial gives the position of the nodes through the year.
The British Library, C.7.c.15

magic. Talismanic images, the magical properties of numbers, the ratios of musical harmonies, all these play their part in the Faustian vision of man elevating himself to the level of a god; magic, in Agrippa's philosophy, 'marries earth to heaven'. In the thought of Campanella, Bruno, Agrippa, and still more among students of the cabala, astrology was part of a mystical belief-system in which the traditional techniques of the horoscope and the related problem of destiny, were secondary to the dazzling vision of conjuring and controlling the powers of the stars. Yet not all Renaissance Neoplatonists were addicted to astrology, and it was, surprisingly, from a follower of Ficino that there came one of the most ferocious attacks on the science ever penned.

Pico della Mirandola (1463–1494) was a young aristocrat and a gifted linguist and scholar, so drawn to mysticism and magic that at the age of twenty-three he was denounced as a heretic and briefly imprisoned. In 1492 Pico was helped by the accession of Rodrigo Borgia as Pope Alexander VI, who looked favourably on astrology, and he wrote a letter absolving Pico of heresy. It was for Alexander that Pinturicchio painted mythological scenes in his private apartments in the Vatican, including a depiction of Hermes himself. The intellectual evolution which Pico experienced during his short life is quite mysterious, for there is no doubt that he was at first a devotee of the arcane doctrines of the cabala, in which astrological symbolism played a definite role. One of his more notorious youthful statements affirmed that 'Nothing proves the divinity of Christ more surely than magic and the cabala', a statement which was partly responsible for the charge of heresy against him. There is a tradition that he turned against magic and astrology having become infuriated when not one but three astrologers predicted that he would die at the early age of thirty-three – he did in fact die at thirty-one. Another and more plausible explanation lies in the undoubted fact that Pico fell under the influence of the religious reformer Savonarola, who was severe in his condemnation of astrology. Whatever the true reason, Pico devoted the last year of his life to composing his extended *Disputationes adversus astrologiam*, which was published soon after his death. This work was notable for the violence of the language it employed, and it became virtually an encyclopedia of anti-astrological arguments, to be repeated again and again by polemicists of the sixteenth and seventeenth centuries:

> When I say astrology I do not mean the mathematical measurement of stellar sizes and motions, which is an exact and noble art…but the reading of forecoming events by the stars, which is a cheat of mercenary liars, prohibited by both civil and church law, preserved by human curiosity, mocked by philosophers, cultivated by itinerant hawkers, and suspect to the best and most prudent men…the most infectious of all frauds, since as we shall show, it corrupts all philosophy, falsifies medicine, weakens religion, begets or strengthens superstition, encourages idolatry, destroys prudence, pollutes morality, defames heaven and makes all men unhappy and uneasy.

The philosophical basis of Pico's anti-astrological stance is evident in his earlier work, the 'Oration of the Dignity of Man'. In an imaginary address to Adam, God informs him that man is the centre of the cosmos, the crown of creation, but that unlike the other creatures, he is not limited to one sphere of existence. Man has the capability to descend to the level of the brutes, or rise to the level of the divine. It follows that man is outside the control of any external natural force, including that of the stars. This view of man as a potential god does not appear overtly in Pico's *Adverusu astrologiam*, which is another reason for supposing that the religious influence of Savonarola was a more likely spur to its writing. Pico was in fact planning a vast work directed against all the enemies of Christian religion – pagans, Jews, Moslems and heretics – of which the anti-astrological text was the first and only-completed part. The whole tenor of Pico's text however is neither religious nor philosophical but rational, critical and empirical. The entire apparatus of astrology – signs, aspects, houses, conjunctions and so on – are questioned and condemned as arbitrary and illogical. How can future events, years or even decades hence, be caused by the configuration of the skies now? By what mechanism can the rays of the stars be imprinted upon nature to cause such effects? How can a 'fortunate' nativity work on the life of a man years after the astrological moment has passed? Pico accepts that the heavens may have universal

The sensual, pleasure-loving character of Venus, from a German woodcut.
Private collection

effects on nature, for example on seasons, tides or weather, but he argues that they cannot at the same time have particular effects. The influence of the Sun, Moon or stars should either be identical on all men, or it should be non-existent: the doctrine that minute changes in stellar positions may cause massive changes in effect is absurd. Like Oresme before him, Pico denied that any demonstrable force emanated from the stars and planets, other than light and heat: there were no occult forces. The special characters of individuals arose from natural causes in the environment – heredity, biology, culture and geography – and not from the skies. The astrologer, Pico claimed, 'consults signs that are not signs and examines causes that are not causes'. Pico replaces a pagan, animistic universe of signs and energies, with a mechanical one in which naturally interacting forces are governed by God alone. He presses home his rationalist arguments by demanding to know the sources of astrology. It cannot claim to be an empirical art, for its predictions are more often false than true, nor can it claim divine authority, for the Bible condemns it. Its defenders urge that it was revealed to the Egyptians and Chaldeans, but they were pagan, idolatrous nations, so why should we believe the science inherited from them, any more than we believe in their myths or their rituals? When he posed this question, Pico had evidently freed himself entirely from the Neoplatonism of his teacher, Ficino, with its faith in a perennial philosophy and in the authenticity of the Hermetic doctrines.

Pico's attack on astrology was rational, detailed and well-informed, and it evoked many responses, both for and against. Yet there is no indication that tracts like these had the slightest effect in loosening the grip which astrology had upon the European mind. Savonarola's connection with Pico was underlined when the stern reformer published an epitome of Pico's work, just one year before his own downfall. When Savonarola was dead and disgraced, Lucio Bellanti penned *De astrologia veritate*, in which he blamed religious fanaticism for corrupting Pico's intellect. The poet and essayist, Giovanni Pontano, also defended astrology against Pico's censures, arguing that all fields of knowledge have their imperfections, astrology included, but that this is not allowed to invalidate an entire sci-

The three-level world of astrology: the twelve mundane houses surround the twelve Zodiac signs and the seven planets, with the earth at the centre. The entire system is shown to be under God's control.

The British Library, C.54.c.9.

ence. Pontano upheld the classical doctrine that the heavens' influence over the course of life on earth was a matter of nature. Pontano was also the author of *De Fortuna*, one of the many Renaissance works to examine the puzzling phenomenon of Fortune. There seems little doubt that the people of the Renaissance believed in the reality of a force which they called Fortune, just as the Greeks had been in thrall to the cult of *Tyche*. Nature seemed to have selected certain men as children of fortune, and to have ignored others, and the fortunate were like poets or prophets, imbued with some divine power which guided their lives, although it might also desert them. In the dangerous world of the Renaissance courts, this cult of fortune provided an attractive framework to explain the rise and fall of princes, courtiers, statesmen, artists or generals. It was natural that astrology came to be seen as a key to interpreting the mystery of fortune, and Pontano theorised that God had endowed the stars with power over all inferior things except the human will, and therefore fortune became a partner with the will in shaping human events. This synthesis preserved the freedom of the will alongside divine providence, and this kind of discussion was popular in the Renaissance. It shows that astrology was seen as a powerful tool to elucidate the riddles of character, fortune and success. It explains astrology's unfailing appeal to those grasping after power and influence in society.

In this atmosphere, astrologers became sought-after figures in the centres of political power, and even one accurate prediction could send their reputation soaring and make their patrons desperate for more. The career and predictions of Luca Gaurico, for example, are quite well-documented. He predicted the downfall of Giovanni Bentivoglio, tyrant of Bologna, for which he was imprisoned, but nevertheless his prophecy proved true. He foretold that Alessandro Farnese would become pope, and when Farnese was elected as Paul III in 1534, he brought Gaurico to Rome and showered him with honours, and always maintained a strong interest in astrology. Gaurico is said to have predicted the exact date of Farnese's death. He later warned John Hamilton, Archbishop of St Andrews, that he would end his life on the gallows, and Hamilton was indeed executed for his part in the murder of Darnley, husband of Mary Queen of Scots. Gaurico prophesied correctly that two Medicis, Giovanni and his cousin Giulio,

Nostrodamus displaying to Catherine de Medici a procession of future kings in a magic mirror. Nostrodamus did practice as an astrologer, but his famous gnomic predictions did not claim to be astrologically derived.
Private collection

would both be elevated to the papacy; one became Leo X in 1513, the other Clement VII in 1523. Gaurico's fame spread through Europe, and he spent some time in France at the court of Catherine de Medici, where however he erred in predicting a long life for her husband Henri II, who was accidently killed at the age of forty. This does not seem to have shaken Catherine's faith in astrologers, for she continued to patronise them, most famously Nostrodamus, who was portrayed in a celebrated picture displaying to the queen images of the future, conjured in an enchanted mirror. Nostrodamus certainly practised as a physician and astrologer, but the cryptic prophecies which have made him so famous have no overtly astrological content, nor is it even certain that they were astrologically derived. Nostrodamus was a self-professed seer and a maker of riddles, and he is interesting as one of history's intellectual vagabonds, but his place in the history of astrology is slight.

The Renaissance interest in the astrological dimension to fortune, character and destiny was fed by a genre of literature which had to some extent existed for centuries, but which was given a new impetus by the medium of printing – horoscopes of the famous, analysed to illustrate general principles. There were many such collections, expounding the reasons for the greatness or infamy of kings and statesmen, but also offering astrological insights into lives of artists, poets or religious leaders. One of the most influential works of this kind was the *Geniturae* by Girolamo Cardano, which gave the horoscopes of figures such as the Emperor Charles V, King Henry VIII of England, Cicero, Petrarch and many others. Cardano (1501–1576) was renowned as a physician and mathematician, but his passion for astrology led him into deep controversy and he was imprisoned in 1570 for the crime of casting the horoscope of Christ. He was released after abjuring his heresies, but he was deprived of the chair of mathematics in Bologna, forbidden to publish, and forced to live in Rome, under the watchful eye of the Inquisition. Cardano undoubtedly published these celebrity horoscopes to display the virtuosity of his art, and to build his own reputation, but in his writings he was unusual in drawing attention to the difficulties and possible sources of error inherent in astrology. Almost to a man, astrologers relied on tables of pre-calculated celestial positions, and rarely glanced at the heavens themselves. Cardano however encouraged astrologers to familiarise themselves with the heavens, to learn to gauge planetary positions and to determine the time. He noted that conjunctions and other events often took place days before or after their predicted times, and that the tables were often several degrees out in the positions which they gave. The implications of such errors for the casting of nativities were of course enormous, and potentially serious enough to destroy their credibility entirely. Cardano concluded that the observational astronomy of his time needed much greater precision. This kind of attention to astronomy was rare among professional fee-taking astrologers, who would never acknowledge that their work might be undermined through its reliance on data which was simply inaccurate.

It was not only the psychology and destiny of individuals to which astrology seemed to hold the key. The astrological theories of history which had been developed during the middle ages, especially by Islamic scholars, were given intense and renewed relevance by events in the sixteenth century. The European crises in church and state convinced many observers that they were living in an apocalyptic age, and astrology became part of a wider flood of prophecy which embraced biblical interpretation, numerology, and natural portents. This movement commenced around the year 1500 – itself an ominous date – and did not cease for almost two centuries. Many of the competing factions in the Reformation, and in the armed conflicts which sprang from it, all regarded themselves as agents of a general purification, and their actions as the necessary prelude to a time of judgement; in this context, celestial events were believed to presage divine anger, an apocalypse, or a new era. In the very year which saw the dawn of the Reformation, 1517, the attention of astrologers began to be focussed on the Great Conjunction of all the planets in the constellation Pisces which would take place in February 1524. Under the doctrine of the Great Year (see above p.66) this was even more significant than other great conjunctions, for it was widely held that that the world had begun when all the planets were in conjunction in Aries, the starting-point of the Zodiac, and it therefore seemed possible that the world might end when such a conjunction recurred at the end of the Zodiac, in Pisces. In hundreds of tracts anticipating the event, a cataclysm was predicted, and the character of Pisces suggested that it would take the form of a flood of biblical proportions. Alternatively a metaphorical flood was predicted: social unrest and rebellion against civil and ecclesiastical powers. The flood did not of course materialise, but the terrible and bloodthirsty Peasants' War in Germany did, so that both the astrologers and their critics were able to congratulate themselves.

It is not clear whether attitudes towards astrology were significantly affected by the Protestant Reformation or not. Like Savonarola before them, Luther, Calvin and Zwingli were all opposed to astrology, the sole exception in their ranks being Philip Melancthon, who maintained a strong belief in astrology throughout his

The predicted floods of 1524: the Great Conjunction of all the planets in the constellation Pisces which occurred in February 1524 was the subject of intense interest, and various disasters were anticipated, especially a universal flood.
The British Library C.71.h.14.

life. The reformers gave much greater attention to combating witchcraft, and the dramatic growth of the European witch-craze, and its sudden cessation at precisely the same time that belief in astrology declined, suggest that there must have been intellectual and social links between them, although such links have never been fully explained. It is certain however that the post-Reformation Catholic church, after centuries of mere disapproval of astrology, now began to harden its stance considerably. Indices of forbidden books began to appear from 1550 onwards, which condemned demonic magic of the kind practised by Cornelius Agrippa, but not specifically astrology. Cardano's arrest in 1570 was exceptional, arising from his horoscope of Christ. However the link which Renaissance

Cardano's Horoscope of Christ

IN 1552 Girolamo Cardano, the great Italian mathematician, physician and astrologer, composed a commentary on Ptolemy's *Tetrabiblos*, the great source-book of classical astrology. In order to illustrate Ptolemy's principles, Cardano included in his work a number of sample horoscopes which he had cast, the most remarkable of which was nothing less than a horoscope of Christ himself. Bearing in mind that the medieval astrologer, Cecco d'Ascoli, had been executed for the crime of casting Christ's nativity, Cardano's publication, even in the changed atmosphere of the Renaissance, might still be highly dangerous. In Christian thought, the incarnation of Christ was the supreme act of divine grace, and to suggest that it was in any way a natural or predictable event was to elevate the fatalistic power of the stars above that of God. What then did Cardano say in this horo-scope, and how did he justify his choice of such a perilous subject?

Before answering these questions, it is worth noticing that earlier Christian thinkers had already ventured into this sensitive area. No less a figure than Albertus Magnus had affirmed that the configuration of the stars at Christ's nativity did indeed reveal his divine nature; the stars were not causes, but they were signs of his greatness. In the book of nature, the stars were letters in which God's power might legitimately be read. This view was echoed by Pierre d'Ailly, archbishop and cardinal of the church, who affirmed that so far as Christ's elemental bodily nature was concerned, he was subject to the stars. So Cardano evidently had an intellectual tradition on which to build, even if it was a controversial one.

What of the horoscope itself? The first problem is the date, and the moment chosen by Cardano was midnight on 24 December 1 BC, thus confirming the date sanctified by tradition. We now know that the true date of Christ's

birth must have been some years earlier, and also that the December timing has no historical basis, but was chosen in order to Christianise certain pagan winter festivals. It is therefore inconceivable that the horoscope given by Cardano is that of Christ. In Cardano's favour, it must be said that the celestial positions which he computed for that moment are quite close to the true ones, as calculated by modern astronomers, so that he has the planets in all the correct signs. Having established a map of the heavens for the desired moment (leaving aside the fact that it was the wrong moment) what significant portents did Cardano see there? The most obvious is that in the ascendant sign of Libra, he place a comet, for this was his interpretation of the star of Bethlehem, 'a comet of such brightness that it announced a disturbance of the whole world'. The force of this omen was strengthened by the presence of Jupiter, promising a character which blended nobility and justice. Added to this was the proximity of Spica, the brightest star in the constellation Virgo, a star which Cardano claimed would impart the qualities of wisdom and love. A second fixed star singled out for comment is Castor in Gemini, which stood in the midheaven, which shared the nature of Mars, and therefore foretold that Christ's life would be marked by violence. The Sun's position near the *immum coeli*, the lowest heaven, foretold a famous death, while the presence there of Mercury rising announced genius. Mars was in the sign of Aries, in opposition to Jupiter and thus an enemy to the ascendant, signifying that the subject would be exposed to plots and grave danger, and would finally suffer a cruel death. Saturn, Venus and Jupiter lay in the trine aspect, shedding a beneficent influence on the subject, bestowing beauty of body and of mind. Most ominously, Cardano traced the course of the prorogator, in this case the

Moon, and found that it indicated that the gifted and noble subject of this horoscope chart would nevertheless die at the age of thirty-three.

Cardano made many further points of detail concerning the celestial positions on this chart, but his message is clear: at this chosen moment, the heavens announced the birth of an exceptional personality, whose life would be marked by nobility, love and justice, and who would die a violent death, but not before he had promulgated a new law which would last for thousands of years. It all sounds

his miracles or the sanctity of his life or his promulgation of the law *depends* upon the stars; but the most excellent and glorious God embellished his horoscope with the best and most wonderful disposition of the stars... Christ's nativity was wonderful, and nature granted him as much as could be imagined by an arrangement of the heavens'. So, through the doctrine that the stars were signs and not causes, Cardano hoped to escape serious trouble, and indeed he did so for many years, although his publication was castigated by his critics as madness,

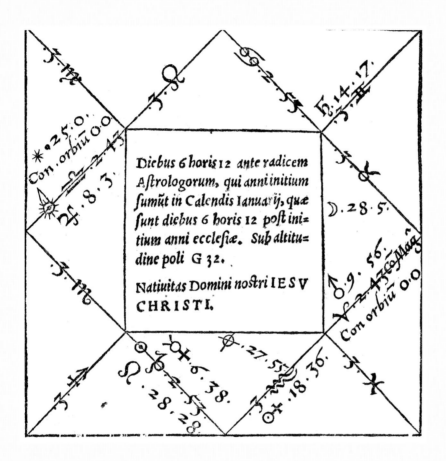

very convincing; but of course this was not a prophecy, but an interpretation after the event. Put simply, Cardano had found what he wanted to find; but he had fulfilled another purpose too, namely to validate the principles of classical astrology by a striking historical example. This was the true purpose of these celebrity horoscopes: to show that the complex rules and axioms concerning the influence of the stars and planets had been established by experience, and might be tested in the same way.

How did he seek to deflect the possible charges of heresy or blasphemy which he must surely have anticipated? By repeating the escape-clause formulated by Albertus Magnus and D'Ailly: 'I do not wish you to understand me to say that either the divinity of Christ or

impiety and vanity. Why he was finally seized and imprisoned for blasphemy in 1570, fifteen years after the horoscope was published, no one can say. Cardano escaped with his life, but he was prohibited from teaching or publishing again, and he was ordered to Rome, where he lived the last five years of his life under the watchful eye of the Inquisition. In the second edition of his commentary on Ptolemy in 1578 (two years after the author's death) the horoscope of Christ was deleted. Cardano had sought to validate astrology in the most audacious way possible, but in doing so he overreached himself, and fell victim to the church's constant uncertainty whether astrology was a genuine science or a heresy.

Prima facies ariet̃ ē mar tis ꝫ ē facies audacie:forti tudinis:altitudinis:ꝫ inue recundie.

Secunda facies est solis ꝫ est nobilitat̃:altitudinis: regni ꝫ magni dominij.

Tercia facies est veneris et est subtilitatis in ope:ꝫ man suetudinis:ludoꝛ:gaudioꝛ ꝫ limpidationum.

In primo gradu arietis Ascēdit vir dextera tenēs falcē: ꝫ sinistra manu balistam.

Homo cum capite canino dex tera sua extensa:ꝫ in sinistra ba culum habentem.

⊂Homo aliquādo laboꝛat:ali quando vero bella exercet.

⊂Homo litigiosus erit et inui dus vt canis.

f

thinkers had developed between astrology and magic clearly troubled the church, and in its vast Tridentine survey of heresy generally, astrology was not likely to escape. The Papal Bull *Coeli et Terrae*, issued by Sixtus V in 1586 was the culmination of this process. Its doctrinal basis was the familiar argument that God alone can know the future, and it condemned judicial astrology and divination generally, while still allowing some role for natural astrology in, for example, weather prediction. In the human realm, it proclaimed that there were no true arts for predicting contingent and human events, except those given by devils, and the casting of horoscopes was at last expressly condemned. This document claimed that each human soul was possessed of a guardian angel, among whose duties was not merely the protection of the soul from demons, but to ward off the malign influences of the stars – a puzzling idea which seems to admit that the stars did indeed have power over men. The Inquisition was charged with prosecuting those who would seek to limit human free will, and the Bull does seem to have succeeded in repressing astrology to some extent in Italy, with many astrologers moving abroad. Judicial astrology ceased to be taught at universities like Bologna, and an interesting example of a recantation is provided by Giambattista della Porta. Della Porta was a Neapolitan scholar, and a leader of an 'Academy of the Secrets of Nature', who had published an influential book on natural magic and astrology. In the 1590s he was investigated by the Inquisition, and in a new work of 1603, he renounced his belief in astrology, attributing human character to the humours and other natural causes. His book gave a full exposition of the leading, and now forbidden, doctrines of astrology from Ptolemy onwards, yet it escaped condemnation because della Porta now abjured them. Whether his change of heart was real or feigned we cannot know. In 1633 the Papal decree was reinforced in even sterner language in a new Bull *Inscrutabilis* of Urban VIII, where astrological predictions concerning changes or crises in church and state were particularly condemned. The astrological tradition, which had co-existed with the Catholic Church for four centuries, was now unmistakably branded as a heresy, and its extinction where the Inquisition held sway – in Italy and Spain – was inevitable.

The sense of crisis in the sixteenth century, and the vogue for prophecy focussed even more attention than before on comets, meteors, violent storms and the like. Among the many writers who commented on the comet of 1531 (which was in fact Halley's comet) was the great physician, alchemist and mystic, Paracelsus. He witnessed the comet at St Gallen in Switzerland, which at that time was experiencing economic hardship from failed harvests, and near civil war between Catholics, Reformers and Anabaptists. Paracelsus firmly believed that 'Each destruction of a monarchy, or the raising of one at God's behest, is announced by indications and signs from heaven, so that everyone will be able to recognise the destruction and ruin, and have forewarning of their fall and rise.' He then relates the civil unrest and the comet to epidemic diseases which he had witnessed in the vicinity, the whole complex of events being illuminated by apocalyptic texts from the Bible. Lest this view of comets should be dismissed as a mere medieval survival, we should recall that no less an astronomer than Tycho Brahe drew astrological conclusions from the comet of 1577, predicting 'Great alteration and reformation both in the spiritual and secular regimes'. Tycho's interest in astrology was considerable, and he eagerly anticipated – though he did not live to see it – the conjunction of Saturn and Jupiter in Aries which was expected in 1603. He called this 'the seventh revolution of the fiery trigon', considering that it had occurred only seven times since the founding of the world, and that it might usher in a new age, 'the eternal Sabbath of all creation'. Astrological ideas of historical cycles and turning-points also proved attractive to Renaissance historians and social theorists who were seeking to detect patterns in the rise and fall of nations. Jean Bodin (1530–1596) the French theorist of law and government, proposed a hierarchy of historical causation, with God at the head and the human individual at the receiving end. In between lay the intermediary causes which God employed to govern the universe, principally the power of the stars. This

Horoscope types by Johannes Engel, 1488. These little images show a horoscope and indicate the likely character of the subject such as the curious one on the right: 'This man was quarrelsome and as unpopular as a dog.' The three figures above are the decans of Aries.
The British Library
IA.6670

power was directed not arbitrarily but mathematically, because the motions of the heavens embodied perfect numerical proportion and ratio, in a Platonic manner. The stars in their turn did not operate on individuals in a direct, simplistic way, but shaped the entire natural environment – the climate, the fruits of the earth,

A fanciful picture of Mercury personified.

MS.Canon Misc.280 f.68
The Bodleian Library, Oxford

the psychological temperament, which Bodin believed made up the 'commonwealth', or what we should call culture. Personal, judicial astrology carried little conviction with Bodin, but this over-arching, cosmic astrology was as appealing to him as it had been to Hellenistic philosophers fifteen centuries before. Alongside his secular, political theories of enlightened government, constitutional monarchy and natural law, Bodin felt the need for this cosmic law to explain and underpin his vision of an ideal society. This example of Renaissance historiography offers some interesting parallels to Renaissance science: a new note of rationalism and empiricism does not exclude a turning-back to metaphysical concepts – in this case the ancient belief that the stars determine events on earth – which are then used as organising principles to bind ideas and data together.

So astrology penetrated deep into the intellectual and political life of the Renaissance. It was, as it had always been, a spacious philosophical structure, somewhere between a science and a religion, offering a unifying perspective on questions of cosmology and physics, medicine and biology, and above all on human destiny. This much had been inherited from the middle ages, but to it was now added a new psychological dimension, as Humanism and Hermetism promoted a new understanding of man's central place in the universe. The orthodox religious view of human life as a progress from sin to redemption appeared bleak and uninspiring beside the far more exciting vision of the power and knowledge promised by Hermetism and occult science. At the same time, astrology's role as a key to wealth and power in a purely worldly sense had never been more eagerly pursued. It would perhaps be misleading to describe astrology's triumph as evidence of secularisation in Renaissance society, for the Hermetic philosophy could hardly be called secular, but that it represented a formidable challenge to the Christian world view is unquestionable. The Renaissance was about nature, paganism, the centrality of man, and the rediscovery of a philosophy older and more exciting than Christianity, one made more enticing by its hints of the forbidden. At what level these things were truly believed, or whether they may have been metaphors for new ways of looking at the world, we cannot say for certain. But one effect, among many others, was that the religious barriers to astrology were progressively dismantled, and the language of astrology became the universally-accepted idiom of the time, as Newtonianism did in the eighteenth century, or Darwinism in the Victorian age.

ASTROLOGY IN ENGLAND 1550–1700

In the Elizabethan Renaissance, England shared fully in the European vogue for astrology, and the new currents of scientific and magical philosophy served to reinforce an already strong medieval inheritance. Robert Recorde's work *The Castle of Knowledge*, 1556, is a textbook of astronomy written entirely from a geocentric point of view, although giving the first account in English of the Copernican theory. In his preface, Recorde reminds the reader of the astrological dimension to astronomy:

> So there never was any great change in the world, neither translation of Empires, neither scarce any fall of famous princes, nor dearth or penury, nor death and mortality, but God by the signs of heaven did premonish man thereof, to repent and beware betime, if they had any grace. The examples are infinite and all histories full of them…and who that can skill of their natures (i.e. understand the stars) and conjecture rightly the effect of them and their menacings, shall be able not only to avoid many inconveniences, but also to achieve many unlikely attempts, and be a governor and ruler of the stars, according to the vulgar sentence gathered of Ptolemy:
>
> > The wise by prudence and good skill
> > May rule the stars to serve his will.

From the modern perspective, the Copernican revolution was one of the decisive events in destroying the world-view upon which astrology was built, yet it is clear that the first stirrings of this scientific revolution had no immediate impact upon the astrologers. Another mathematician, Thomas Digges (d.1595) is credited with first drawing out one of the most far-reaching implications of Copernicanism, namely that the stars should now be understood as being scattered throughout infinite space and that, by implication, the celestial sphere was a fiction. Thomas Bretnor, a mathematician and astrologer of the early seventeenth century, explained the altered sense of cosmic space which follows from Copernicanism,

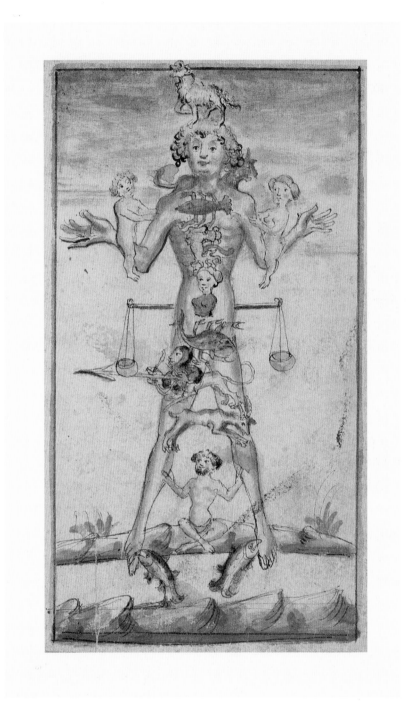

The Zodiac Man from a medieval manuscript composed in Germany in 1446. The power which each Zodiac sign was believed to wield over parts of the body was one of the clearest links between man the microcosm and the universe the macrocosm.

The British Library
Add.MS.17987 f.96

by pointing out that 'the Sun in Aries' should be re-phrased as 'the earth in Libra', and he gives an example of astrological language corrected along Copernican lines:

> This brumal season, commonly called winter, and usually taken for the first quarter of our astronomical year, took its beginning the eleventh of December last, for then, according to the old dotage, did the Sun enter the

first scruple of the cold and melancholic sign Capricorn, or rather according to verity, this earthly planet, entering the first minute of Cancer, and furthest deflected from the Sun's perpendicular rays, did then receive the least portion of Sunshine, and greatest quantity of shadow.

Digges had been a pupil of the man most associated with science and magic in Elizabethan England, John Dee. Dee (1527–1608) studied mathematics and cosmography at Cambridge, Louvain and Paris, and became a convinced Copernican. Dee is often said to have been the court astrologer to Queen Elizabeth, but there is no evidence that such a position officially existed, and throughout his career, Dee's petitions for some ecclesiastical or civil post by which to support himself were unsuccessful. What is true is that Dee was consulted by the queen and her advisers on a number of occasions. The Earl of Leicester commissioned him to determine an astrologically propitious date for the queen's coronation in 1559. Dee is also reported to have given private lessons in astrology and the occult sciences to the queen. In 1577 the court was alarmed by the appearance of the comet, and Dee was summoned to Windsor to discuss its possible significance. At about the same time he was urgently required to ward off a possible occult threat to the queen, when a wax image of her with a needle in its breast was found in Lincoln's Inn. Dee was greatly interested in navigation and the exploration of the New World, and in 1580 he drew up a great world map for the queen, in order to indicate her possible title to overseas territories. In 1575 the queen and a party of courtiers visited Dee's house, where she was shown his famous magic glass, in which he claimed to see distant of future events. By this time Dee's interests had veered sharply towards alchemy, magic and conversing with spirits, aided – and duped – by the fraudulent medium, Edward Kelley. Dee acquired an evil reputation as a necromancer, to the extent that, during his absence abroad in 1583, a mob broke into his house and destroyed many of his books and instruments. It is beyond question that Dee was a serious scientist, and an equally serious student of the occult, two aims which still went hand in hand at this period. His fundamental belief seems to have been that everything in the world radiated energy to all other things and received rays back from them. There were also relations of sympathy and antipathy between all things, and these rays – 'species' or 'virtues' in the language of the time – occupied a spiritual realm which existed alongside the physical. The rays of virtue from the heavenly bodies far surpassed in subtlety and power the visible light which they emitted, and each star and planet had its own individual character. Dee placed a new scientific obligation on the astrologer by arguing that precise study of mathematical astronomy and optics was required to compute the strength of these rays. Dee's conviction was that 'We daily may perceive that man's body, and all other elemental bodies, are altered, disposed, ordered, pleasured and displeasured by the influential workings of the Sun, Moon and other stars and planets', a succinct expression of astrology's central doctrine, in line with the classical science of the four elements.

In spite of all his learning and scholarly earnestness, it cannot be pretended that Dee advanced the cause of astrology in England, for his involvement with magic and his consequent ill-fame led to suspicions of witchcraft which fatally damaged his career. Very different was the influence of Francis Bacon, the theorist of Elizabethan science and apologist for a new empirical approach to nature. Bacon proposed a reform of astrology, as he did of all knowledge, for in his *Advancement of Learning*, 1605, he wrote 'As for astrology, it is so full of superstition that scarce anything sound can be discovered in it. Notwithstanding, I would rather have it purified than altogether rejected.' This purified or reformed astrology turns out to be partly a re-statement of the old distinction between natural and judicial astrology, but a re-statement founded on reason rather than on religious scruples. 'I do not hesitate,' continues Bacon, 'to reject as idle superstition the doctrine of horoscopes and the distribution of houses, which is the very delight of astrology, and has held a sort of Bacchanalian revelry in the heavenly regions… The doctrine

The Castle of Knowledge.

The Sphere of Destinye.

The wheele of Fortune.

Sphæra Fati

Sphæra Fortunæ.

QVI MODO SCANDIT, CORRVET STATIM.

whose governour is Knowledge.

whose ruler is Ignoraunce.

To KNOWLEDG is this Trophy set,
All learninges friendes will it support.
So shall their name great honour get,
And gaine great fame with good report

Though spitefull Fortune turned her wheele
To staye the Sphere of Vranye,
Yet dooth this Sphere resist that wheele,
And fleeyth all fortunes villanye.
Though earthe do honour Fortunes balle,
And bytells blynde hyr wheele aduaunce,
The heauens to fortune are not thralle,
These Spheres surmount al fortunes chance.

Title page of Robert Recorde's Castle of Knowledge, *1550.
To Recorde, the twin sciences of astronomy and astrology, seen on the left, lead to a true understanding of destiny, which then easily overthrows all notions of blind fortune, on the right.*
The British Library
C.124.f.4.

of nativities, elections, inquiries and the like frivolities, have in my judgement for the most part nothing sure or solid, and are plainly refuted and convicted by physical reason.' Bacon then proposes four novel principles by which astrology may be purified. First the 'greater revolutions', the influences of the stars on world history, should be retained, while the 'smaller revolutions' of horoscopes timed to the hour of the individual's life, must be rejected. Second they affect masses, for the amount of celestial influences reaching any individual is negligible. Third, these influences operate over long periods, and therefore predictions of specific effects on individuals on a given day are vain. Fourth, 'There is no fatal necessity in the stars; they incline but do not compel.' Bacon held it certain that the stars did emit forces other than heat and light, but they operated only according to the limiting rules which he had laid down. Exactly how these forces

Astrologer at work: the practitioner is seated at his desk before his open books, but turns his gaze to the stars.
Herzog August Bibliothek, Wolfenbuttel

worked, Bacon claimed to 'lie concealed in the depth of Physic, and require a longer dissertation', which he himself never wrote. Bacon agreed with Dee that the distances, speeds and sizes of the planets needed careful study to determine their influences, and this reformed astrology would make its judgements not on the basis of the superstitions and arbitrary rules of tradition but of verifiable experience only. This plea – that the scientific study of the planets might underpin a new, rationalised astrology – would be voiced by many other seventeenth-century writers, but it was never put into practice. The application of this new form of astrology would, claimed Bacon, lie in the study and prediction of 'comets, meteors, inundations, droughts, heats, frosts, earthquakes, fiery eruptions, winds great rains, the seasons of the year, plagues, epidemics, diseases, plenty, famine, wars, seditions, sects, transmigrations of peoples, and all commotions or great innovations of things natural or civil.' Astrology applies therefore to the world of nature, and to human history in its collective sense, but not to the life and fortune of any individual. Bacon regards personal divination by astrology, as by omens, dreams and the like, as mere delusion. Bacon has no time for astrological magic of any kind, or for the philosophy of macrocosm-microcosm which underlay it, nor, strangely, does he deal with the most prevalent form of natural astrology, namely medicine. Yet the man who has often been hailed as the prophet of modern, empirical science, still grants considerable scope in his world-view to astrology. Having accepted the basic premise of astrology, that the stars do emit forces other than light and heat which determine events on earth, Bacon proposed a programme of empirical research to establish the science on a new, rational footing.

For a most extreme and non-Baconian form of nature mysticism, we must turn to his exact contemporary, Robert Fludd (1574–1637). In Fludd's cabalistic system, astrology was an accepted component as he developed the macrocosm-microcosm link into a labyrinth of symbols and images. The aim of the cabala was to reveal and tap spiritual powers beyond the natural forces of the cosmos, and the influence of stars was just one part of this numinous system. Metaphysical categories of mind, spirit, space and time were brought together by Fludd, and shaped into

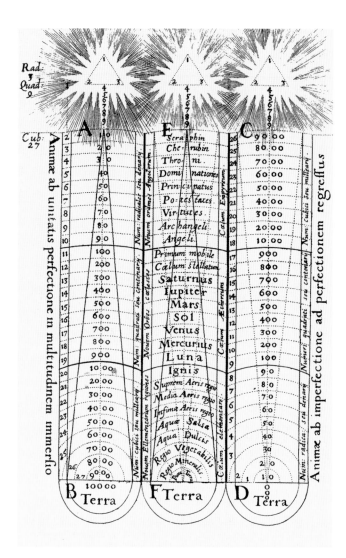

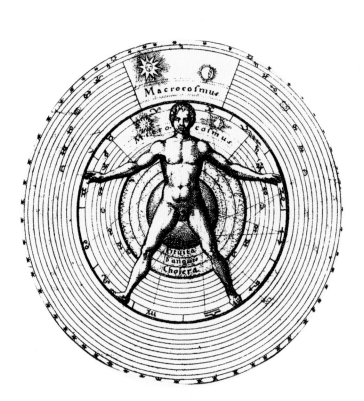

The title-page of Robert Fludd's Utrisque Cosmi, *1617, showing man the microcosm as the focus of universal forces emanating from the stars and planets.*
The British Library L.32/65

Right. *The hierarchy of the universe by Robert Fludd, 1617. The soul descends from perfect unity in the heavens to multiplicity on earth, but seeks to re-ascend. The cosmos is divided here into three realms – the elemental, the celestial and the spiritual. To Fludd, the spheres of the planets were both real places and stages in a spiritual progress.*
The British Library L.32/65

an edifice which was a curiosity even in its own day, and which attracted few disciples. Kepler, who himself spent his life searching for the hidden symmetries and connections of the universe, scorned Fludd's works with their fantastical illustrations as 'pictures forged from air'.

Dee, Bacon and Fludd represent in their different ways the undiminished appeal of astrology as a philosophic system. But Elizabethan England witnessed at this same time a very different development, namely the vulgarisation and commercialisation of astrology at the hands of the fee-taking astrologers who haunted both the court and the back-alleys of London and other cities. These were men virtually without education, with none of the high philosophical ideals which had characterised the astrological tradition from Ptolemy onwards, but who pandered to their clients' desire to peer into the future in matters of wealth, sex or social position, and who frequently became involved in the resulting intrigues. The careers of some of these men – Simon Forman and William Lilly for example – are known in intimate detail, thanks to the survival of many of their original papers, and their study leaves an impression of astrology debased into a trivial, sordid and fraudulent business.

From 1580 until his death in 1611, Simon Forman was a physician and astrologer in London, but he was frequently in and out of prison for practising without a licence. During the various processes against him, he was found to be laughably ignorant of medicine and astronomy, but answered that he used no other diagnostic aids but the planetary ephemerides. He was said to have invoked angels and spirits to assist him in his healing. Many of his clients were women, and he seduced a considerable number of them, leaving a large illegitimate family when he died. Despite his unsavoury reputation, he was evidently a charismatic man, and he succeeded in charming some highly-placed friends, mostly female. A few years after his death, some lurid details of his practices came to light in a murder trial, when one of the accused was shown to have obtained magical love-philtres from Forman, and indecent wax images of the persons concerned, made by Forman, were brought into court. A contemporary poet bore witness to his reputation:

> Forman – that fiend in human shape,
> That by his art did act the devil's ape.

It is clear from his papers that Forman did make some study of astrology: he kept full notes of his cases, and he transcribed texts on medicine, alchemy and related sciences. His personal diaries give a fascinating insight into Elizabethan social life, but their frank immorality shows that astrology was for him not an intellectual system but a ticket into society, wealth and pleasure. We know that at the height of his practice, Forman was drawing up more than a thousand horoscopes each year, answering questions on love, fortune, property, sickness and so on. In the light of the serious mathematical demands involved in erecting even one accurate horoscope, it is plain that Forman was a rank amateur, if not a complete charlatan. Ben Jonson mockingly called him 'Oracle Forman', and probably had Forman in mind when he drew the character of Subtle in his play *The Alchemist*. In intellectual terms, Forman's place in the history of astrology is rather like that of a spectre at a feast. He was a cynical careerist who profited from a society where, as one contemporary complained, 'astrology was ravened, embraced and devoured of many'.

Marginally more respectable and more interesting than Forman was William Lilly (1602–1681) the pre-eminent practitioner of astrology's last great period. Like Forman, Lilly was entirely self-taught, and came to astrology simply as a profitable career. He 1644 he published his first almanac, which he sub-titled *The English Merlin Revived, or a Mathematical Prediction upon the Affairs of the English Commonwealth*. It was indeed the English Civil War and the Interregnum which caused a surge of interest in prophecy of all kinds, gave a renewed impetus to astrology, and made Lilly's fortune. Lilly was a Parliamentarian, and early in 1645 he told Oliver Cromwell's advisors that if they could avoid battle until after 11 June, they would win a great victory. Lilly was highly gratified when the Battle of Naseby was won on 14 June. From 1648 Lilly was awarded a government pension of £100, and in the same year he was ordered to attend the Parliamentary army engaged in the siege of Colchester, to encourage them with predictions of victory. It was said that if the King could have brought over Lilly to his side, he would have been worth more than half a dozen regiments. In 1651, Lilly published *Monarchy or no Monarchy*, in which he foretold that 'England should no more be governed by a king', and it was in this work that two enigmatic pictorial figures appeared, which Lilly claimed signified a plague and a fire which would engulf London, although he did not say when. There is ample evidence that Lilly was regarded seriously and was much consulted by leading Parliamentary figures, and not merely for the sake of propaganda. It seems that the Puritans' and Levellers' strong interest in prophecy cancelled out any religious scruples which we might imagine them to have had about astrology, and indeed Lilly had chosen the title

The Christian Astrologer for the textbook which he published in 1647. It is a conventional statement of the main techniques of astrology, with the usual assurances that the science is entirely consistent with the Christian faith. He was later to argue that astrology could not predict God's miracles, among which he classed the biblical flood, for in these events, God overruled nature. This was in contrast to the long-held doctrine that events such as the flood, and perhaps even the birth of Christ, were astrologically determined because God operated through nature. Lilly excused his failure to predict the execution of King Charles on the same grounds, that it was a miracle of providence.

Comet over London, 1666. The years of the English Civil War, the Commonwealth, the Plague and Great Fire, saw an upsurge in prophecy and astrology, in an effort to make sense of these cataclysmic events. The motto on this medallion reads 'Thus God punishes', leaving no doubt that London's misfortunes had a heavenly cause.
Department of Coins and Medals
The British Museum

At the Restoration, Lilly was held in custody and questioned about his activities, but he took the oath of allegiance to the new king, and somehow survived. In October 1666 he was examined again by the Parliamentary committee which investigated the Great Fire of London, who wished to know the basis of Lilly's prediction of 1651. Here the ambiguity which characterised so many of his predictions came to his aid, and he was able to convince the committee that his prediction, although valid in general terms, did not spring from any prior knowledge of the exact date or extent of the fire. Lilly's fame was enormous, and clients came from Spain, Italy and the West Indies to consult him. He cast even more horoscopes than Forman, and published an almanac each year for almost forty years. The personal subjects on which he was asked for judgements included missing husbands, love affairs, expected legacies, buried treasure, lost property and career advancement, while during the Civil War there were many military and political questions: would a certain town be taken, would foreign troops be brought in, what would happen to property confiscated by the armies, and so on. Lilly's income was swelled still further by teaching pupils the science of astrology, one of them offering him several hundred pounds for some very advanced techniques which Lilly wished to keep secret.

The overriding question raised by the careers of Forman and Lilly, and the many others who flourished at this time, is whether they really have any place at all in the philosophic tradition of astrology? Was there any intellectual basis to their practice, or were they simply opportunists. The answer lies in the prevalent role which elections and interrogations played in their work: the sheer number and triviality of the questions they answered plainly rules out any intellectual dimension. A philosophic system whose origins lay in the belief that man was, in the depths of his being, linked to the cosmos, had descended in their hands to answering questions about lost property, faithless lovers and career prospects. Forman, Lilly and the others like them may conceivably have believed in what they were doing, but their practices took astrology into new territory, both intellectually and socially, and although they did not realise it, it was dangerous territory, where their very success would eventually prove fatal to their art.

Forman and Lilly were by no means the only astrologers practising at this time, and the years 1640–1670 seem to have witnessed a last frantic outburst of astrological activity in England. Turbulence in the political and social world may partly explain this, nor was there as yet any clearly-defined gulf between science and occultism. Daniel Defoe asserted that in the years around the Plague and the Great Fire, 'the people were more addicted to prophecies and astrological conjurations than ever they were before or since.' As late as 1673 King Charles II consulted Elias Ashmole to seek astrological advice about his relations with Parliament, while the participants of the so-called Meal-Tub plot of 1680 against the king, consulted the astrologer John Gadbury to select a suitable time and to check the character of their accomplices. There is a knockabout, Hogarthian quality to the careers of the English astrologers at this time which is highly amusing but intellectually depressing. They would arrive in London penniless, then discover the attractions of astrology as a career, master the technique of casting horoscopes, and proceed to manipulate gullible women, hover on the fringes of political factions, perhaps be prosecuted for fraud and fall out with their friends, but always surface once more to compose philosophical tracts in their own defence, and always succeed in captivating new clients. Gadbury was entirely typical: a friend of Lilly and of Ashmole, the Oxford scholar, he was a prolific author

A 17th century astrologer with his client.
The British Library
718.g.44

and commentator on the events of his time. Yet he quarrelled so badly with Ashmole that the latter defaced his copy of one of Gadbury's books, inking his portrait and scrawling beneath it the words: 'His father a knave, his mother a whore, himself the most malicious tailor and besotter (?) who ever breathed – a bold impudent scorpionist'. The subject-matter of Gadbury's astrological treatises centres entirely on worldly and mercenary ambitions: how determine whether a client will receive honours or preferment, an expected legacy, a beneficial marriage or a profitable business transaction. From being a royal art, astrology had been democratised, and no aspect of bourgeois life was outside the influence of the stars.

Even after the Restoration, as the scientific revolution was gathering pace, astrological theory was still capable of development. Francis Bernard wrote to Lilly in 1664 describing a new discovery which he had made which correlated known fires in London's history with the astrological pattern of the heavens, enabling him to draw up a form of horoscope for the city , and to predict future fires. Bernard claimed to have discovered that city fires were analogous to fevers in the life of the individual. The religious and civil conflicts of the period seem to have fed the well-established awe of comets, eclipses and other celestial omens, never more so than on 'Black Monday' – the solar eclipse of 29 March 1652.

Sermons and pamphlets had been warning of the event for months past, and on the day itself there was near-hysteria. The diarist John Evelyn wrote that 'Hardly any would work, and none stir out of their houses, so ridiculously were they abused by knavish and ignorant star-gazers'. People loaded up their belongings to escape from London, while quack doctors sold magical remedies to ward off the effects of the eclipse. The panic seems to have begun as a piece of Royalist propaganda, for the original 'Black Monday' tract had been issued in December of the previous year, predicting divine vengeance on the regicide nation. In the event, Monday 29 March was a fine day, and not a few commentators mocked at the lost reputation of the astrologers. This reaction, however logical, was premature, for no single event of this kind, no failed prediction, seems to have been able to undermine popular faith in astrology.

Johann Heinrich Alsted's chart of astrological history, 1624. Alsted was a distinguished Calvinist theologian, who sought to harmonise the great events of biblical history with astrological events, especially the great conjunctions. He foretold the dawn of a new age in 1694.
The British Library, 799.c.1.

The entire structure of astrological medicine for example, remained intact until almost the end of the seventeenth century. It centred on the theory of 'critical days' when a sickness would reach its crisis. These days were astrologically determined of course, and followed from the patient's natal horoscope, and more specifically from his 'decumbiture' – the moment of the onset of sickness. The progress of the planets, especially the Moon, was charted over succeeding days, with little or no observation of the patient himself, indeed the staunchest astrologer-physicians would claim that they did not even need to see the patient. The Moon exercised a special influence over the mind, as Thomas Vicary had declared in 1577:

> Also the brain hath this property, that it moveth and followeth the moving of the Moon; for in the waxing of the Moon, the brain followeth upwards, and in the wane of the Moon, the brain descendeth downwards, and shrinketh together in itself, and is not so fully obedient to the spirit or feeling, and this is proved in men that be lunatic or mad.

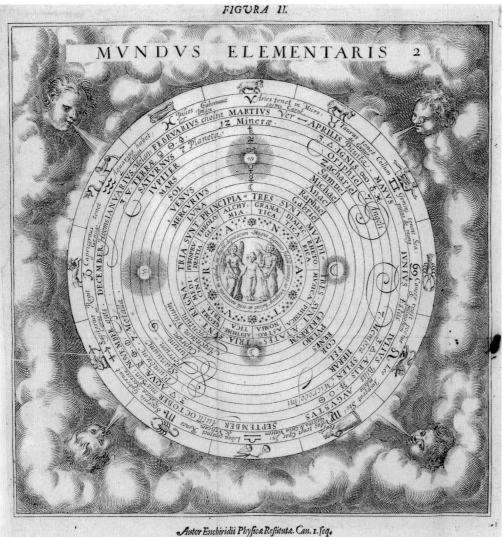

§.1. Deus est Ens Æternum, Unitas Infinita, Radicale Rerum omnium Principium: Cujus Essentia est Lux Immensa: Potestas Omnipotentia: Voluntas Bonum Perfectum: Nutus Opus absolutum. Plura desideranti occurrunt stupor, Silentium & Abyssus Gloriæ profundissimæ. §. 2. Mundum ab Æterno in Archetypo suo descriptum fuisse Sapientum plurimi duxerunt: Archetypus autem Ipse qui Totus Lumen est, ante Universi Creationem in se complicatus, ceu liber sibi soli illuxit, in Mundi vero productione quasi parturiens se aperuit & explicuit, Opusq; suum in Mente, velut in matrice, prius occultum, quadam sui Extensione manifestum fecit ac Mundum Idæalem, quasi duplicatâ Divinitatis Imagine, actualem & materialem eduxit. Hoc annuit *Trismegistus*, dum Deum formam suam mutasse ac Universa subitò revelata & in Lucem conversa fuisse refert: Nihil aliud quippe est Mundus, quam patens occultæ Divinitatis Imago. Hunc Universi ortum intellexisse videntur Antiqui per Palladem suam è Jovis Cerebro, Vulcani, nempe Ignis sive Luminis Divini Ope extractam. §. 3. Æternus Rerum Parens, non minus in Ordinando Sapiens, quam in creando potens Organicam Mundi molem in tam præclarum ordinem digessit, ut summa Imis & ima summis citra confusionem intermixta & analogiâ quadam similia sint; Unde Extrema Totius Opificii, secreto quodam nexu, per media insensibilia strictissimè inter se cohærent, ac sponte omnia in supremi moderatoris Obsequium. Et inferioris Naturæ Commodum consentiunt, Solo nutu Ejus qui colligavit, solvi se passura. Rectè itaque *Hermes id quod inferius est, simile esse Ei quod est superius*, affirmavit. §. 4. Qui summum jus Universi in Naturam transfert aliam à Divina Natura, Deum negat: neque enim aliud in creatum Naturæ Numen, aut in producendis aut in conservandis Expansæ hujus Machinæ Individuis, agnosci fas est, præter Spiritum illum Divini Opificis, qui primis aquis incubuit & confusa in Chao rerum semina de potentia in Actum eduxit, educta per constantem alterationis Rotam versans componendo & resolvendo hæc inferiora Geometrice tractat.

The only treatment prescribed by these doctors was to bleed the patient in order to restore the balance of the humours, and to use those herbs which tradition taught were related to beneficent planets. 'It hath been many times experimented and proved', said one textbook, 'that that which many physicians could not cure or remedy with their greatest and strongest medicines, the astronomer hath brought to pass with one simple herb, by observing the moving of the stars'. By the late seventeenth century however, many doctors were becoming sceptical about the astrological theory of disease, or at least were coming to believe that it must be supplemented by direct medical intervention to combat dangerous symptoms. Even the convinced astrologer-physician was aware of the damage done to his profession by quack-doctors. William Ramsey, a physician to Charles II, defended astrology as 'the most necessary discipline of all the rest', but went on to warn:

Not as it is commonly practiced (and indeed abused) by broken mechanics and illiterate novices, bringing shame and contempt upon that noble art, which, because of its excellent use in physic, they under that colour deceive men of their moneys and fool them out of their lives; there being more empirical impostors pretending to astrology than there are very idiots...I say it is not this I allow, but the pure astrology of the ancients; for men's bodies alter in their temperatures with the seasons, which change according to the motion and places of the several constellations and celestial bodies, whence follow many infirmities and diseases. Ergo, whosoever is ignorant of astrology is ignorant of the cure.

Popular faith in astrology was fed by a publishing phenomenon of the seventeenth century, the yearly almanac, in which a cascade of miscellaneous information was added to a basic calendar and to astrological predictions for the coming year – about weather, harvests, unusual natural or civil events such as floods, epidemics or the death of great men. There were dozens of competing almanacs, each selling in their thousands, and it has been estimated that they exceeded even the Bible in their popularity and authority, no literate person of any social class being without at least one almanac. 'Who is there,' asked one commentator, 'that maketh not great account of his almanac, to observe both days, times and seasons, to follow his affairs for his best profit and use?' Such was their hold that 'people scant would ride or go any journey unless they consulted with these blind prophets'. The traditional role of astrology as a royal art was upheld as late as 1603, when Christopher Heydon wrote that astrology 'had not much conversed at any time with the mean and vulgar sort, but hath ever been most familiar with great personages, princes, kings and emperors.' When this was written it was a hopelessly anachronistic viewpoint, for the printed almanac had brought astrology into the lives of millions.

But for this there was a price to be paid, and that price, as Doctor Ramsey saw very clearly, was the vulgarisation of astrology and a loss of intellectual respectability. A current of resistance to popular astrology is detectable from the late sixteenth century onwards, and the number of dissenting voices raised against it steadily increased. Of course there had always been resistance to astrology on high religious grounds, as we have seen with the Paris condemnation of 1277, or in the work of Oresme and Pico. But these later seventeenth-century polemics were not philosophical: they did not rehearse the traditional religious problems of freewill and divine providence; nor were they scientific, focussing on the nature of the celestial influence or on the mathematics of house-division. Instead they were satirical, mocking the triviality and the ambiguity of astrological predictions. This mockery appeared not in scholarly treatises, but in polemical squibs, in drama and in verse, where it reached the widest public. Pamphlets appeared with titles like *The Madness of Astrologers*, *The Detestable Wickedness of Magical Sciences*, *The Anatomy of Abuses*, *A Defensative against the Poison of the Supposed Prophecies*, and so on. These tracts are full of invective and personal mockery directed at the astrologer as a social parasite, and at the clients who are so foolish as to support him. One such tract, John Melton's *Astrologaster* of 1620, gives a new definition of astrology:

A satirical picture of the astrologer in his consulting-room, casting horoscopes and weighing his money-bags.
Private collection

> Astrology is an art whereby cunning knaves cheat plain honest men; that teacheth both the theory and the practice of close cozenage; a science of instructing all the students of it to lie as often as they speak, and to be

believed no oftener than they hold their tongues; that tells truth as often as
bawds go to church, witches or whores say their prayers...

Where in the 1590s, Marlowe had filled his plays with references to destiny,
astrology and the occult, so that the phrase 'the stars that reigned at my nativity'
became almost a cliché, and where Spenser had used astrological symbolism to
write lyrically of the procession of the months, seventy years later the prevailing
tone was set by Samuel Butler's *Hudibras*, the great popular poem of the age:

> There's but the twinkling of a star
> Between a man of peace and war,
> A thief, a justice, fool and knave,
> A huffing officer and slave,
> A crafty lawyer and pickpocket,
> A great philosopher and blockhead..
> ..As if men from the stars did suck
> Old age, diseases and ill luck,
> Wit, folly, humour, virtue, vice,
> Trade, travel, women, claps, and dice,
> And draw with the first air they breath,
> Battle and murder and sudden death.
> Are not these fine commodities
> To be imported from the skies?

From Ben Jonson's *The Alchemist* of 1610, the stream of satire against astrology
continued, to be enriched by writers such as Dryden, Congreve and Swift, and by
numerous less famous wits. In 1708 Swift issued a burlesques set of predictions
under the pseudonym Isaac Bickerstaff, in which he pretended to foretell the
imminent death of the astrologer and almanac-publisher John Partridge. The
unfortunate Partridge was forced to print advertisements assuring his clients that
he was still alive and that his rival's prophecy was a hoax. The public revelled in
this proof of the absurdity and commercialism to which astrology had descended,
and after this episode, even the satirists lost interest in the subject. Underlying
this body of satire and invective, which was one hundred years old by the time
that Swift became involved, there were two elements: social contempt of the
back-street charlatan and the fools on whom he preyed; but also an intellectual
contempt for the beliefs which sustained the whole system. The first is easy to
understand, but the origin of the second requires more explanation: some intellectual shift had evidently occurred during the seventeenth century which the
satirists do not overtly explain, but which is unmistakably embodied in their
work.

THE SCIENTIFIC REVOLUTION AND THE DEATH OF ASTROLOGY

Why did astrology die at the end of the seventeenth century? It had persisted in so
many cultures for almost 2,000 years, and had become so integrated with philosophy, religion and science that it was part of Europe's intellectual landscape.
What happened between 1650 and 1700 to render astrology incredible or irrelevant to the children or grandchildren of those who had universally believed in it?
It seems clear that astrology's demise must be related to the revolution in science
which occurred at exactly this time. The work of astronomers and physicists from
Tycho to Newton created both a new understanding of the universe and a new,
rigorous approach to scientific method. The post-Newtonian era was consciously
an era of science, rationalism and enlightenment, an era in which, as we now see,
astrology could not possibly survive.

However there are two great difficulties about making this connection, obvious
and attractive as it now appears. The first is that there is virtually no contemporary

SHAKESPEARE'S OWN intellectual beliefs – about religious or scientific matters – scarcely emerge at all in his plays, but there is one such subject which he mentions rather often, and that is astrology. The use which he makes of it is more than rhetorical, and it is worth asking whether some definite belief in astrology is discernible in the Shakespearean canon? The difficulty is that the many statements about it come not directly from the author, but from his characters, whose words have a dramatic rather than an intellectual purpose. Perhaps the best-known text is Edmund's speech from *King Lear*:

> This is the excellent foppery of the world, that when we are sick in fortune, often the surfeit of our own behaviour, we make guilty of our disasters the sun, the moon and the stars; as if we were villains on necessity, fools by heavenly compulsion, knaves, thieves and treachers by spherical predominance, drunkards, liars and adulterers by enforced obedience of planetary influence; and all that we are evil in, by a divine thrusting-on: an admirable evasion of whoremaster man, to lay his goatish disposition to the charge of a star.

This seems to be as clear an attack on astrology as one could find. But the speaker is a villain – selfish, cruel and treacherous, and claiming to be above all law; therefore his mockery of the stars might be seen as an aspect of his pride and arrogance. In the same play, the characters of Cordelia and her sisters differ so sharply that Kent exclaims:

> It is the stars,
> The stars above us govern our conditions,
> Else one self mate and mate could not beget
> Such different issues.

Again an unmistakably clear statement, but this time on the side of astrology. Shakespeare also makes use of astrology in comic situations:

> GLENDOWER: At my nativity
> The front of heaven was full of fiery shapes
> Of burning cressets; and at my birth
> The frame and huge foundation of the earth
> Shak'd like a coward.
>
> HOTSPUR: Why, so it would have done at the same season, if your mother's cat had but kitten'd , though you yourself had never been born.
>
> – *Henry IV Part 1*

This is almost as damning of astrology as Edmund's speech, but it reflects Hotspur's roughness of speech, rather than Shakespeare's considered view.

These statements taken from different plays appear to contradict each other, but it is important to recall that there were different levels of astrological belief, and in particular that there was a long-standing distinction between natural and judicial, or personal, astrology. Shakespeare made frequent references to natural astrology, and to the appearance of omens in the skies:

> Hung be the heavens with black, yield day to night!
> Comets, importing change of time and states,
> Brandish your crystal tresses in the sky,
> And with them scourge the bad, revolting stars
> That have consented unto Henry's death!
>
> – *King Henry VI Part 1*

The same idea is put more simply in *Julius Caesar*:

> When beggars die there are no comets seen:
> The heavens themselves blaze forth the death of princes.

Medical astrology, linking human health with the planets, especially the Moon, is also found in the plays, as when Othello laments:

> It is the very error of the moon;
> She comes more near the earth than she was wont,
> And makes men mad.

At its highest, natural astrology affirmed that the heavens governed all the cycles of nature that occur on earth, including human life and death. Lear summed up this belief when he exclaimed:

> By all the operations of the orbs
> From whom we do exist and cease to be.

But what of judicial astrology, with its central device of the horoscope to predict the individual's future – what does Shakespeare have to say about that? The answer is almost nothing. Romeo and Juliet are described as 'star-cross'd', meaning that their destinies were irreconcilable from birth. In *The Winter's Tale*, Hermione, the wronged queen, laments:

> There's some ill planet reigns:
> I must be patient till the heavens look
> With an aspect more favourable.

Clearly she sees her plight as a temporary misfortune, not as her destiny. The only specific reference to a horoscope expressing a decree a fate seems to be in *Henry VI, Part 2*, where the Duke of Suffolk becomes terrified when he discovers that his captor is named Walter Whitmore:

> A cunning man did calculate my birth.
> And told me that by water I should die.

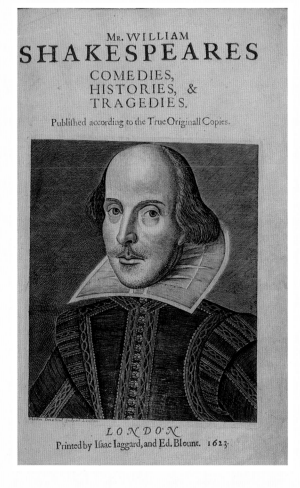

Mr. WILLIAM
SHAKESPEARES
COMEDIES,
HISTORIES, &
TRAGEDIES.

Published according to the True Originall Copies.

LONDON
Printed by Isaac Iaggard, and Ed. Blount. 1623.

Glou. These late Eclipses in the Sun and Moone portend no good to vs : though the wisedome of Nature can reason it thus, and thus, yet Nature finds it selfe scourg'd by the sequent effects. Loue cooles, friendship falls off, Brothers diuide. In Cities, mutinies ; in Countries, discord ; in Pallaces, Treason ; and the Bond crack'd, 'twixt Sonne and Father. This villaine of mine comes vnder the prediction; there's Son against Father, the King fals from byas of Nature, there's Father against Childe. We haue seene the best of our time. Machinations, hollownesse, treacherie, and all ruinous disorders follow vs disquietly to our Graues. Find out this Villain *Edmond,* it shall lose thee nothing, do it carefully : and the Noble & true-harted Kent banish'd ; his offence, honesty.'Tis strange.*Exit*

Bast. This is the excellent foppery of the world, that when we are sicke in fortune,often the surfets of our own behauiour, we make guilty of our disasters, the Sun, the Moone,and Starres,as if we were villaines on necessitie, Fooles by heauenly compulsion, Knaues, Theeues, and Treachers by Sphericall predominance. Drunkards,Lyars,and Adulterers by an inforc'd obedience of Planatary influence; and all that we are euill in, by a diuine thrusting on. An admirable euasion of Whore-master-man, to lay his Goatish disposition on the charge of a Starre, My father compounded with my mother vnder the Dragons taile, and my Natiuity was vnder *Vrsa Maior,* so that it followes, I am rough and Leacherous. I should haue bin that I am, had the maidenlest Starre in the Firmament twinkled on my bastardizing.

His fears are justified, and Walter murders him. If Shakespeare was uninterested in horoscopes, and was not drawn to fatalism, there is every sign that he shared the contemporary belief in Fortune, that the rise and fall of great men was subject to some external power, with which they might negotiate. This is Prospero in *The Tempest*:

> I find my zenith doth depend upon
> A most auspicious star, whose influence
> If now I court not but omit, my fortunes
> Will ever after droop.

This seems to be the very opposite of fatalism, and it embodies the typically Renaissance belief that men are free to shape their own destinies. Perhaps the reason that Shakespeare's plays are of such lasting appeal, is that his characters' fortunes spring from their own psychology and not from any destiny imposed upon them. In this sense, despite their absence of overt intellectual argument, the plays may be seen as part of a new era of humanism, an era in which natural astrology was an acceptable source of poetry and metaphor, but in which judicial astrology and fatalism appeared irrational.

support for it: surprising as it seems, none of the scientists of the seventeenth century turned their attention to mounting a critical attack on astrology in the light of the new knowledge. The connection between the demise of astrology and the scientific revolution is one that has been made only by later historians. The second problem is more general, namely to identify exactly *how* the new science impacted upon astrological beliefs. Astrology's basis had always lain in the belief in forces which were invisible and intangible, but nonetheless real, and a central part of the new science was also to reveal the existence of hitherto unsuspected forces, such as magnetism, electricity, atmospheric pressure, and, most important of all, gravity. It can hardly be argued therefore that stellar influence suddenly became incredible because it was invisible. This point acquired greater force when we recall that many of Newton's contemporaries found it difficult to accept the concept of gravity because it entailed 'action at a distance'. Gravity seemed to them to be a wholly occult force: it did not consist of rays, or particles or waves, yet it was claimed to operate across empty space, so what was it? And yet, in spite of these objections, the concept of gravity became scientific orthodoxy within a few decades, while astrology died.

The difficulty of pinpointing the exact point of conflict between astrology and science is well seen in the variety of theories which have been advanced to solve this problem. Firstly, is has been argued that astrology functioned as a universal law of nature, and that this role was taken over by Newton's theory of gravity. The theory, authorised by Aristotle, that all action and movement of earthly elements, all generation and corruption, sprang from the forces exerted by the heavenly bodies, had reigned for centuries as an article of faith; but it could not survive the precise, quantitative formulation of the law of gravity as nature's central governing power. Secondly, the telescopic revolution has been singled out. Galileo showed that the heavens were not as they had always been imagined to be: some planets had satellites, the Moon had mountains and (supposedly) seas, nebulae were really star-clusters, and there were infinitely more stars than had previously been imagined. If the structure of the universe which astrology had always assumed was now proved to be simply wrong, how could astrology itself be expected to survive? Thirdly, the Copernican revolution suggested the possibility that the universe might be infinite, an idea which followed from the absence of stellar parallax, which should have been observable as the earth moved along its orbit. Astrology and its parent doctrine of the macrocosm-microcosm correspondence depended on a finite, enclosed Ptolemaic universe; how could man be a microcosm of a universe which was infinite and largely unknown? In the post-Copernican universe, the constellations of the Zodiac became merely accidental patterns of stars determined by the earth's position in space patterns, which in reality have no special qualities or characteristics. Fourthly, one very specific scientific discovery has been suggested as the cause of astrology's demise, namely the periodicity of comets, hammered out by Newton and Halley. Comets had always been regarded as the most dramatic and visible omens through which the heavens foretold crisis or change on earth. But if comets were an explicable part of the solar system, moving in regular, predictable orbits, how could they also be divine portents of the future? Finally, rather than any one astronomical discovery, the scientific method itself has been identified as the key to astrology's decline. This method had two guiding principles: the search for laws of physical causality and the demand for verification, and in both these principles measurement or quantification was essential; conceptual links were no longer enough. So here are four of five distinct theories about the relation between astrology and science, all of them plausible. Is just one of them the truth, or do they all contain part of the truth? What emerges from these overlapping theories is that there was no direct confrontation, no single, crucial point of evidence or belief upon which contemporaries seized to discredit astrology.

The boundaries between occult science and natural science in the years 1550–1700 are by no means easy to understand, for it is well known that, while the foundations of modern science were being laid, many of the leading thinkers retained a strong interest and belief in the occult, including astrology. Tycho Brahe, who initiated the observational reform of astronomy, continued to cast horoscopes all his life, and subscribed to the doctrine that comets and planetary conjunctions signified turning-points in human history. Kepler's view of astrology underwent several changes. He too cast numerous horo-scopes, and he coined the famous metaphor that astron-omy was a wise but poor mother, who must starve if her daughter astrology did not support her. Yet he was capa-ble of dismissing all judicial astrology as worthless, super-stitious fantasy that preyed on people's credulity. He did finally reject the conventional apparatus of the horoscope – the signs, the houses, the decans, the lots and so on – while striving to find some deeper basis for natural astrol-ogy. This he thought he had found in his doctrine of mathematical harmony, in which the astrological aspects were all-important. Kepler seems to have arrived at the view that astrological effects were caused by the harmony or disharmony of the heavenly bodies, by which he meant that at certain times their speeds, orbits and posi-tions would achieve precise mathematical ratios with each other, on the analogy of music, which achieved its harmonies through the intervals between the notes. On the celestial level he believed that when the correct ratios were achieved, powerful astrological forces were released. This system functioned because mathematical laws had been built into the fabric of the universe: 'Geometry is one and eternal', he wrote, 'shining in the mind of God; that share in it accorded to men is one of the reasons that man is the image of God'. The quest for these laws of harmony underlay all Kepler's thought, and when he dis-covered the law which related the periodicity of the plan-ets to their orbits, he exclaimed ecstatically:

> I give myself up to sacred frenzy... I have stolen the golden vessels of the Egyptians to make from them a tabernacle for my God far from the land of Egypt.. I am indeed throwing the dice and writing the book, either for my contemporaries or for posterity to read, it matters not which; let the book await its reader for a hundred years, if God himself has waited six thousand years for his work to be seen.

The gold of Egypt was the joint science of astronomy-astrology, which Kepler, like many others, imagined to be an Egyptian invention. Kepler's theory of astrol-ogy was subtle and arcane, and it had little influence upon later generations. Moreover it suffered from one serious defect, namely that the harmony upon which it concentrated refers only to the solar system. Kepler's successors were more and more inclined to believe that the Sun was but one star in an infinite uni-verse, and therefore the grandiose theory of cosmic harmony broke down.

Kepler was exceptional in combining a passionate quest for the divine geometry of the universe with an insistence that astronomy should be based on rigorous observation. By contrast the theorists of the occult sciences such as Agrippa, Dee, Paracelsus or Fludd, became enmeshed in a labyrinth of symbols. To these men, nature was not of interest primarily for its own sake, but was seen as a system of symbols which pointed to some transcendent reality; science to them was not physical but metaphysical. Natural science only advanced from this impasse as the concern with the transcendent diminished, and nature was analysed and meas-ured for its own sake. After Galileo had published his discovery of the moons of

HARMONICIS LIB. IV. 149

Kepler's theory of aspects: Kepler considered that astrology was really the science of celestial harmony, which worked because at certain moments the planets formed harmonious patterns. In his work on the harmony of the universe, he expanded the normal canon of aspects by adding the octile and the dectile.
The British Library, 48.e.15.

IN ENGLAND the years 1640–1670 appeared, for obvious reasons, to be years of crisis and catastrophe, and as a result this period witnessed a final flourish of astrological activity. If one episode from these years has been more widely repeated than any other, it is probably that William Lilly predicted the Great Fire of London, and perhaps the Plague too, fifteen years before they occurred. The truth is not clear-cut, and this episode demonstrates the equivocal nature of astrology when it became involved in the dangerous world of politics.

In 1651 Lilly published a work entitled *Monarchy or No Monarchy*, which contained prophecies concerning the future of England, embodied in a series of pictures which Lilly termed 'hieroglyphics', and whose exact meanings were not explained. Four of these pictures were later to attract much attention: two showed a mass burial of diseased corpses, while two others showed a city in flames, and then a pair of twins falling into a fire; Gemini was the Zodiacal sign associated with the city of London. After the Fire, which burned from 2 to 6 September 1666, rumours about its possible cause were rife, including plots, conspiracies and the use of occult powers. Perhaps Lilly's pamphlet of 1651 would not have been recalled, but for an event which had occurred in April of the same year, five months before the Fire. That event was mentioned in Pepys's diary:

> W.Hewer dined with me and showed me a Gazette in April last (which I wonder should never be remembered by anybody) which tells how several persons were then tried for their lives, and were found guilty of a design of killing the King and destroying the government; and as a means to it, to burn the City, and that the day intended for the plot was the 3rd of last September. And that Fire did indeed break out on the 2nd September – which is very strange methinks – and I shall remember it.

The plot referred to was that of eight former Parliamentarian soldiers, led by John Rathbone, who had been charged with conspiracy against the King and the government:

> The better to effect this hellish design, the City was to have been fired and the Portcullis let down to keep out all assistance…the third of September was pitched on for the attempt, as being found by Lilly's almanac, and a scheme (i.e. horoscope) erected for that purpose, to be a lucky day..

The eight soldiers had all been found guilty and executed, and now five months later, the details of the case came back into peoples' minds, and the coincidence of the September dates clearly spelled trouble for Lilly. At the end of October 1666, Lilly was summoned to appear before a Parliamentary committee to explain how he could possibly have foreseen the Fire. Lilly was extremely worried, for it was well known that he had supported the Parliamentary cause, and had made many prophecies of its success. The committee had done their homework, for when Lilly appeared before them on 25 October, they already knew that the almanac referred to at the Rathbone trial was irrelevant, since it actually made no mention of the downfall of a monarch. But they had studied some of Lilly's other works, and had seen the pictures in *Monarchy or No Monarchy* and had interpreted them as clear predictions of the Plague and the Fire. The worst moment of the hearing came when the committee hinted that Lilly might have started the Fire himself in order to demonstrate his power as a prophet. Lilly denied that he had ever foreseen either the extent of the Fire or the exact year in which it would happen. He explained himself in terms that would sound politically acceptable to the committee, saying that after the execution of King Charles, the government had failed to bring peace to the nation, that the people were in turmoil, so that he feared that the country would soon by overwhelmed by disasters, and that this premonition was confirmed by the stars, but in ways which he could not precisely foretell. He said he thought it:

> …most convenient to signify my intentions and conceptions thereof in Forms, Shapes, Types, Hieroglyphics etc., without any commentary, so that my judgement might be concealed from the vulgar, and made manifest only unto the wise… Having found, Sir, that the City of London should be sadly afflicted with a Great Plague and not long after with an exorbitant Fire, I framed these two hieroglyphics as represented in the book, which in effect have proved very true.

Lilly tried to appear helpful to the committee by adding that since the Fire, he had attempted to discover by astrological means whether it had been deliberately caused, but without success. He concluded piously that 'It was the finger of God, but what instrument he used thereunto, I am ignorant.' His political obsequiousness, and the claimed vagueness of his foreknowledge, saved Lilly. He was thanked by the committee and allowed to go, his reputation greatly enhanced by the fame of his prediction. Lilly was immensely relieved, and he must have known that he had had a narrow escape, for he withdrew to his country home at Hersham in Surrey, and recorded in his memoirs that 'Since that time no memorable action hath happened unto me, my retirement impeding all concourse with me'.

One of the things that strikes us about this episode is the absence of any *astrological* discussion at this enquiry.

None of the committee saw fit to ask Lilly exactly what it was in the heavens which led him to predict the Plague and the Fire. Their suspicion seems to have been that Lilly may have had some foreknowledge of a purely political conspiracy. The methods and validity of his astrology were never tested, and the question whether he did or did not predict the Great Fire was never finally answered. Lilly predicted calamities for England, among them fires, sickness and death, but is that the same thing as saying that he predicted the Great Fire of 1666? Plague and fire had been twin curses of European cities for centuries, and Lilly, as a professional astrologer, knew well that his public demanded sensational reading, and that predictions that nothing unusual would happen did not sell pamphlets. So the problem remains unresolved: was Lilly a seer, or a cunning publicist with an eye for an ambiguous headline? He was certainly pre-eminent in the crowded world of London astrologers, so that one elegist lamented after his death:

> Our Prophet's gone; no longer may our ears
> Be charmed with music of the harmonious spheres.

Jupiter in 1611, a group of astrologers in Perugia wrote to him expressing their doubts whether these moons could really exist, because they had no place in the astrological tradition, and no astrological influence from them had ever been detected. Galileo replied ironically to this, inviting them to check all their earlier predictions with regard to Jupiter, and suggests that if they had ever been in the slightest degree inaccurate, then perhaps those defects might be attributable to the influence of the moons. Galileo evinced far less interest in astrology than did

A visually dramatic image of the threefold universe of the Hermetic tradition: God and his angels inhabit the highest heaven, while an unmistakably Christ-like figure rules the Zodiac, which pours down its rays upon the world of man, governed by secular rulers. From Athanasius Kircher's Ars Magna Lucis, *1646.*
The British Library, 536.l.25

Tycho or Kepler; he did not attack it outright, but his attention as a scientist was clearly elsewhere.

Galileo's case is most revealing, for what seems to have happened in the post-Copernican, telescopic era was that astronomers became increasingly absorbed in exploring the physical reality of the heavens. The task of observing and describing the new heavens which the telescope now revealed to them, was so huge and the physical mysteries were so great, that ideas of occult influence permeating the heavens became simply irrelevant. Mankind, it seemed, did not even know what the heavens were, so any theories of their innermost workings could only be seen as baseless fantasy. In other words, a separation between astronomy and astrology was finally achieved, and as knowledge advanced, astrology was left behind, left to the non-scientist. It is this separation which surely lies at the heart of astrology's demise: it lost contact with its foundation in science, in natural philosophy, in the intellectual consensus of the day, and it could no longer survive, except as a vulgar superstition. Man's vision of the universe, of what the heavens actually were, changed profoundly between 1550 and 1700 – between Copernicus and Newton. Changed too was the understanding of how the heavens should be studied – with the telescope, with the laws of physics, and with the language of mathematics. Astrology had indeed been entirely dependent on the enclosed, finite universe of

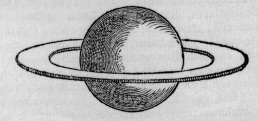

Saturn's rings observed by Christian Huygens in 1659. No one had ever seen Saturn in this way before, and this little picture sums up the problem presented to astrology by the scientific revolution: the heavenly bodies were now the object of telescopic scrutiny, and their imagined role in an ancient belief-system became suddenly irrelevant.
The British Library, 60.a.28.

Aristotle and Ptolemy, and belief in that universe had permeated downwards from the intellectual elite to the rest of society. The birth of modern, observational astronomy created a vast new field of inquiry which left astrology in the hands of the amateurs, the quacks and the almanac-makers like Forman and Lilly, and it could only be a matter of time before they were discredited, as popular beliefs caught up with those of the elite. Moreover the idea that there could be no knowledge without demonstration was one of the cardinal tenets of the Scientific Revolution, and the search for a verifiable chain of cause and effect would clearly prove fatal to astrology. Arguably it was the same demand for proof, for connections which could be demonstrated, which led to the sudden decline in witchcraft convictions at exactly this time. The age demanded testable propositions about the real world, not claims of unseen powers which rested on age-old belief-systems.

It is noticeable too that the graphic schemes and diagrams so beloved of medieval scholars did not long survive the Copernican revolution. After 1600 it became increasingly difficult, except to Cabalists such as Fludd, to imagine that the reality of a possibly infinite universe could be encapsulated in a symbolic diagram. Put simply, astrology had been part of the scientific tradition during the long centuries when science had been non-empirical; when science became empirical, astrology lost its place.

It was with the stated aim of presenting a new, scientific approach to astrology that one of the last great treatises on the subject was written, the *Astrologia Gallica* of Jean-Baptiste Morin, which appeared in 1661. Morin (1583–1659) seems to have occupied a position in French court circles similar to that John Dee in England: he was not officially court astrologer, but he was consulted by royal and noble clients, and a famous (though unsubstantiated) story tells how he was concealed in a closet in the royal apartments at the moment when Louis XIV was conceived, in order to cast his horoscope. Morin's claim at the outset of *Astrologia Gallica* was that he would reform astrology along scientific lines by taking account of contemporary advances in astronomy. This claim, despite his lengthy, quasi-scientific arguments, he fails entirely to fulfil. He rejects the Copernican theory, and affirms that the first heaven, the *primum mobile*, is indeed a real body which imparts motion to the rest of the universe, and pours its influence like a world-soul throughout the cosmos. Likewise the planets, although now believed to be compound bodies just like the earth, also possessed a celestial nature, and emitted 'virtues' capable of acting on man and upon the earth. The star of Bethlehem was not a comet, claims Morin, but was an angel in a luminous cloud, so that this event has no astrological implications. He contends that the science of astrology was revealed by God to Adam, and transmitted via the secret traditions of the Cabala, although it had suffered from many false additions and perversions. The bulk of Morin's work is an exposition of classical astrology, certain features of which he rejects as spurious, but most of which he expounds in an entirely conventional way. He has doubts about interrogations, has no time for astrological talismans and the like, and attempts to clarify the vexed problem of mundane house division. But virtually everything which he writes about the planets, the signs, casting horoscopes or astrological medicine, might have been set down at any time in the preceding four centuries. He is aware of contemporary science, referring to the discoveries of the telescope and the Copernican theory, but his claim to have harmonised that science with astrology remains entirely unfulfilled. Morin's work is densely textured and immensely long. The Bodleian Library in Oxford holds a copy of *Astrologia Gallica* which belonged to William Lilly, presented to the Library by him in the very year of its publication. This fact, and its clean, crisp pages, make it certain that, if Lilly ever began to read the book in the hope of finding something new there, he soon gave up.

With astrology deprived of its intellectual base, the harm done to astrology by the Forman–Lilly school became ever clearer and more damaging. The kind of questions which popular astrology answered, the class of people frequenting the astrologers, the character of the astrologers themselves, all these alienated serious thinkers in the seventeenth century. Thus astrology suffered a process of social destruction as well an intellectual one, and the importance of the first should not be underestimated. Astrology came to be seen as a vulgar pursuit, which could only appeal to the ignorant, and which was manipulated for gain by quacks and charlatans. In Restoration England specifically, there was the additional problem that astrology was associated with the fanaticism and vogue for wild prophecy of the Puritan period, and so stood doubly condemned. The whole tenor of the attacks on astrology made by its seventeenth-century enemies, most of whom of course never mentioned Copernicus or Newton, was that it was vulgar, credulous and sensationalist, so that no civilized person could countenance it. This note of scorn is very much in evidence in the very few written attacks upon astrology made by scientists of this time. In France there was Pierre Gassendi, mathematician and empirical philosopher, while in England there was John Flamsteed, the first Astronomer Royal.

Gassendi (1592–1655) derided astrology in the course of his principal work *Syntagma Philosophicum*, and his hostility was based on his philosophy of knowledge – that true knowledge of nature came only through the senses, and that astral influence, the central tenet of astrology was an unprovable fantasm, as was most metaphysical philosophy. Astrologers did not even observe the heavens, but used unreliable, second-hand tables, thus standing doubly condemned in the eyes of the empiricist Gassendi. The origin of astrology was easily explained claimed Gassendi: 'In no age have men not been greedy to know the future, and in none have there been wanting impostors to boast that they know it.' So strongly did Gassendi feel the contrast to be between scientific knowledge and astrological fantasy, that he suggested that there might have been two Ptolemies, one of the author of the rigorous, mathematical *Almagest*, the other responsible for the false and credulous *Tetrabiblos*. Gassendi published a lofty dismissal of Fludd's arcane philosophical works, with their misty science, their angels and daemons, and their magical symbolism, which Gassendi clearly recognised as belonging to an era of thought that was now passing away.

Flamsteed's criticism of astrology was rooted more specifically in science than in philosophy. In 1674 he composed a polemic which he entitled 'Hecker' (after the German astronomer whose tables he used). Flamsteed had previously taken an active interest in astrology, calculating the nativities of many of his friends, but he explains here that he became disenchanted with its pretensions. He emphasises the role of the telescope in exploding the old image of the universe, and mentions the contemporary discussion about the possibility that the universe is infinite. If this were so, he ponders, how pathetically man-centred astrology would be, as if the heavens were of importance merely for their supposed influence on mankind, and not for their own splendours and mysteries. He concluded that 'There was no reason in nature why the planets should have any influence upon our actions or our thoughts.' He dwelt at length on the incompetence of modern astrologers, their ignorance of the mathematics needed to cast a horoscope accurately, their venality, and the inconsistencies of their methods and their predictions. He attacked the almanacs and their makers, exclaiming that 'the vulgar have esteemed them the very oracles of God', and his contempt is evidently both intellectual and social. Intriguingly, this work was never printed, and it seems possible that, having written it, Flamsteed decided that the subject was simply not worth dignifying by a public attack. Another rare testimony from a disillusioned scientist, some years before Flamsteed wrote, was penned by the mathematician Henry Briggs, who said that as a young man he had been greatly drawn to astrology, for he 'thought it a fine thing to be of God's council, to foreknow secrets'. But his study of astrology convinced him that there was 'no certainty in it', and he turned his attention to pure mathematics, becoming a professor at Oxford and pioneering the use of logarithms.

The case of Isaac Newton, the supreme scientist of the age, is revealing in a purely negative way. We know that Newton's interest in occult science and learning was long-lasting, and that he devoted many years to alchemy and to unravelling the symbolic language of biblical prophecy. It has sometimes been claimed that he was also a clandestine student of astrology too, on the basis of an anecdote allegedly found in Brewster's *Memoirs of the Life of Sir Isaac Newton*, to the effect that, when Edmond Halley once spoke disparagingly of astrology, Newton silenced him, saying 'Sir, I have studied these things – you have not'. As told, this story is a mere fable, for Newton and Halley were speaking here of religion, and not of astrology at all. The truth is that Newton evinced no interest whatever in astrology. He neither attacked nor defended it, but, in common with almost all the scientists and intellectual elite of his time, he simply ignored it.

CHAPTER FIVE

UNDEFEATED:

ASTROLOGY IN THE MODERN ERA

Astrology did not vanish entirely, in England at least, during the eighteenth century. As late as the 1760s, in his novel *Tristram Shandy*, Laurence Sterne thought it worthwhile to invent a rather detailed satire on the subject, centring on the horoscope of Martin Luther, a satire which could not have been written without a fair knowledge of astrological language, and which also assumes such knowledge in its readers. The traditional almanacs continued to appear, still under the names of their founders, such as Lilly, Gadbury, Partridge or Moore, and they continued to sell in large numbers; at the very end of the eighteenth century, Moore's almanac was still selling each year between a quarter and a half a million copies. There is evidence that a few astrologers were still offering their services in London and in some provincial cities, and books explaining the principles of astrology were still published occasionally, although they merely repeated earlier works. This was true of the most comprehensive work of its period, Ebenezer Sibly's *The Complete Illustration of the Celestial Art of Astrology*, a huge and detailed textbook of astrology first published in 1784, and many times thereafter. Sibly was an eccentric scholar and amateur scientist, but he had nothing new to say about astrology, and his work shows the extent to which the art had become fossilised. One contemporary critic discovered in it 'all the faults of old John Gadbury, introduced without correction or distinction in the very language of Bedlam'. In France, Italy and Germany however, even these signs of life were lacking. Astrology had lost its scientific basis and its intellectual respectability; after the long centuries during which it had been part of the intellectual mainstream in western Europe, it had declined to the status of a vulgar superstition.

This may be clearly seen in the only detached and considered accounts of astrology written in the eighteenth century, namely the encyclopedias, which now became so popular in England and France. Louis Moreri's *Grand Dictionnaire Historique* of 1674 stated bluntly that judicial astrology was a delusion, and rehearsed some of the classic arguments against it, while not even mentioning natural astrology. Pierre Bayle's celebrated *Dictionnaire Historique et Critique*, 1697, was entirely biographical and therefore did not deal explicitly with astrology. However Bayle's opinions may be inferred from some of the comments which he made on the famous figures in the history of astrology, such as Jean-Baptiste Morin, whom he branded little short of mad. Bayle's judgement on Agrippa was typically derisive: 'After all, if he was a magician, he is strong proof of the impotency of magic, for never any man miscarried more frequently than he, nor was oftener in fear, or want of bread.' However the great *Encyclopédie* of Diderot and D'Alembert, 1751, gave a surprisingly large space to natural astrology, judging it to be an integral part of physics, and citing Robert Boyle in support of the opinion that atmospheric phenomena and climate are indeed influenced by the heavens. Personal, judicial astrology however, was damned as mere superstition, which 'even today has resisted complete eradication'. By the time we come to the first edition of *Encyclopedia Britannica* in 1771, the entry on astrology is brief, cold and dismissive: 'A conjectural science which teaches to judge the effects and influences of the stars, and to foretell future events by the situation

Consider the Heavens, the work of thy fingers, the Moon & the Stars which thou hast ordained. Psal. VIII. 3.
They fought from Heaven, the Stars in their courses fought against Sisera. Judges V. 20.

The frontispiece of Sibly's Celestial Science, *1790, showing the symbols of astrology in a picturesque eighteenth-century setting. Sibly's book was an immensely long recapitulation of traditional astrology, with no reference to its intellectual position in an age of science.*
The British Library
8610.e.4

and aspects of the heavenly bodies. This science has long ago become a just subject of contempt and ridicule.'

In this context, it is not surprising that a major event like the discovery of the planet Uranus in 1781, which finally shattered the classical cosmos which the astrologers had inhabited, had no great impact upon the astrological community, for there was no community for it to impact on. Later however, in the nineteenth and twentieth centuries, opponents of astrology would seize on this and on the subsequent discovery of Neptune in 1846, as proof that the universe of the astrologers was illusory, outdated and unscientific, and that the great authorities of the past, from Ptolemy onwards, had not even suspected that these planets existed. For later astrologers, these new planets, and Pluto too, would pose many problems as they attempted to define their natures. They had a few outstanding characteristics: they were remote, slow-moving and mysterious; this suggested that they might tend to influence long epochs of time rather than single moments, and people *en masse*, rather than individuals. The naming of all these

A angel waves the horoscope of the newly-independent America, dated 4 July 1776. Published in 1790 by Ebenezer Sibly in his Complete Illustration of the Celestial Science of Astrology, *this is a reminder that the pursuit of astrology had not entirely vanished in eighteenth-century England.*

The British Library
8610.e.4

planets was a rather arbitrary process, decided by the astronomical community, yet astrologers have tended to use their names as reliable guides to their natures – Neptune exercising power over the sea, and Pluto over the underworld. They have also sought to find a significance in the moment when these planets were discovered: Uranus, discovered on the eve of the Industrial Revolution, is said to be associated with science and technology and perhaps also with revolutionary wars; Neptune's rule over the limitless and changing sea has been connected with the emergence in the 1840s of evolutionary theory and early socialism, while Pluto is seen as symbolic of the destructive events of the 1930s – the splitting of the atom, Fascism, war and genocide.

After almost a century of steady decline, the years from 1780 onwards witnessed the faint beginnings of a revival of astrology, for reasons which are not easy to explain. Was this revival connected in some way with Romanticism, with the cult of nature or of the past? The evidence is very slight; Goethe is probably the only serious European writer of this period to mention astrology, giving some details of his own horoscope in the course of his autobiography, yet it plays no part in his dramas, even where we might expect it, in *Faust*. Sir Walter Scott is known to have considered using astrology as the mainspring of the plot of a novel, on the basis of a story told by an old servant of his father's, fifty years earlier. But as Scott pondered the plot of the novel which became *Guy Mannering* (1815) he was forced to admit that 'Astrology…does not now retain influence over the general mind sufficient even to constitute the mainspring of a romance'. Astrology did indeed appear in the final book, but was given a much reduced role. With these few exceptions, none of the major poets or theorists of Romanticism in England, Germany or France seem to have been at all drawn to astrology as a subject of study, or as a theme upon which to base imaginative works. The French Revolution and the Napoleonic Wars, although they dominated the historical consciousness of Europe for thirty years, did not awaken any great prophetic or astrological fervour, and only one or two isolated attempts were made to read the times by looking at Napoleon's horoscope.

The astrological revival of these years seems to have been non-intellectual and to have taken place predominantly among the lower middle classes. Magazines of astrology, some of them short-lived it is true, began to be published, and professional astrologers once again began to advertise their services. *The Astrologer's Magazine* first appeared in August 1793, as a new incarnation of *The Conjurer's Magazine*. Its contents were mainly devoted to matters of horoscopy, in sufficient detail to show that the writers had mastered these techniques well, but articles also appeared on more esoteric subjects such as the making of astrological talismans. One expert, William Gilbert, proposed to teach this art for the fee of £150 per annum, a very high figure indeed for its day. Pamphlets and magazine-literature from these years confirm the impression that astrology had a strongly mercenary element, that its practitioners were fee-taking professionals, who saw their business to be the sale of specialist knowledge. The published books, pamphlets and magazines were used to a large extent as publicity-vehicles for their authors, who were thus able to advertise their expertise, as John Worsdale did in his *Astronomy and Elementary Philosophy* of 1820, where he claimed that if readers would inform him of the time and place of their birth, he would 'Point out and ascertain the time and quality of every important event during the life of the individual, both past, present and to come.' Neither the philosophical infrastructure of astrology, nor the religious and scientific implications of the art are discussed: the system is presented as entire and self-sufficient. It was in the 1840s that astrological literature began to appear in America: *The Horoscope*, published in Philadelphia, was probably the first American journal of its kind, carrying articles on the aims and techniques of astrology which were essentially similar to those now appearing in England.

Whether coincidentally or not, it was in 1824 that astrology became for the first time a crime in English law. An Act against 'Disorderly persons, rogues and vagabonds' included in its scope 'persons pretending or professing to tell fortunes, or using any subtle craft, means or devise by palmistry or otherwise to deceive and impose on any of His Majesty's subjects'. For the next hundred years, the charge of charlatanism was all the easier to make, and it was always possible for astrologers' enemies to invoke the law against them. Astrologers took refuge

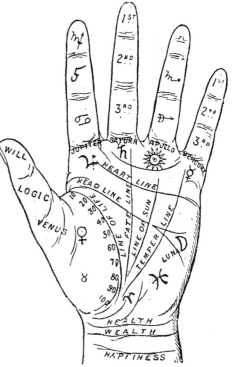

Palmistry makes contact with astrology. Palmistry is generally believed to have originated in India, and to have reached Europe during the Renaissance. As a direct, accessible technique for foretelling the future, its popularity was huge. But exactly how the signs and planets came to be imposed on the map of the palm is impossible to explain.
The British Library
pp.1556.da

behind resonant pseudonyms like Zadkiel, Raphael or Sepharial, and despite the law, many of them used entrepreneurial skills to build up considerable businesses conducted by post. In the 1820s and 1830s the most successful of these astrological journalists was Robert Cross, or 'Raphael', who edited the annual *The Prophetic*

Messenger. Cross's success with this journal was such that, when he died in 1832 there was a considerable conflict among his associates as to who should succeed him, and they were particularly anxious that his death should not be generally known, so that 'Raphael' should survive and prosper into the future.

Still more successful than Cross was Richard Morrison, or 'Zadkiel', who edited *The Herald of Astrology* then *Zadkiel's Almanac*. Morrison was a retired naval officer, educated, socially well-connected and a practising Christian, who for forty years combined astrological journalism with the life of a prosperous Victorian gentleman, although the threat of controversy, prosecution or at least public ridicule always hung over him. He had been singled out for attack in *A Complete Refutation of Astrology* by T.H.Moody, published in 1838, in which astrology was condemned principally because it was irreligious: 'Astronomy', wrote Moody 'connects the mind with heaven, but astrology associates it with the demons of darkness'. In the 1840s Morrison was in the habit of sending horoscopes to the royal family, until doubts about his reputation prompted a delicate rebuke from Windsor to the effect that these were no longer welcome. He had become involved in crystal-ball gazing in high society, employing children as mediums to foresee future events. Morrison appears to have used the circle of acquaintances which he gained through astrology to raise finance for a number of dubious business ventures, and it is difficult to decide whether he was fundamentally a charlatan. In 1862–3 he became embroiled in a major scandal because he had predicted in print that a possible misfortune would befall Prince Albert during August 1861. When the Prince Consort died suddenly in December of that year, this prediction was widely commented upon, and his critics poured scorn upon him in the press for claiming credit in such melancholy circumstances. One of his fiercest critics was Admiral Sir Edward Belcher, who denounced him as a fraud, 'a crystal globe seer who has gulled many of our nobility.' Morrison felt obliged to initiate a libel action against Belcher, which he won, but the court was deeply unsympathetic to him, awarding him a derisive twenty shillings in damages and no costs, and he emerged with his reputation severely tarnished. The articles in Zadkiel's magazines included not only horoscopes and the techniques of astral science, but astro-meteorology, astrology in other cultures such as India, the significance of the new planet Neptune, and some very mundane applications of astrology, such its role as a guide to horse-racing. Morrison scored the occasional outstanding hit with predictions of historic events. Writing in 1864 he predicted that the American Civil War would come to an end in the following spring, and that the peace would be associated with an eclipse of the Moon; on 10 April 1865, the day of the eclipse, Robert E. Lee surrendered to General Grant.

To what extent this revival of astrology sprang from the same roots as other Victorian cults such as spiritualism, phrenology, theosophy and so on, is difficult to say. It would be tempting to claim that all these things represented a flight from rationalism, from the growing dominance of science, or from the monotony of conventional religion. It seems clear that there did exist a growing underworld of these alternative or esoteric beliefs in Victorian England, which may indeed have sprung from a genuine sense of spiritual alienation, but which were always likely to be exploited and to descend into charlatanism. It was no doubt from a mixture of worldly and genuinely spiritual motives that certain individuals encouraged these forms of mystic and occult interests after a century and a half in which such beliefs had been unknown in England. In such a setting, astrology could and did begin to flourish once more, despite the absence of any philosophical underpinning specific to astrology itself. Theosophy acquired some astrological content, although of a curious kind involving some Indian doctrines, and it was typical of this realm of beliefs in disclaiming any novelty of doctrine, affirming that it was merely the rediscovery of an ancient spirituality, obscured by the science and religion of the modern day. Mainstream educated opinion might remain hostile to astrology, as to theosophy or spiritualism, but this could not prevent its widening appeal. Theosophy did at least succeed in giving some kind of intellectual framework to astrology in the nineteenth century, which it had hitherto lacked. The obvious point of contact was that the destiny which was revealed in an individual's horoscope could be linked with the eastern doctrine of karma, which was central to theosophy. Madame Blavatsky, the controversial founder of theosophy, wrote: 'Those who believe in karma have to believe in destiny, which from birth to death man is weaving round himself as a spider weaves his web; and this destiny is guided either by the heavenly voice of the invisible prototype, or by the intimate astral or inner man, who is too often our evil

Facing page. *Title page of* The Astrologer of the Nineteenth Century, *an anonymous work published in 1825, dealing very much with the occult aspects of astrology, especially the conjuring of spirits. This undercurrent of occultism was to grow much stronger in the nineteenth-century.*
The British Library
718.g.22

genius'. The most influential figure to interweave theosophical ideas with astrology was Alan Leo, who would claim that 'It was not until the light of Wisdom Religion (i.e. theosophy) gave illumination to the ancient symbology, that a few astrologers, turning the rays of that light upon astrological symbols, were able to penetrate beyond the veil of the horoscope.' The same vogue for the esoteric was

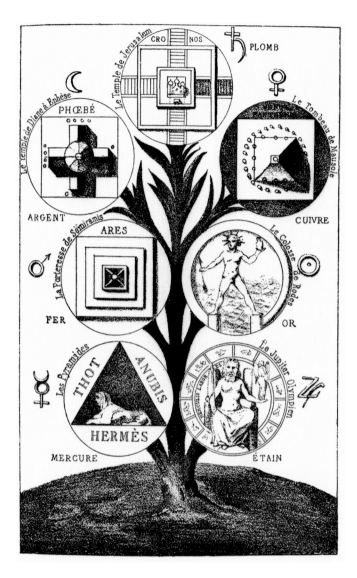

Right. *The Tree of Life by Eliphas Levi, 1855. Levi was the central figure in the esoteric revival in France. Astrology was part of his system, which revived the ancient doctrine of correspondences, for example between planets and metals. The tree of life joining earth and heaven was a religious symbol drawn from ancient Mesopotamia.*
The British Library
8631.cc.46

Facing page. *Indian astrologers at work in the 1830s. India experienced no scientific revolution, so that her tradition of astrology reaches back to the era when first Babylonian omens and then Greek mathematical astrology reached the sub-continent.*
The British Library
MS.Or.5259 f.29

discernible in France before the birth of theosophy, where Eliphas Levi composed his highly influential *Dogme et rituel de la haute magie* in 1856, a compendium in which magic, numerology, cabalistic symbolism, alchemy and astrology were entwined in a system as rich and complex as it was opaque. According to Levi, the Tree of Life had its branches in the heavens and its roots in the earth, and astrology was the study of links and affinities between the one and the other. In this atmosphere, as in the Hermetism of the Renaissance, astrology was but one manifestation of an entire system of magical relationships by which man could penetrate nature's secrets.

The nineteenth-century link between astrology and the esoteric is well illustrated in the judgement which Alfred Russell Wallace, the great naturalist, made on a practising astrologer whom he knew: 'I am quite satisfied,' wrote Wallace, 'that there are astrologers who do give very striking readings of character, and sometimes of events... My conclusion is that the care, labour, attention and study

required to draw out accurate results, offer conditions which enable spirits to impress on the astrological student the results he gets, or thinks he gets from the completion of the figures; *the astrologer is in fact a medium.*' It should be remembered that Wallace, like many other sober Victorians from the 1850s onwards, had become attracted to psychical research, but this scientist's grave assertion that the true key to the mysteries of astrology lay in spiritualism, is truly remarkable.

Alan Leo (1860–1917) was the most successful popular astrologer in England since William Lilly, continuing the tradition in which astrology flourished through journalism. From humble beginnings, with no education or financial backing, Leo, a rather solitary misfit, had by the year 1900 built up a business which employed a dozen people and maintained offices in Paris and New York. Its twin bases were the magazine *Modern Astrology*, and the supply of horoscopes to clients by post. It was the volume of these horoscope-requests which prompted

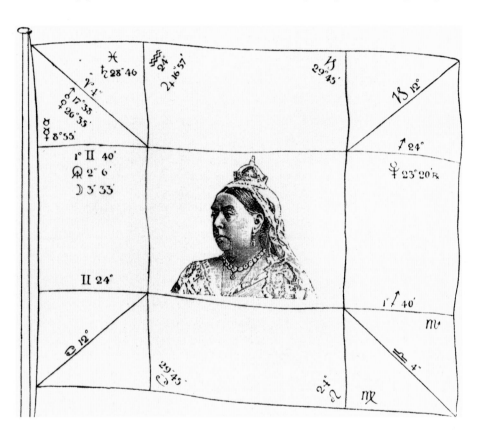

The journal Modern Astrology *was founded in 1895 by Alan Leo and it became the focus of astrology in Britain. In the first issue this horoscope of Queen Victoria was published, and a prize of three guineas was offered for the best reading of it. One wonders how fair a test this was, since astrologers had by then had sixty years to read the queen's character.*
The British Library
pp.1556.da

Leo to develop a quick method of nativity-casting in which the client's birth-date was shortened to 'March: Sun in Pisces', or 'July: Sun in Leo', and so on. This was the earliest origin of the Sun-sign system, which was to become all-pervasive in astrological journalism. Leo and many others like him evidently tapped a large and growing appetite for astrology, but its triumphant return to universal public consciousness came when newspapers and journals in Britain and America in the 1930s began to publish regular star-predictions. It was obviously impossible to offer the public horoscopes that were in any sense personal or individual, and it was for this reason that the Sun-sign system became indispensable. The idea that the most important astrological fact about any individual is the sign of the Zodiac in which the Sun stood at the moment of his or her birth is quite without foundation in classical astrology. It was conceived as a way of classifying people into large, homogeneous groups to whom an instant or collective horoscope could be applied. It was evidently a triumph of journalism for it has flourished ever since, but it has undoubtedly obscured in the popular mind the true complexity of classical astrology. Leo wrote several textbooks of astrology, was prosecuted a number of times as a fortune-teller, undertook a pilgrimage to India, and made a great deal of money. Like many astrologers he was a business man and an opportunist, but he was a genuine esotericist too, and he exercised a formative influence on modern popular astrology.

It is noticeable that astrology had never entirely died out in England after the rise of science, but had maintained a tenuous existence throughout the eighteenth century. In France and Germany, by contrast, it had to be rediscovered within the context of the nineteenth-century revival of esoteric philosophy. In Germany there was no popular astrological journalism before the 1920s, and the re-emergence of astrology was very much part of the fin-de-siecle occultism to be found among a small semi-artistic elite, a movement which also produced the anthroposophy of Rudolf Steiner. The great upsurge in German astrology came only after the catastrophic events of 1919, when social and psychological dislocation

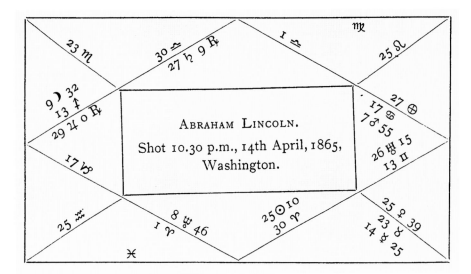

A horoscope cast for the moment of Lincoln's assassination. The Sun is in the sign of Aries which rules the head, and is in opposition to the malefic planet Saturn. Lincoln was shot in the head while attending a theatre. The Sun is also in the fifth house, which rules places of amusement, while the other malefic planets Mars and Uranus are in the seventh house, often associated with enemies. According to the author of this horoscope 'These positions exactly describe the event'; but of course the horoscope was cast and interpreted retrospectively.
The British Library, pp.1556.da

created a feverish desire to be able to predict and perhaps control historical events. The German-speaking contribution was to prove vital in adding a new psychological dimension to astrological theory.

When compared with the classical, medieval and Renaissance tradition, the astrology of the post-scientific revolution had been intellectually sterile: it existed outside science, outside, religion and outside philosophy. It needed a new intellectual basis, a cultural framework to re-connect it to the mainstream of ideas. Theosophy, oriental philosophy and esotericism had provided one possible point of contact, but they were arcane and obscure, and their practitioners were just as open to the charge of charlatanism as astrologers themselves. A new and valid basis emerged however in the science of psychology, and in particular in the serious attention which psychology paid to mythology and symbolism, and the idea that beliefs which were ancient, obscure or pre-scientific had in fact a psychological validity. Freud himself did not analyse astrology in these terms, but it was Carl Gustav Jung who became convinced that both astrology and alchemy were symbolic expressions of psychological patterns. Astrology provided an excellent illustration of one of Jung's characteristic concepts, the archetype, for he could readily argue that the zodiacal and planetary types could be seen as archetypes of the human personality, embodying all the positive and destructive potentialities of human character. In a sense, this concept had already been summed up in Alan Leo's doctrine that 'character is destiny'. On the specific causal connection between the stars and the human world, Jung was elusive, preferring to coin the terms 'synchronicity', by which he meant that significant patterns did recur, that certain elements in the natural and human worlds did correspond, but not in a

way which science could accept as cause and effect. Jung was sufficiently moti-
vated to make some statistical studies of the horoscopes of married couples, and
found that traditional affinities and enmities were indeed confirmed.

It would be wrong to claim that Jung had single-handedly restored astrology to
the intellectual mainstream. What happened was more general: as psycho-analytical

*A Zodiac from Burma,
mid nineteenth-century.
From India astrology spread to
many other Asian countries,
with the Zodiac figures
adapted, as here, to suit the
local culture.*
The British Library
Bur.MS.203 f.17

concepts and theories penetrated western intellectual life, it became accepted that
there were indeed deep, unconscious forces and patterns in the human mind,
some of which had been embodied in ancient myths and typologies. This realisation was seized upon by later astrologers to validate their art, and it resulted in a
conscious transformation of the language of modern astrology. What the stars are
now said to reveal is couched in terms such as self-fulfilment, creativity, conflict,
affinity, crisis, harmony, self-discovery, and so on. This is a language which psychology has made universally appealing; it is the language of the post-Freud,
post-Jung journey into the true self, and this is surely what makes modern astrology so irresistible to many of its followers. This is a world away from the death of
kings, the famines, the plagues, the dreams of wealth, the predestined blows of
fate, which filled the predictions of ancient and medieval astrologers. The language and the focus of interest of astrology must always be to some extent socially
conditioned, or to put it more simply, astrology tends to tell its public what it
wishes to hear, in the language of the day. Astrology has moved away from its traditional field of prediction, with the stigma of fortune-telling and charlatanism,
and into the field of character analysis and personal counselling. Some German
practitioners even coined the more sophisticated terms astro-biology or cosmo-
biology for this modern incarnation of astrology; *Kosmobiologie* was the title of an
intellectually demanding journal of astrology founded in Germany in 1928. This

brand of astrology really came into its own in America after World War Two, when it took its place among the many pathways, scientific, mystical or emotional, towards the hallowed modern goal of self-discovery. Few astrologers now claim to predict the future in any literal sense, and the emphasis has shifted to psychological analysis, from which the individual's future will inevitably grow.

It has generally been imagined that German astrology was dragged down from these austere heights into the mire of Nazi mythology. It is true than in the 1920s some of the minor figures in the Nazi party were directly involved with astrology, and it is also true that some Nazi leaders such as Himmler and Hess did resort to astrologers. But the story that Hitler himself never did anything without astrological advice is quite without foundation, and officially the Nazis were hostile to astrology: within a year of their seizure of power, astrological publishing was suppressed in Germany as decadent and demoralising. There is no inconsistency in the Nazis' policy of attacking astrology, while some of its leading figures still maintained their personal interest in it: in a totalitarian state, what was permissible for the elite was often denied to the people at large, and there is an exact parallel here with the Roman emperors' decrees against the use of astrology, while still resorting it to themselves. Goebbels was certainly interested in the possible use of astrology in black propaganda directed against the allies, and it is known that he believed the prophecies of Nostrodamus to be suitable for this end. One of the astrologers whom Goebbels pressed into service for this work was a Swiss, Karl Ernest Krafft, who in the 1920s had pursued some highly original research aimed at validating astrology by statistical methods. Krafft examined the horoscopes of thousands of people from well-defined professions such as music, and believed he had found a strong statistical link between their birth-signs and their careers. Krafft coined the impressive phrase 'typocosmic science' to describe his new, sophisticated approach to astrology, and published *Influences cosmiques sur l'individu humain* in 1923, and *Traité de l'astrobiologie* in 1939. Krafft came to the attention of the Nazi authorities by predicting in November 1939 the attempt which was made on Hitler's life in the Munich beer-hall explosion. Krafft was first interrogated, then, having convinced the Nazis that he was not a conspirator, was recruited to produce predictions which Goebbels men used as propaganda. Some knowledge of Krafft's activities reached London, and this seems to have been the origin of the widespread but mistaken belief that Hitler was in thrall to the astrologers. For some time the British government even retained an astrologer especially to 'shadow' Krafft, to analyse astrologically the course of the war and the personality its leaders, and to predict the predictions which Krafft was believed to be feeding to Hitler. In 1941 the Nazis intensified their persecution of astrology and imprisoned many practitioners; the reason was the widely-known enthusiasm which Rudolf Hess had displayed for astrology and the possible role which astrology may have played in his partial mental collapse and his bizarre flight to Britain. Krafft's work failed to satisfy his masters, and he died in a concentration camp.

Krafft's approach was the forerunner of several considered attempts to construct new scientific bases for astrology. On the one hand, statistical studies have been made of the traditional personality types associated with the planets and the Zodiac signs; while on the other, biological processes have been related to external forces such as the earth's magnetic field, which is in turn affected by the Sun. Probably the most interesting writer in this field was the French statistician Michel Gauquelin, who initially repeated Krafft's statistical analysis, and concluded that both Krafft's methods and his results were entirely wrong. Gauquelin devised his own statistical procedures and again analysed thousands of horoscopes. Gauquelin himself was surprised that the results tended to confirm that professional groups did share the same ascendant signs, and also reflect the traditional astrological attributes of those signs, sportsmen showing the influence of Mars, actors of Jupiter, scientist of Saturn and so on. Lunar cycles and sunspot cycles have also been shown to produce definite effects on human biochemistry.

The results of some of these studies are interesting, but no one could possibly

ALAN LEO launched the monthly journal *Modern Astrology* in 1895, and under his editorship it became for many years very much the focus and the voice of astrology in England. To some extent it fulfilled the role of a superior almanac, since each month's issue contained predictions of coming events and horoscopes of public figures – in fact the very first issue published the horoscope of Queen Victoria, and offered a prize of three guineas for the best interpretation of it. The tone of the articles – most of them presumably written by Leo himself- was serious, dignified and philosophical: articles on astrology's compatibility with the Christian faith, on astrology in the eastern traditions, astrology and science, and so on. Historically, one of the most valuable functions of this journal is to show the astrological community reacting to the First World War, attempting to explain its causes and to foresee its eventual outcome.

With the benefit of hindsight, the year 1914 did not begin impressively for the astrologers, for the January and February issues both confidently predicted that no European war would occur in that year, indeed that international tensions would ease. This tone was maintained throughout the spring and early summer, and absolutely no hint was given of the catastrophe to come. Then, in June, the journal and editor were plunged into a crisis of their own: Leo was arrested and charged with fortune-telling, which was the legal trap in which astrologers could always be caught, although astrology itself could not be outlawed. Leo was tried in court and acquitted of the charge, and the whole of the July and August issues were taken up with reports of the case, and with discussion of its implications for the status of astrology in England. Thus, during the fateful month of July, while the governments of Europe drifted helplessly towards catastrophe, the attention of English astrologers was fixed elsewhere. War was declared on 5 August, and *Modern Astrology's* special war issue finally appeared in October, on its cover, inevitably, a picture of the god Mars.

The obvious first question to be addressed was 'What were the astrological causes of the war?' There were several possibilities, and, rather oddly, one event singled out had occurred in 1910 – a conjunction of the Sun with Uranus at the first New Moon of that Year – which was said to have ended one era of history and to have inaugurated another, although the precise reasons for this dramatic judgement were never completely spelled out. However this event was not regarded as an implacable decree of fate, rather it created the potential for portentous and destructive events: war was certainly not inevitable. Why had *Modern Astrology* not warned of the danger before? The answer given by Leo was that 'We have always held that it is unwise to make definite predictions that are evil'. What then had turned the tide of events fatally towards war? This is Leo's answer:

> In the solstitial map (i.e.21 June 1914) for the Sun's entry into Cancer, Mars is rising in the ascending sign of Leo, with Jupiter in opposition, thus densifying the war clouds. This unfortunate map is followed by the eclipse of the Sun on August 21, which falls exactly on the place of Mars in the solstitial map! In the east of Europe, Mars was rising and Jupiter setting. Both the June and August maps are very evil indeed...and over the whole of Europe, Saturn is rising: it denotes downfall and disaster for monarchs.

As to the expected course of the war, this was handled entirely in personal terms by examining the horoscopes of the European leaders – King George V, Kaiser Wilhelm, Czar Nicholas II and the Emperor Franz-Joseph of Austria. The greatest interest seems to have centred on the Kaiser's ominous horoscope, which had the malefic planets Mars and Neptune in the mid-heaven. This was contrasted with that of Bismarck, and the two men were characterised as the 'maker and breaker of Germany'. The Czar's horoscope was also unfortunate, while King George's was that of a magnanimous warrior and peace-maker. These horoscopes – or rather the interpretations given to them – obviously suggest that patriotism was dictating astrology here, an impression reinforced by the repeated assertions that England's ultimate victory was not in doubt. This bias did not pass without criticism, and, remarkably, Leo gave

'When will the war end?' was discussed, and certain astrological signs were examined, but none was identified as being decisive, and no positive prediction was ever made – for obvious reasons. It was repeatedly claimed that 'the cosmic forces favoured England', while the war was darkly described as 'the greatest crisis in the history of

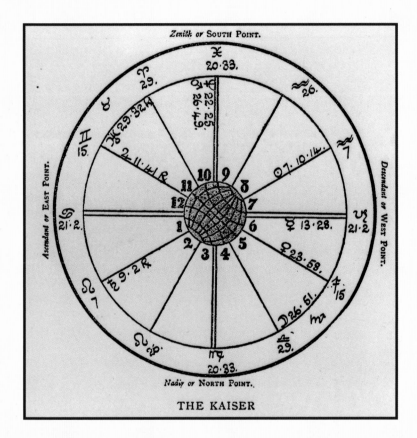

THE KAISER

space in the December issue for a German astrologer to reply; Wilhelm Beck gave horoscopic readings which largely exculpated the Kaiser, and which were much more favourable to Germany. Perhaps the most striking of these horoscopes however was not that of a king but of a philosopher, Friedrich Nietzsche, which was included because he was 'held by many to be the evil influence of Germany...the apostle of war'. In fact the interpretation given here of Nietzsche's horoscope was a generous one – that he was a thinker of high ideals whose reputation as a war-monger was a myth.

At various times of course the great question

humanity since the struggle with the Dark Forces in Atlantis', and also that 'dark forces were utilising the German nation'. Alan Leo did not witness the resolution of the crisis, for he died in August 1917, and his widow employed new assistants to edit the journal, which continued to flourish throughout the 1920s and 1930s. The articles in *Modern Astrology*, when they relate to contemporary events like the Great War, show once again that the language of astrology evolves and adapts itself to the culture around it: patriotism, psychology and commercialism were all in evidence, alongside Leo's genuine passion for esoteric philosophy.

claim that they are in any way conclusive. Firstly the gulf between certain minor physiological changes and the systematised doctrines of astrology is huge; secondly, statistical claims for astrology's validity lead immediately to the old problem of how the stars and man may be linked: by what conceivable and verifiable mechanism can the stars and planets affect events on earth? Why should material bodies, composed of familiar chemical elements, millions of miles distant, produce effects here on earth because they happen to lie on arbitrary arcs – the Zodiac signs and the houses – of a non-existent circle – the ecliptic? In answer to this, astrologers have often pointed out that science deals with many effects and forces which are invisible or inexplicable – gravity, quantum physics, relativity, genetic mutation and so on. Has not science often been forced to discard cherished doctrines in favour of results which are far more complex, or even inexplicable? But to be inexplicable is not the same thing as being unverifiable. We may not understand why genetic mutations or quantum leaps occur, but that they do occur has been verified thousands of times. The problem for astrology is – as it has always been – that there is no testable chain of cause and effect between a celestial event and its claimed consequences. Even if an astrological prediction happens to be fulfilled, its status is still that of a random event, which cannot be explained by any hypothesis. It is for this reason that, since the end of the seventeenth century, astrology has never regained the place in the intellectual mainstream which it had enjoyed for almost two thousand years. Astrology has proved enduring and protean; it has been synthesised with many systems of thought, with Greek science, with Christian theology, with Renaissance magic, and with modern psychoanalysis; but its function is now personal and subjective, and it seems impossible that it can ever to reclaim its place in the intellectual tradition.

However, this book has not been concerned with the truth or otherwise of astrology. True or false, the history of the subject is important and intriguing in its own right, as crossing the boundaries between science, philosophy and religion. During the entire twentieth century, the century of science, astrology stubbornly resisted all the rational and scientific arguments against it, in a manner which reminds one of astrology's progress through the universities and courts of medieval Europe in the teeth of all the theological objections to it. The outstanding fact about astrology is that for centuries people *wanted* to believe it: they longed for it to be true, and around that longing they created an elaborate intellectual edifice. The desire or the intuition that lay behind astrology was that mankind and the cosmos must be linked, that, at some profound level of his being, man *belonged* in the universe. From this intuition there sprang a system of thought and practice which became elaborated, mathematised and mythologised in ways which are often completely inexplicable. And yet, if we compare astrology to other belief-systems, and to all that has been engendered by western religion and western science – the causes and the cruelties, the dreams and the destruction they have inflicted – astrology may perhaps claim that it was at least untainted by blood or by authoritarianism. Its guiding principle has constantly re-appeared through the centuries, and it evidently remains still a vital force in men's minds as the twenty-first century dawns.

The reality of the planets, studied and analysed by modern astronomy: in an age of science, is there still room for a form of astral symbolism, drawn from the esoteric beliefs of ancient civilisations?
Julian Baum /
Science Photo Library

BIBLIOGRAPHICAL NOTE

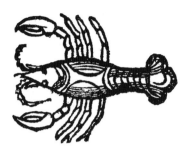

The only good general work is S.J.Tester: *A History of Western Astrology*, 1987, which is however a good deal less comprehensive than its title suggests. The framework of classical astronomy, from Babylonia to the sixteenth century, can be found in C.Walker, ed: *Astronomy Before the Telescope*, 1996.

The classic works on Babylonian astral religion are B.L.van der Waerden: *Science Awakening, Part Two: the Birth of Astronomy*, 1950 and 1974, and O.Neugebauer: *The Exact Sciences in Antiquity*, 1969. A more recent summary is David Pingree: *Astral Science in Mesopotamia*, 1999.

For Greece and Rome, the texts of Manilius's *Astronomicon* and Ptolemy's *Tetrabiblos* have both been translated in the Loeb Classical Library. All the Greek horoscopes are collected in Neugebauer and van Hoesen: *Greek Horoscopes*, 1957. Tamsyn Barton: *Ancient Astrology*, 1994, is a recent discussion of the classical period, while most of the Roman evidence was collected in F.H.Cramer: *Astrology in Roman Law and Politics*, 1954.

There is no general history of astrology in Islamic culture. The best introduction is the articles by David Pingree and others on the Islamic scholars such as Abu-Mashar in the *Dictionary of Scientific Biography*. The background of Islamic science can be found in Howard Turner: *Science in Medieval Islam*, 1995. On the contacts between Mesopotamia, India and the Islamic world, see David Pingree: *From Astral Omens to Astrology*, 1999. The astrolabe is well explained in the article on Islamic celestial mapping by E.Savage-Smith in J.B.Harley and D.Woodward: *The History of Cartography Vol.Two Part One*, 1992.

For the Latin middle ages, every writer of any importance on astrology is described in Lynn Thorndike's massive *A History of Magic and Experimental Science*, 8 vols,1923–58, but Thorndike has almost nothing to say about the social history of astrology. The detailed mathematics of the medieval horoscope can be studied in John North: *Horoscopes and History*, 1987. The politics of medieval astrology was researched in H.Carey: *Courting Disaster*, 1992.

The classic account of Renaissance magic, including astrology, is Frances Yates: *Giordano Bruno and the Hermetic Tradition*, 1964, perhaps supplemented by W.Shumaker: *The Occult Sciences in the Renaissance*, 1972. The career of a leading Renaissance astrologer is the subject of a recent study, A.Grafton: *Cardano's Cosmos*, 1999. The early modern period can be approached through Keith Thomas: *Religion and the Decline of Magic*, 1971. Astrology in the time of the English Civil War is described in P.Curry: *Prophecy and Power*, 1989. There have been a number of important essay-collections on the intellectual fall-out from the Scientific Revolution, for example B.Vickers: *Occult and Scientific Mentalities in the Renaissance*, 1989; P.Curry: *Astrology, Science and Society*, 1987; C.Webster: *From Paracelsus to Newton*, 1982. For the nineteenth and twentieth centuries, two excellent works are P.Curry: *A Confusion of Prophets*, 1992, and E.Howe: *Urania's Children*, 1967. Among the English translations of Michel Gauqelin's works are *The Truth About Astrology*, 1979.

INDEX